EARLY STATE ECONOMICS

Political and Legal Anthropology Series

Myron Aronoff, Series Editor

Political and Legal Anthropology
Volume 8

EARLY STATE ECONOMICS

Edited by

Henri J.M. Claessen and Pieter van de Velde

Transaction Publishers
New Brunswick (U.S.A.) and London (U.K.)

Third printing 2009

Copyright © 1991 by Transaction Publishers, New Brunswick, New Jersey.

Library of Congress Catalog Number: 90-11294
ISBN: 978-0-88738-402-8 (cloth); 978-0-88738-885-9 (paper)
Printed in the United States of America

Library of Congress Cataloging-in-Publication Data

Early state economics / edited by Henri J.M. Claessen and Pieter van de Velde.
　　p. cm—(The Association for political and legal anthropology; vol. 8)
　Papers from the Conference on "the Political Economy of the Early State", held during the 12th International Congress of Anthropological and Ethnological Sciences at Zagreb, Yugoslavia, July 28 and 30, 1988.
　Includes bibliographical references and index.
　　1. Economic anthropology—Congresses. 2. Society, Primitive Congresses. 3. Economics, Prehistoric–Congresses. I. Claessen, H. J. M. II. Velde, Pieter van de. III. Conference on "the Political Economy of the Early State" (1988 : Zagreb, Croatia) IV. Series.

GN448.E25　　1991
306.3—dc20
　　　　　　　　　　　　　　　　　　　　　　　　　90-11294
　　　　　　　　　　　　　　　　　　　　　　　　　　　CIP

Contents

Preface

The foundations for this volume were laid during the conference on The Political Economy of the Early State which was held during the Twelfth International Congress of Anthropological and Ethnological Sciences at Zagreb, Yugoslavia, July 28 and 30, 1988. For two days, an international group of scholars discussed a series of papers on problems of the (political) economy of the early state. It there appeared useful to place the phenomenon of political economy in the wider frame of the economy of the early state in general. This approach is, therefore, followed in this volume too. In order to better relate the papers to each other, the editors wrote an introduction, in which several of the problems that were discussed during the Zagreb meetings were placed in a wider perspective.

We greatly regret that not all colleagues who accepted our invitation to participate in the conference actually attended. For various reasons Dr. hab. Michal Tymowski (University of Warsaw, Poland), Professor Ronald Cohen (University of Florida at Gainesville, U.S.), and Dr. Edward Ch.L. van der Vliet (University of Groningen, The Netherlands) could not join us. Their papers, however, were presented in Zagreb. It was possible for the papers of Cohen and Tymowski to be included in the volume.

We are proud that, apart from those whose papers have been gathered into this volume, a large number of scholars attended our conference and contributed to the discussions. We would like to mention in this connection especially Professor Donald V. Kurtz (University of Wisconsin at Milwaukee, U.S.), Professor Edward I. Steinhart (Texas Tech University at Lubbock, U.S.), Dr. Peter Skalník (University of Cape Town, South Africa), Dr. Thomas Bargatzky (University of Munich, G.F.R.), Professor Dietrich Treide (University of Leipzig, G.D.R.), Professor Jean-

Claude Muller (University of Montreal, Canada), and Dr. Hans-Jürgen Hildebrandt (Deutsche Forschungs Gemeinschaft, G.F.R.).

As usual, it is impossible to name all who have contributed in some way to the realization of this book. From them we want to mention especially Dr. Franklin Tjon Sie Fat for his help in many ways. Our sincere thanks to Peter Deunhouwer of the Institute for Prehistory (University of Leiden) for making most of the maps and figures for us.

The editors feel honored by the positive judgement of the manuscript by the editor of the Political Anthropology Yearbook, and by its acceptance by Transaction Publishers for publication.

HENRI J.M. CLAESSEN
PIETER VAN DE VELDE

University of Leiden

Introduction

Henri J. M. Claessen and Pieter van de Velde

The Problem

This book discusses the political economy of early states. Central in the discussion will be an analysis of the ways in which the income of the central government is organized. This will be discussed in connection with the ways in which the income is spent by those in government. These movements, in turn, will have to be placed against the economy of early states in general, for without some insight in the general situation the specific problems of political economy cannot be understood clearly.

This way of approaching political economy is reflected in the contributions to this volume. Three of the chapters have a more theoretical or general approach, to which we will return presently, and the other nine concentrate on specific early states or regions. In some respects this collection seems composed in a rather haphazard way: the cases discussed are mainly from Africa, Polynesia, and the Americas; the only case from Asia is the chapter on Nepal by Joanna Pfaff-Czarnecka. The American cases comprise a discussion of only archaeologically known Cahokia by Patricia O'Brien, two chapters on the highly developed Aztec Empire by Elizabeth Brumfiel and Frederic Hicks, and a chapter on the Maya by Rien Ploeg. Two of the African cases form the ethnographic core in more general chapters by Aidan Southall

1

and Albert Trouwborst (Kongo and the Interlacustrine states, respectively); the other two (Bornu and Wolof) are discussed by Ronald Cohen and Michal Tymowski. The chapters devoted to Polynesia both have a comparative character. In the one Marin van Bakel compares the economy of Hawaii and Samoa, and in the other Henri Claessen compares the situation in Tahiti with the situation in the Tonga Islands. Though this seems a rather arbitrary sample, it meets a number of qualifications. The cases can be divided quite satisfyingly over the three categories of early states as distinguished in *The Early State* (Claessen and Skalník 1978): the inchoate, the typical, and the transitional early state. To the category of the inchoate (or emergent) early states belong Hawaii, Tahiti, Tonga, and Cahokia. Typical early states are the Interlacustrine states, the Wolof, Kongo, and the Maya. As transitional early states the Aztecs, Bornu, and Nepal can be considered. Moreover, the cases are spread over several continents, and—with the exception of the Interlacustrine states—there are no (regular) connections between the cases mentioned; hence, they can be regarded as independent instances. The cases are well documented and the data are based on recent findings. Finally, viewed historically, they range from twelfth century Cahokia to nineteenth century Bornu.

The theoretical chapters contain a discussion of the concept of political economy (M. Estellie Smith), an analysis of early state economy in terms of modes of production (Aidan Southall), and a discussion of the role of the central government in the economy of the early state starting from the situation of the Interlacustrine states of Africa (Albert Trouwborst). Here we will first present some more general views on the economy of the early state and on the relations between state, economy, and political economy. In doing this we will draw on the contributions to this volume, on the existing literature on early states, and on economic anthropology. In the last section we will return shortly to the three theoretical contributions.

A Multitude of Models

For quite some time debates in economic anthropology have revolved mainly around the question: Which of the various paradigms should be preferred—the formalist, the substantivist, or the Marxist? Each of the paradigms had its protagonists. Scott Cook (1973, 1974) and Raymond Firth (1967) defended the formalist's point of view; George Dalton (1969, 1978), and Marshall D. Sahlins (1972) stood for the substantivist approach; scholars such as Maurice Godelier (1966), Maurice Bloch (1983), and Ludmilla Danilova (1971) represented the Marxist tradition. In its briefest form the view of the formalists is that (modern) economic theory can be applied to any society. Everywhere input-output problems, maximization principles, competitive decision-making processes, and so forth can be found. Thus "economic analysis will be applicable to some extent in all societies" (Cook 1973, 799). Substantivists, however, hold that modern economic theory applies to modern, capitalist societies only and say that for the analysis of primitive or early economies different tools are needed. They follow the lead of Polanyi, who stated that the economy of precapitalist societies should be analyzed in terms of reciprocity, redistribution, ports of trade, and so forth (on Polanyi see Humphreys 1978). Marxist anthropologists approach the ethnographic world with concepts such as social classes (Terray 1975), exploitation, tribute, mode of production, and many others developed originally to analyze the capitalist mode of production (but, see Marx 1964).

At first sight the substantivist approach seems best qualified for the analysis of the economy of early states. A number of books and articles have been published by scholars of this view, and their works are very useful (for example, Ekholm 1977; Hodges 1982; Janssen 1975, 1987). As will be demonstrated below, concepts such as reciprocity, redistribution, prestige goods, and so forth are powerful tools for the analysis of the economic phenomena of early states. But, is this a sufficient reason not to consider views of rivaling paradigms? Gledhill and Larsen (1982), for example, demonstrated the existence of private trade in Assyria, circa 1800 BC (see below pp. 18–19); Hicks (1987) analyzed Aztec economic policy in terms of market integration; and the economy of Capetian France can be analyzed easily in modern terms (Claessen 1985). Moreover, the social relations in France in that period showed aspects of emergent classes (to say the least), and there is no reason not to consider the relations of production in ancient Hawaii in terms of exploitation and class antagonism (Van Bakel 1989, and chapter 11). This situation gives reason to assume that concepts from the three paradigms can be applied when analyzing the economy of early states; this notwithstanding the fact that in many respects the views of the substantivist school will be dominant. Now this may seem a kind of opportunistic eclecticism. There are, however, several reasons not to confine ourselves to the views of only one school of thought. In the first place, the early state underwent considerable transformations in the course of its development. The inchoate early state differed in many respects from the transitional. The influence of the central government increased, economic life became more complex in the course of this process, the division of labor changed, there were differences in income and expenditure of the state, and so on. This already justifies the application of various paradigms. There is more, however. Phenomena such as social classes—demonstrated by the existence of slaves, tenants, smallholders, landlords, and so forth—exploitation, as demonstrated by the existence of tribute and taxation, are found to exist already in inchoate early states. Socioeconomic relations here can be expressed in terms of relations of production and mode of production, as well as in terms of reciprocity and redistribution. This means that concepts from the Marxist toolkit can and will be applied, together and side by side with concepts derived from the substantivist denomination. The same arguments hold for the application of concepts from modern economic theory, side by side with those from marxism and substantivism.

One conclusion of these considerations must be that the various paradigms do not exclude one another. This also holds for the models distinguished by Brumfiel and Earle in their recent overview of specialization and exchange in complex societies (Brumfiel and Earle 1987). Apart from the question whether the term "model" was appropriate—"approaches" might have been more apt—they give a virtually exhaustive overview of the ways in which early state economies can be analyzed. Their main models are the commercial development model, the adaptationist model, and the political model.

In the commercial development model, "increases in specialization and exchange are seen as an integral part of the spontaneous process of economic growth" (Brumfiel and Earle 1987, 1). Rulers assume no special role as economic actors. Even though such developments may conceivably take place, they think that cases "of special complexity originating through commercial development must be relatively few." Still, cases are known where social or political changes were brought about as a consequence of economic development without the interference of political leaders. The development of the large irrigation works in traditional Bali is a case in point. Local farmers constructed dams and terraces and created institutions for maintenance and controling committees without the political overlords being involved. Yet Balinese society was influenced deeply by these waterworks (Grader 1984; Geertz 1980).

In most instances, however, political leaders actively interfered with development; the basis for the two other models of Brumfiel and Earle. In the adaptationist model "political elites are supposed to intervene in the economy; in fact, the ability of political leaders to organize a more effective subsistence economy is considered the raison d'être of powerful leaders" (Brumfiel and Earle 1987, 2). This can be done via redistribution, via the facilitation of market exchange, the centralized management of production, or the sponsoring of long distance trade. According to Brumfiel and Earle, the enlarging or improving of the resource basis of the commoners should have been the objective of such measures, but in several cases the primary object was the financing of governmental institutions or the extension of political power (Brumfiel and Earle 1987, 3). This observation seems correct and realistic. There is no reason to suppose that the benefit of the commoners ever was the sole impulse for a government to undertake large and costly activities. Neither, however, is there reason to assume that the benefit of commoners always was left out from the considerations; very often governmental measures were of a mixed character. When the somewhat naive ideological requirement of benefitting commoners is left out of the definition, this model contains valuable elements for the analysis of the economic life in early states. When all is said and done, however, the remains of the adaptationist model would fall under the third model, the political. Here the interests of the rulers come to the fore undisguised. The catchword of the model is mobilization, "the transfer of goods from producers to political elites" (Brumfiel and Earle 1987, 3). This model also has several versions: mobilization via a monopoly over foreign commerce; mobilization via monopolizing food crops, tools or weaponry; and mobilization via the control and manipulation of wealth—especially prestige goods. The main aspects of these versions are specialization in production, exchange, and social complexity. The authors of this article cover every possibility! The problem is that the various models and versions do not exclude each other. The promotion of irrigation works can be found combined with control of long distance trade or with a monopoly of prestige goods—a situation described for the early state in Sri Lanka by Gunawardana (1981).

In view of the intentions of the present volume—to describe the economy of the early state in connection with the political economy—a somewhat different approach seems feasible. Instead of looking for an all-encompassing theory of economics, or trying to find a model that covers every possibility in this field, we will consider the economic aspect as a part of a more complex whole. A complex whole, comprising the sociopolitical organization, the ideology, and the societal format. It is our contention that there exists a great amount of interaction between these phenomena. An interaction to such an extent that the understanding of one of the factors is seriously hampered when the other components are not considered as well. This view is based on the Complex Interaction Model, which we presented in earlier publications (Claessen and Van de Velde 1985, 1987; Van Bakel 1989). Where, in these earlier studies, the sociopolitical organization was the center of attention, in this volume the economic component will be central. This means that the focus lies on the economy, and the other components will be included only as far as they are relevant for understanding the economy. To illustrate these views, we first give a detailed example of the complex interaction occurring between the economic life, the ideology, the societal format and the sociopolitical organization.

We will use for this example Van Bakel's analysis of the sociopolitical systems of five Polynesian societies: traditional Hawaii, Mangareva, the Marquesas Islands, Rapa, and Samoa (Van Bakel 1989). In many respects the ideological background of these societies was identical: a shared common Polynesian origin. Also the economic basis of the five societies showed many similarities with only minor differences (see the chapters 11 and 12). Yet there were important differences among the types of sociopolitical organization. Where the Hawaii Islands qualified as early states, traditional Samoan societies never developed further than the village organization. The Marquesas Islands had a more complex structure, but here the individual qualities of the leaders played a dominant role which made them more similar to Melanesian big men than to Polynesian chiefs (in the sense of Sahlins 1963). Rapan society was divided in a number of well-organized autonomous entities. Mangareva, finally, was organized into one system, with sharp distinctions between elite and commoners. Van Bakel even speaks here of "social classes" (1989, 231). The differences in sociopolitical organization developed in a complex interaction with the societal format (the number of people in relation to the means of production and the spatial distribution of the population; Claessen and Van de Velde 1987, 6) and the ideology. The ideological factor appeared to be relatively adaptive to the local situation, though always remaining within the general pattern of the Polynesian world of thought. Very different patterns of sociopolitical organization were legitimized with basically the same ideology. The problem then became the question why and how such a variety of forms, all rooted in the same basic culture, developed. The answer lies, according to Van Bakel, in a tension between the means of production and the number of inhabitants. Where, as in traditional Samoa, the number of people in relation to the means of production was low, there was abundance, and nobody could be forced to obey the local potentates. Only a small surplus was produced, and this was not sufficient to sustain a complex political apparatus. With a number of early states, the Hawaii Islands had the most complex organization in Van Bakel's sample. There was a high population density and a highly developed agricultural production. A large surplus was produced, which helped to sustain a hierarchy of officials. For the commoners there was no chance here, as in Samoa, to escape the burden of taxation and labor, since there was no open space left. Indeed, there are indications that the population had reached its maximum size. In contrast, Mangareva had only a small population and very limited resources, yet a political hierarchy had developed there as well. The commoners were subject to a harsh and demanding—but yet legitimized—government. The fact that the population lived in small groups on a number of dispersed small beaches prevented cooperation and made it possible for the rulers to maintain their sway. This was a society in decline, and soon after the arrival of the Europeans it collapsed. The situation in the Marquesas Islands was not so very different from Mangareva. Groups of people lived in small valleys, each under the leadership of a big man. The rugged nature of the mountains made it difficult to contact other groups, and lack of a reef made contacts by sea dangerous. Climatic disasters repeatedly damaged harvests and the only way to survive in such cases was warfare to get food. The limited resources and the great isolation of the valleys made it impossible for aspiring leaders to build a sufficient powerbase, while the formation of an all-embracing unity of island chiefs was also seriously hampered. Rapa, finally, showed a stable situation. The comparatively great population density made an intensive horticulture necessary; the fairly stable climate made a high production possible. This enabled the Rapans to develop small, well-organized chiefdoms, but then developments came to a standstill. Each of the chiefs lived with his people in a virtually impregnable mountaintop fort. This defensive isolation of the groups prevented unification and further organizational ramification.

Apparently, none of the factors mentioned can be singled out as causative in the political development of the five groups; there is no common factor, nor is only one factor responsible for local change in any of the cases. Economy played a role, but also population pressure, and ideology. The sociopolitical organization was cause as well as result of what happened. The evolution of the Polynesian cultures was occasioned by a complex interaction of a number of factors, economy being one of them.

Redistribution, Reciprocity, Taxation

The emergence of the (early) state is considered usually a qualitative reorganization of society; the state organization is fundamentally different from its predecessors. Tribal organization, therefore, is related to a different category. Though the drawing of the demarcation lines is always a matter of arbitrary criteria (for example, Fried 1979), most scholars will agree with the principle (for a different view, Smith 1985). Yet, the early state organization was not completely new; it evolved from earlier forms of sociopolitical organization, and elements of earlier forms persist for some time in the newer one (Claessen and Skalník 1978, 622).

This holds, among other things, for the economy. In the general economy of the early state, and also in the field of political economy, the changes were generally limited. However, in this volume Van Bakel compares the political economy of Hawaiian early states with the economic organization of Samoa; here the differences were considerable. In Hawaii a clear division of society was found, while Samoan leaders hardly had the possibility to order their people. The Hawaiian early state had coercive power at its center, but in Samoa hardly so. This difference indicates that Samoa was a simple chiefdom (if it could be named a chiefdom at all), and the Hawaii Islands a strongly developed early state (see also Valeri 1985). When comparisons would have been made between a more complex chiefdom, such as the We (Geary 1976), or the Rukuba (Muller 1980), and an inchoate early state such as Ankole (Steinhart 1978, 1985), or the Wolof (Tymowski, chapter 5), the differences would have been much less marked.

It can be assumed, therefore, that the organization of the political economy of inchoate early states had a lot in common with that of complex chiefdoms. The most important common characteristic of these polities was *redistribution*. Several definitions of this concept have been proposed; we will follow the formulation of George Dalton (1980, 31): redistribution will be spoken of when "a sizeable fraction of ordinary and special goods and labour services [is] acquired by the political/religious centre(s) for the material support of the ruler and his elite servants, and allocated by the centre for public services of defence, religious observance, roads, shrines, aid to the needy and such like." As the amount of power to enforce acquisitions in chiefdoms is smaller as in early states—as Van Bakel illustrates in chapter 11—the quantity of goods circulating in the redistributive system of chiefdoms will be smaller too. Generally speaking, redistribution is a form of asymmetric reciprocity (Orenstein 1981). The ruler receives goods,

food, and labour, with which he covers the expenses of government—including the rewarding of his faithful—while those who
contribute his riches are compensated mainly in the ideological
sphere. The ruler "guarantees" fertility of women, cattle, and
land; the ruler "guarantees" peace and prosperity. Also, the ruler
has temples built and irrigation works and roads constructed.
Even when a ruler succeeds in converting his gifts from goods
and food into more ideological returns, his household remains
expensive. Rulers are continually haunted by their followers for
more and higher rewards, and they probably never succeed in
meeting their obligations completely. The tension between income and expenses in, for example, Tahiti (Claessen, chapter 12)
is a point in case. Even gifts for the ruler that were still under
construction or in preparation—canoes, or barkcloth—were already promised to greedy followers, who impatiently waited for
the moment of completion to snatch them away. Similarly, political leaders are known to have been ruined completely by trying
to comply with their obligations toward their followers. This not
only occurred to the nobles in Gaul who tried to bring together
large retinues to combat the Roman legions (Roymans 1987, 146ff.),
but also to the Merovingian kings of early France who, once they
had handed out their landed property found their faithful followers—their retinue—gone too (Claessen 1985, 201).

The obligations of rulers were many, and their income was
often considerably less than their expenses (Cohen, chapter 4).
Janssen (1987, 30) gives an overview of, on the one hand, the
mobilization of goods and labour services, and, on the other, the
types of expenses a ruler should take care of. He divides the
expenses into (1) the maintenance of the political system and (2)
the maintenance of society. In the first category he places the
expenses made for feasts, the building of palaces, the royal tombs,
the costs of the harem, the rewards of the royal servants, and so
forth. In the second category he places the salaries of civil servants, the costs of defense, the costs of the infrastructure (roads,
bridges, irrigation works, and so forth), and "social security,"
including the maintenance of temples, priests, and offerings. It
is not always easy to make a clear distinction between income
and expense: the citizen who fulfilled his military duties paid

taxation-in-labour, but received in return weapons, rations, and the like (Van der Vliet 1987a, 1987b).

An important feature of a redistributive system is that some form of reciprocity lies at its basis. The more the system develops the more reciprocity will become asymmetrical: the government receives goods, food, and services, and the population receives ideological rewards in return. Of course the picture is more complex, for many individuals also receive material rewards, or profit greatly from the roads or from the irrigation works. Conversely, the ruler at the apex of the system sometimes does not profit very much himself. "My treasure is always empty" one of the Merovingian kings lamented, according to Gregory of Tours (1974, 6:46). Yet, reciprocity is the basic characteristic of the system. The ruler hands out—in person or by proxy—a considerable part of the state income. The implications of the "gifts by the king" (Janssen 1984) should be considered more closely here, for they were an expression of the social relations between the ruler and the donee. By accepting the gift the donee demonstrated his being the *minor*; through his giving the ruler proved to be the *major*. From that moment on, the minor was under obligations to the major (Mauss 1970; Sahlins 1965; Janssen 1984, 52). Such gift giving thus had nothing to do with generosity or friendship; gifts were calculated and obligatory. On the side of the citizen, gifts to the ruler contained aspects of taxation: he was not free to give or not to give. On the side of the ruler, gifts were a form of remuneration or an effort to create ties of dependency: he was not free in giving either (see chapters 4, 5, 8, and 9). As long as a state government fulfilled its obligations toward the population in a reasonable way, its legitimacy was not questioned by the population (Kurtz 1984, 303). Even so, the image of the "benevolent lord" was created, the ruler, who cared for the well-being of the population (Claessen 1978, 563–67). "One of the hallmarks of nobility was the ostentatious display of wealth, coupled with openhanded generosity to friends and followers" (Sawyer 1979, 149).

This seems the appropriate place to make a distinction between tax and tribute. But let us be clear at the outset: tribute is what *we* choose to call tribute, tax is what *we* choose to call tax; definitions are arbitrary. On the other hand, there is a set of meanings traditionally and customarily associated with each of these terms (for an overview, see Pershits 1979). Normally, *tribute* is connected with requisitions, occasional as well as on a more regular basis, from conquered groups. Tribute thus is connected with booty: the plunder by a successful army or by a party of raiders. Tribute, however, is somewhat more formal than booty; the defeated population is told what the victor expects them to render yearly (or monthly, or occasionally): maidens, cattle, money, food. The collection of tribute is left to the defeated themselves. *Tax*, in contradistinction, is found in a situation of reciprocity, that is, where redistribution takes place. This means that those who fall within the scope of a redistributive network do pay tax; those outside this scope pay tribute (for a slightly different view, see Trouwborst 1987). This implies that part of the population of an early state is taxed, while another part has tributary obligations (chapters 4, 8, and 10; also, Skalník 1981, 340). This same problem was faced by Willems (1986, 378–80), when discussing the boundaries of the Roman Empire. He divided the state territory into three zones: (1) unified by military action; (2) centralized under uniform civil administration; (3) economically integrated. It seems reasonble to expect tributary relations in zone 1, where subjection and military administration was dominant. Tax began in zone 2, once the subjected groups were placed under civil administration—though a mixture of both forms seems probable here. In zone 3 taxation will be prevalent.

Generally, tax and tribute in early states were paid in goods and services. Most early states lacked monetization (but see chapters 4 and 10). All commerce was barter. Yet, values were regularly expressed in some standard; references were made to quantities of copper, silver, or grain, although usually none of these materials was directly involved in the transaction. Janssen (1975, 177), calls this "money-barter" and adds that such a system is "fairly intricate and poses a number of problems" (to us).

State functionaries formulated their requirements in specific quantities by referring to the equivalents in silver, copper, and so forth. As great quantities of food and goods were handed over as tax or tribute to the state, state officials developed means to handle these too. Serious problems were posed by the often perishable nature of the food and by the quantities of goods which heavily strained both storage and transport facilities. To reduce transport, often food and goods were stored locally or regionally. The ruler and his court, travelling through the realm, visited these depots in turn and consumed the goods on the spot (Kobishchanov 1987). Another solution was found in dividing the collected goods into two categories: staple and wealth. D'Altroy and Earle (1985; also Earle 1987) use this distinction in their analysis of the ways in which the Inca organization was financed. According to them, the greater part of the goods—the staple goods—remained in the local and regional storehouses and never left the region of production (also Moore 1958). It was kept there and used to cover local and regional expenses and as a reserve for times of need or war. Only the choiciest objects—the wealth—went to Cuzco, the governmental center, to finance the expenses of the central government.

The division of state budget into staple finance and wealth finance, was certainly not limited to the realm of the Incas. In many early states a similar system was found, if only for the simple reason that the costs of transport of great quantities of goods over long distances were too high (Drennan 1984). Thus, the complex economy of the Aztecs, for example, was based on this same principle (Hicks 1986, 1987, and chapter 8); Brumfiel 1987 and chapter 7; Bray 1977); even so, the rulers of the Javanese early state of Majapahit distinguished wealth and staple goods (Hall 1985, 234); and the Nepalese rulers let the government servants collect their income from fields in the region where they were stationed (chapter 10).

An Addition to Redistribution: Prestige Goods

The use of wealth as a means of financing the early state can possibly be described under the heading of prestige goods. This concept is extensively used by Kasja Ekholm (1977; see also chapter 2). Referring especially to the kingdom of Kongo, where the ruler converted "money into human beings", she defines prestige goods as "products which are not necessary for material subsistence, but which are absolutely indispensable for the maintenance of social relations" (1977, 119). Here prestige goods were going down the social hierarchy, and women and slaves moved upwards in return (1977, 120). Such a system functions only when the prestige goods can be monopolized by one of the parties. In the case of Kongo, the ruling group dominated the vital connections with the Portuguese. As long as this monopoly could be maintained the prestige goods system flowered. When, however, the Portuguese started to also trade with other persons in the kingdom, the system collapsed and the established hierarchy broke down (Ekholm 1977, 128ff.).

Now the question can be posed whether it is possible to extend the concept of prestige goods, and, for example, to consider landed property as a prestige good too? This question is suggested by the many instances on record, where such transfers were important. For instance, by handing out land to their followers, the Merovingians—and later the Carolingians—converted a possession (not money) into support. Landed property was of tremendous value in early medieval France (McKitterick 1983, 30ff.). It was not only a means of subsistence for the nobility, but it was also indispensable in the maintenance of their social relations. Land was a bridal gift; it was donated to cloisters to guarantee the saving of their precious souls; the possesion of land was above all a matter of prestige. Similar practices are known from other feudal societies, such as Japan and Mughal India (Barnes, 1987; Van der Wee 1984). It seems, therefore, that Ekholm's definition should be rephrased in a more general way: whenever a group controls the use and flow of goods that are indispensable to the maintenance of social relations by the remainder of society, these goods can be called prestige goods, especialy when they command return gifts of social or technical support to the monopolists.

Apart from the nobility, in medieval Europe the clerics were also rewarded lavishly for serving the interests of the ruler. Clerics promoted greatly the ideological foundations of the early state by proclaiming the sanctity of law and by stressing the sacral qualities of the ruler (Claessen 1978, 555–59). In return the ruler protected the Church and contributed lavishly to the maintenance of the clerics. Of course, the better the organization of the Church, the more the ruler had to donate. When the Carolingians took over the government, they needed the help of the Church to construct some form of sacrality as a backing against the sacrality of the Merovingians and also to give an aura of legitimacy to their rebellion (Claessen 1985, 202). The resulting obligations towards Church and nobility induced the Carolingians to a never ending series of wars to conquer land and tribute to pay their debts.

Such interactions between state and church were not limited to Western Europe. Gunawardana, for example, points to the enormous number of Buddhist monks in Anuradhapura, the capital of the early state in Sri Lanka. "At the height of its affluence it is likely that Anuradhapura supported about 10,000 clerics" (Gunawardana 1989, 159). In another article he described the royal gift giving to Buddhist monasteries as a kind of potlatch (1981, 136). Indeed, such gift giving sometimes ruined the economy of the state, and the rulers ended in troubles. In Southeast Asia, similar obligations towards monks and other clerics were met with the same disastrous consequences for the state organization (Hagesteijn 1987, 1989; Kulke 1982). The potlatch is the logical outcome of the vicious circle of prestige and hierarchy construction, as noted long ago by Mauss (1970), Godelier (1966), Friedman (1979), and others.

The need for prestige goods promoted long distance exchange considerably. For example, Haselgrove (1982, 80) points to a prestige goods system found in Britain shortly before the Roman conquest, in which tribal leaders exported slaves, cattle, hides, gold, silver, iron, corn, hunting dogs, and imported ivory necklaces, bracelets, amber, glassware, amphorae filled with wine, olive oil, pickled olives, and the like. There are also known ethnographic cases of luxury goods that were traded over long distances: The Trobriand *kula* (Malinowski 1922) is perhaps the best known case in point, as is the exchange of salt for axes by the Australian Yir Yoront (Sharp 1953). Where, however, powerful political leaders occupied themselves with long distance trade, exchange increased considerably (chapters 6 and 9). In this respect Van de Velde (1985), Champion (1982, 71), and Champion and Champion (1986, 62) point to Central Europe Iron Age early states centered around the *oppida* of the Heuneburg and Mont Lassois. The rich royal burial mounds there contained among other things Greek and Etruscan bronze vessels, Attican red and black painted ware, Greek wine amphorae, coral, and amber. These goods were all connected with long distance trade, especially with the Mediterranean. In exchange were probably given raw materials such as ores, grain, salted meat, and slaves too. Where exchange of such bulky goods is concerned, it is implicit in the argument that transport facilities of some kind existed: roads, carts, horses, oxen, and eventually the possibility of transport by water, as in Cahokia (chapter 6). Where transport facilities were limited to human porters, the amount of goods, as well as the distances covered diminished greatly of necessity (see also Drennan 1984). Such systems of long distance trade were found everywhere. Barrett Jones describes them for medieval Java; Gunawardana (1981, 1985) discusses long distance trade in early Sri Lanka, Elizabeth Brumfiel, and Frederic Hicks describe such a system for the Aztecs, and Rien Ploeg discusses the Early States of the Maya in this perspective (chapters 7, 8, and 9).

War and Income

Notwithstanding the fact that most early states were agrarian and produced considerable surpluses in food and goods (we are aware of the pitfalls of this concept; cf. Haas 1984), the demands of the state organization often could not be met. Reference was made already to the Carolingians, who, in order to meet the demands of Church and nobility, had no other option than an endless series of wars of conquest. Conquered lands were handed out to followers; tributes were handed out to clerics and cloisters; subjugated peoples became the serfs of victorious Franks. As long as the war machine produced a sufficient amount of tribute, the position of the Carolingians was unassailable; however, when their war machine stopped, the collapse of their realm was near at hand. The Carolingians were but one of the many ruling feudal families which, in order to survive, fought endless wars. To get European goods the rulers of Dahomey had to sell slaves, and to catch slaves they had to make war on neighbouring peoples, and to fight these wars they needed more European weapons, and so on (Claessen 1990). The same held for the rulers of Asante, who also became involved in the slave trade, the wish for European goods, and war with neighbouring peoples (Luig 1981; Chazan 1988). Asante, however, was so fortunate that, when the slave trade was abolished, its gains could be replaced by those of trade in other goods such as kola nuts (Wilks 1975). Also the Incas were "forced" to war. In their case wars were occasioned by a mixture of economic and ideological factors. In the Cuzco area, the Incas emerged as the dominant group from a cycle of tribal wars; in their myths, the victory of Pachacutec was decisive. Added to this was an ideological motive: the existence of the royal *panacas* (Conrad and Demarest 1984). It was customary that the descendants of a deceased ruler—except his successor—would remain together, living from the possessions of the deceased. All his belongings were reserved for the *panaca*, obliging his successor to bring together a treasure for his own descendants himself. This meant war and tribute, which caused never ending problems with subjected peoples. War was followed by subjection, and subjection was followed by rebellion. Meanwhile, the rulers in Cuzco concentrated great quantities of wealth in the center, leaving the staple goods in the provinces. However, their legitimacy in the eyes of the subjugated peoples remained weak or nonexistent (Toland 1987; Claessen 1990). The problems connected with war and conquest notwithstanding, many early states took recourse to these means to make ends meet. In this volume examples of this policy can be found in chapters 3, 4, 5, and 10. It is not clear, however, how far this should be considered a general feature of early states. Especially chapter 9, on the Mayas, points to a completely different strategy, namely "pooling" instead of conquering.

Private Enterprise as a Factor

Above, attention has been focused on the ruling elites and their manipulation of the state resources. In the field of economics, however, many developments were triggered by activities of citizens who also followed their own interests and looked for private profits only. Though in some cases traders were governmental functionaries—as in Asante or in the Aztec Empire—they operated side by side with private entrepreneurs. In fact, a whole sector of the economy existed outside the redistributive structure of the state. Even in societies with a relatively underdeveloped economy, such as traditional Tahiti or Tonga (chapter 12), non-state entrepreneurial activities were found: exchanges (barter) of goods, production on demand. This implied that there were specialists. There was also a clear understanding of value-for-money, for, when the British arrived, regular markets were soon established. In other early states economic activities outside the governmental arrangements are attested to. Janssen (1975, 162–65) points to commerce in articles of food, such as bread and wine in Ancient Egypt, and elsewhere he concludes to the existence of markets in the New Kingdom (Janssen 1980).

Though the development of trade and markets could occur very well without interference of the state organization, it is clear that the existence of a more complex political organization could be supportive for these private enterprises. Protection by state functionaries, and the maintenance of law and order in large areas are conditions promoting trade and commerce. On the other hand, the more trade and commerce grew, the more the demands by the state in the form of tolls and taxes increased (chapter 10). Before this would happen, however, trade had to grow so as to become noticed by the rulers; as long as it concerned only a few traders, and the quantity of goods was but limited, the redistributive system—connected with prestige goods—remained dominant. In the Frankish state of the Merovingians, for example, trade and markets were small and of local and, at the most, of regional importance only (Hodges 1982, 38, 53; Sawyer 1979, 144; McKitterick 1983, 20ff.) In early medieval England, on the other hand, efforts by the rulers to promote trade and markets were successful, and already by the seventh century, special royal functionaries charged with the task of controling trade are mentioned (Hodges 1982, 55). While in England the efforts to promote the economy were successful (also Sawyer 1979, 153, 156), conscious efforts by the Carolingians hardly met with success (Hodges 1982, 155). Whether this was occasioned by their weaker governmental organization or by the vastness of their realm is not easy to decide. The fact is, however, that pillage by the Vikings notwithstanding, British trade steadily increased, while trade and commerce in France did not really develop till the twelfth century. That the protection of the state promoted trade and markets considerably is also illustrated by the situation in Assyria and Anatolia, about 1800 B.C. In an analysis of the connections between the Anatolian port of trade Kültepe (formerly Kanesh) and the political centre Assur, archaeologists Gledhill and Larsen (1982) give a description of an intricate and complex trade system. The Assyrian traders had their home base in Assur (Gledhill and Larsen 1982, 209); Kanesh was the main Assyrian settlement in Anatolia, but there were several more. The administrative center for the entire network of commercial establishments was located in Kanesh. There was a town council in Kanesh and a number of administrative functionaries, but still the trade district was directly subordinated to the Assembly of the City of Assur; envoys from Assur regularly assisted in the political and diplomatic activities of Kanesh. The private level is a reflection of the governmental structure. In the mother city there were a number of merchant houses, which were directed by men who clearly formed part of the elite of the city (Gledhill and Larsen 1982, 210). The men and women in Kanesh and the other commercial establishments functioned basically as agents for the Assyrian houses. Also documented are special investments and partnership contracts, which gave a fund of money to an individual trader. The market in Assur remained the transit point where all commercial circuits intersected. Gledhill and Larson continue:

> The texts allow us to describe the caravan transactions in great detail, and there can hardly be doubt that the investments were made by private individuals and firms. Goods bought in Assur are in all cases that can be documented by the texts paid for with private funds— often silver sent back from Kanesh as the proceeds from the sale of previous shipments (1982, 212).

There were obligations to pay tax on the caravan trade, but, as Gledhill and Larsen state, this amounted to only 5 percent of the silver value of the shipment. They concluded that the substantivist views of early state economies as being characterized by the absence of markets and state regulation are contradicted by their findings. The Assyrian trade should rather be interpreted in terms of an interplay of "centralization and bureaucratic forms on the one hand, and decentralization and private economy on the other" (Gledhill and Larsen 1982, 213). A conclusion that is confirmed in our discussion of the early state economy in the second section of this introduction.

Some Comments on the Theoretical Contributions

Several times in the discussion the ethnographic contributions to this volume have been mentioned. In the present section some short remarks with regard to the more theoretical contributions will be made, intended mainly to situate them in relation to the views formulated thus far.

Estellie Smith (chapter 1) gives a short general treatise on the concept of political economy. As a starting point she takes the view that all polities depend on "the crucial building blocks" of accumulation, bureaucratization, and capitalization. According to Smith, political economy can be defined as "economic behavior as affected by political concerns of various competing polities and interrelated, multinational market forces." Since her views are expressed in general terms they should be applicable to the situation in early states. Accumulation of income by the state is crucial; if not available in sufficient quantities, the polity will decline or even collapse (see also, Kennedy 1987). Accumulation can be extended in several ways: by expanding the internal production, by preying on weaker polities, or by seeking additional resources through trade and gifts. Examples of each of these ways have been presented in the preceding sections. The shift from nonstate to state is defined by Smith in terms of the shift from "loyal retainers" to "dedicated civil servants." Though we agree with the idea, we are afraid that the drawing of the line will be difficult. There are on the one hand early states where retainers are found side by side with civil servants, and there are, on the other hand, individual functionaries whose activities lie somewhere in between; under some circumstances they are "dedicated civil servants" and under other "loyal retainers"; the Frankish state of the Capetians being a case in point (see also Guenée 1988). Her use of formalist terms such as "income" and "capital" we can agree with; in fact we have approached early state economies with different paradigms ourselves. Again we agree with a distinction between private and public, but we feel that it is more likely that these labels are applicable to the poles of a continuum, rather than to clear-cut institutional opposition. Fortunately, in her conclusion, Smith states the same feelings of uncertainty in this respect.

Aidan Southall, in chapter 2, discusses the distinction between centralized and noncentralized polities. By (politically) centralized he means that "institutions of power are significantly gathered at the center" and, in fact, "exercise ultimate authority

throughout the territory of the state." But few of the preindustrial
states—early states—were truly centralized, in his opinion. The
main concept with which to analyze and describe centralization
is the Asiatic mode of production. He contrasts this mode to the
feudal mode of production, with decentralization as its main characteristic. The two complex, competing tendencies—centralization and decentralization—"are bound to occur at least in all
large precapitalist state societies where power is unequally distributed." We agree, though we wish to point out that the difference between the Asiatic mode and the feudal mode is more
a matter of different relations between the people concerned,
than of a different political structure (Claessen and Van de Velde
1981). As Smith does, Southall also points to the crucial difference
between state and nonstate societies, especially in the field of
economics. He asks for more and better data on this shift that
must have taken place over and again, in order to better understand how early states have arisen. Though we do agree with him,
we will not elaborate this problem here, as it falls outside the
scope of this volume.

Albert Trouwborst (chapter 3), finally, tries to find an answer
to the question whether the early states of the Interlacustrine area
of East Africa "could be said to posses each a political economy
and to what extent their economies were administered and controlled from the center." As in his earlier studies (Trouwborst
1987), his concepts of tax and tribute differ slightly from the
definitions proposed in our present introduction. This, however,
is of no consequence to his central questions. Regarding centralization, Trouwborst states that the king in a sense "acted as
the centre of distribution"; in practice, however, much of "the
tribute and corvée-labor remained at local levels," a situation we
found in the majority of early states. Royal control of the districts
was minimal, and the same was found at all levels of administration. Still, much of the economic activities took place "in the
name of the king" and was legitimized in that way. The junction
of long distances, lack of infrastructure, lack of a control apparatus, and so forth inevitably had to result in this form of political
economy. On these points, Smith, Southall and Trouwborst fully
agree—and we concur too. Under such circumstances the man-

agerial role of the rulers was of necessity limited—though not completely absent (as Trouwborst also states).

References

Bakel, Martin A. van
1989   *Samen leven in gebondenheid en vrijheid; Evolutie en ont-
            wikkeling in Polynesië.* Ph.D.thesis, University of Leiden.
Barnes, Gina L.
1987   The role of the *be* in the formation of the Yamato state.
            In *Specialization, exchange, and complex societies*, ed. E.
            M. Brumfiel and T. K. Earle, 86–101. Cambridge: Cam-
            bridge University Press,
Barrett Jones, Antoinette M.
1984   *Early tenth century Java from the inscriptions.* Dordrecht:
            Foris. [Verhandelingen of the Royal Institute of Linguis-
            tics and Anthropology No. 107].
Bloch, Maurice
1983   *Marxism and anthropology.* Oxford: Oxford University
            Press.
Bray, Warwick
1977   Civilising the Aztecs. In *The evolution of social systems*,
            ed. J. Friedman and M. J. Rowlands, 373–400. London:
            Duckworth.
Brumfiel, Elizabeth M.
1987   Elite and utilitarian crafts in the Aztec state. In *Speciali-
            zation, exchange, and complex societies*, ed. E. M. Brum-
            fiel and T. K. Earle, 102–18. Cambridge: Cambridge Uni-
            versity Press.
Brumfiel, Elizabeth M. and Timothy K. Earle, eds.
1987   *Specialization, exchange, and complex societies.* Cam-
            bridge: Cambridge University Press.
Champion, Sara
1982   Exchange and ranking: the case of coral. In *Ranking, re-
            source, and exchange*, ed. C. Renfrew and S. Shennan,
            67–72. Cambridge: Cambridge University Press.
Champion, Timothy and Sara Champion
1986   Peer polity interaction in the European Iron Age. In *Peer
            polity interaction and socio-political change*, ed. C. Ren-
            frew and J. F. Cherry, 59–68. Cambridge: Cambridge
            University Press.
Chazan, Naomi
1988   The early state in Africa: the Asante case. In *The early
            state in African perspective*, ed. S. N. Eisenstadt, M. Abit-
            bol, and N. Chazan, 60–97. Leiden: Brill.

Claessen, Henri J. M.
1978   The early state: a structural approach. In *The early state*,
               ed. H. J. M. Claessen and P. Skalník, 533–96. The Hague:
               Mouton.
1985   From the Franks to France. In *Development and decline;
               The evolution of sociopolitical organization*, ed. H. J. M.
               Claessen, P. van de Velde, and M. E. Smith, 196–218.
               South Hadley: Bergin and Garvey.
1990   Alleen staten voeren oorlog. In *Beschermers en bedreigers;
               Militairen en de vroege staat*, ed. H. J. M. Claessen, 187–
               99. Leiden: Instituut voor Culturele Antropologie [ICA
               Publ. 85].
Claessen, Henri J. M. and Peter Skalník, eds.
1978   *The early state*. The Hague: Mouton.
Claessen, Henri J. M. and Pieter van de Velde
1981   Een intercultureel model voor het feodalisme. In *Evo-
               matica; Een bundel opstellen rond het onderwerp evolutie*,
               ed. P. van de Velde, 203–15. Leiden: Instituut voor Cul-
               turele Antropologie [ICA Publ. 42].
1985   The evolution of sociopolitical organization. In *Develop-
               ment and decline; The evolution of socio-political organi-
               zation*, ed. H. J. M. Claessen, P. van de Velde, and
               M. E. Smith, 1–12, 126–40, 246–63. South Hadley: Ber-
               gin and Garvey.
1987   Introduction. In *Early state dynamics*, ed. H. J. M. Claes-
               sen and P. van de Velde, 1–23. Leiden: Brill.
Conrad, Geoffrey W. and Arthur A. Demarest,
1984   *Religion and empire; The dynamics of Aztec and Inca ex-
               pansion*. Cambridge: Cambridge University Press.
Cook, Scott
1973   Economic anthropology: problems in theory, method, and
               analysis. In *Handbook of social and cultural anthropology*,
               ed. J. J. Honigman, 795–860. Chicago: Rand McNally.
1974   "Structural substantivism": a critical review of Marshall
               Sahlin's Stone Age Economics. *Comparative Studies in
               Society and History* 16:355–79.
Dalton, George
1969   Theoretical issues in economic anthropology. *Current An-
               thropology* 10:63–102.
1978   The impact of colonization on aboriginal economies in
               stateless societies. *Research in Economic Anthropology*
               1:131–84.
1980   Anthropological models in archaeological perspective. In
               Pattern of the past, ed. I. Hodder, 17–48. Cambridge:
               Cambridge University Press.

D'Altroy, Terence N. and Timothy K. Earle
1985   Staple finance, wealth finance, and storage in the Inka political economy. *Current Anthropology* 26:187–206.
Danilova, Ludmilla V.
1971   Controversial problems of the theory of precapitalistic societies. *Soviet Anthropology and Archeology* 9:269–327
Drennan, Robert D.
1984   Long-distance transport costs in pre-Hispanic Mesoamerica. *American Anthropologist* 86:105–12.
Earle, Timothy K.
1987   Specialization and the production of wealth: Hawaiian chiefdoms and the Inka empire. In *Specialization, exchange, and complex societies*, ed. E. M. Brumfiel and T. K. Earle, 64–75. Cambridge: Cambridge University Press.
Ekholm, Kasja
1977   External exchange and the transformation of Central African social systems. In *The evolution of social systems*, ed. J. Friedman and M. J. Rowlands, 115–36. London: Duckworth.
Firth, Raymond, ed.
1967   *Themes in economic anthropology.* London: Tavistock.
Fried, Morton H.
1979   Economic theory and first contact. In *New directions in political economy; An approach from anthropology*, ed. M. B. Léons and F. Rothstein, 3–18. Westport, Conn.: Greenwood Press.
Friedman, Jonathan
1979   *System, structure and contradiction: the evolution of "Asiatic" social formations.* Copenhagen: National Museum of Denmark.
Geary, Christraud
1977   *We. Die Genese eines Häuptlingtums im Grasland von Kamerun.* Wiesbaden: Steiner.
Geertz, Clifford
1980   *Negara. The theatre state in nineteenth century Bali.* Princeton: Princeton University Press.
Gledhill, J. and M. Larsen
1982   The Polanyi paradigm and a dynamic analysis of archaic states. In *Theory and explanation in archaeology*, ed. C. Renfrew, M. Rowlands, and B. A. Segraves, 197–229. New York: Academic Press.
Godelier, Maurice
1966   *Horizon, trajets marxistes en anthropologie.* Paris: Presses Universitaires de France.

Grader, C. J.
1984   The irrigation system in the region of Jembrana. In *Bali;
              Studies in life, thought, and ritual*, ed. L. J. Swellengrebel,
              267–88. Dordrecht: Foris Publications [Reprints on In-
              donesia, Royal Institute of Linguistics and Anthropology].
              (orig. ed. in Dutch 1939).
Gregory of Tours
1974   *The history of the Franks*. Ed. L. Thorpe. Harmonds-
              worth, Middlesex: Penguin Classics. (orig ed. 593).
Guenée, Bernard
1988   *States and rulers in later medieval Europe*. Oxford: Black-
              well.
Gunawardana, R. A. L. H.
1981   Social function and political power: a case study of state
              formation in irrigation society. In *The study of the state*,
              ed. H. J. M. Claessen and P. Skalník, 133–54. The Hague:
              Mouton.
1985   Total power or shared power? A study of the hydraulic
              state and its transformations in Sri Lanka from the third
              to the ninth century A.D. In *Development and decline; The
              evolution of sociopolitical organization*, ed. H. J. M. Claes-
              sen, P. van de Velde, and M. E. Smith, 219–45. South
              Hadley: Bergin and Garvey.
1989   Anuradhapura: ritual, power and resistance in a preco-
              lonial South Asian city. In *Domination and resistance*, ed.
              D. Miller, M. Rowlands, and Chr. Tilly, 155–78. London:
              Unwin Hyman.
Haas, Siegfried
1984   *Surplus—eine relative Grösse in der Gesellschaft; ein Bei-
              trag zur Wirtschaftsethnologie*. Vienna: Verlag der Oes-
              tereichischen Akademie der Wissenschaften.
Hagesteijn, Renée
1987   The Angkor state: rise, fall and in between. In *Early state
              dynamics*, ed. H. J. M. Claessen and P. van de Velde,
              154–69. Leiden: Brill.
1989   *Circles of kings; Political dynamics in early continental
              Southeast Asia*. Dordrecht: Foris Publications [Verhan-
              delingen of the Royal Institute of Linguistics and Anthro-
              pology No. 138].
Hall, Kenneth R.
1985   *Maritime trade and state development in early Southeast
              Asia*. Honolulu: University of Hawaii Press.
Haselgrove, C.
1982   Wealth, prestige and power: the dynamics of late Iron Age
              political centralisation in South-east England. In *Ranking,*

resource and exchange, ed. C. Renfrew and S. Shennan, 79–88. Cambridge: Cambridge University Press.

Hicks, Frederic
1986   Prehispanic background of colonial political and economic organization in Central Mexico. In *Supplement to the Handbook of Middle American Indians*, ed. V. R. Bricker. Vol. 4, *Ethnohistory*, ed. R. Spores, 35–54. Austin: University of Texas Press.
1987   First steps toward a market-integrated economy in Aztec Mexico. In *Early state dynamics*, ed. H. J. M. Claessen and P. van de Velde, 91–107. Leiden: Brill

Hodges, Richard
1982   *Dark age economics; The origins of towns and trade AD 600–1000*. London: Duckworth.

Humphreys, S.
1978   *Anthropology and the Greeks*. London: Routledge and Kegan Paul.

Janssen, Jac. J.
1975   Prolegomena to the study of Egypt's economic history during the New Kingdom. *Studien zur altägyptischer Kultur* 3:127–85.
1980   *De markt op de oever*. Leiden: Brill.
1984   Het geschenk des konings. In *Macht en majesteit; Idee en werkelijkheid van het vroege koningschap*, ed. H. J. M. Claessen, 51–59, Utrecht: De Bataafsche Leeuw.
1987   Redistributie in vroege staten. Een model. In *Verdelen en heersen? Redistributie en andere aspecten van het economisch bestel in en van vroege staten*, ed. M. A. van Bakel and E. Ch. L. van der Vliet, 23–38. Leiden: Instituut voor Culturele Antropologie [ICA Publications 77].

Kennedy, Paul
1987   *The rise and fall of the great powers*. New York: Vintage Books.

Kobishchanow, Yurii M.
1987   The phenomenon of *gafol* and its transformations. In *Early state dynamics*, ed. H. J. M. Claessen and P. van de Velde, 108–28. Leiden: Brill.

Kulke, Hermann
1982   State formation and legitimation in early Java. *Working Paper*. Bielefeld: University of Bielefeld.

Kurtz, Donald V.
1984   Strategies of legitimation and the Aztec state. *Ethnology* 23:301–14.

Luig, Ute
1981   Konstitutionsbedingungen des Ashanti-Reiches. In *His-*

torische Konstitutionsbedingungen des Staats, ed. E. Hanisch and W. Titzlaff, 118–86. Giessen: Europa Verlag.
Malinowski, Bronislaw
1922   *Argonauts of the Western Pacific*. New York: Dutton.
Marx, Karl
1964   *Pre-capitalist economic formations*. Ed. E. Hobsbawn. London: Lawrence and Wishart.
Mauss, Marcel
1970   *The gift* London: Cohen and West. (orig. ed. in French 1925).
McKitterick, Rosamund
1983   *The Frankish kingdoms under the Carolingians, 751–987*. London: Longman.
Moore, Sally Falk
1958   *Power and property in Inca Peru*. New York: Columbia University Press.
Muller, Jean-Claude
1980   *Le roi bouc émissaire*. Quebec: Fleury.
Orenstein, Henry
1981   Asymmetrical reciprocity: a contribution to the theory of political legitimation. *Current Anthropology* 21:69–91.
Pershits, Abraham I.
1979   Tribute relations. In *Political anthropology, the state of the art*, ed. S. L. Seaton and H. J. M. Claessen, 149–56. The Hague: Mouton.
Roymans, Nico
1987   *Tribale samenlevingen in Noord-Galliē: een antropologisch perspectief*. Ph.D. Thesis, University of Amsterdam.
Sahlins, Marshall D.
1963   Poor man, rich man, big man, chief: political types in Melanesia and Polynesia. *Comparative Studies in Society and History* 5:285–303.
1965   On the sociology of primitive exchange. In *The relevance of models for social anthropology*, ed. M. Banton, 139–236. London: Tavistock [ASA Monographs, no. 1].
1972   *Stone age economics*. Chicago: Aldine.
Sawyer, P. H.
1979   Kings and merchants. In *Early medieval kingship*, ed. P. H. Sawyer and I. N. Wood, 139–59. Leeds: School of History.
Sharp, Lauriston
1953   Steel axes for Stone Age Australians. In *Human problems in technological change*, ed. E. H. Spicer, 69–91. New York: Rusell Sage Foundation.
Skalník, Peter
1981   Some additional thoughts on the concept of the early state.

In *The study of the state*, ed. H. J. M. Claessen and P. Skalník, 339–52. The Hague: Mouton.

Smith, M. Estellie
1985   An aspectual analysis of polity formations. In *Development and decline: The evolution of sociopolitical organization*, ed. H. J. M. Claessen, P. van de Velde, and M. E. Smith, 97–125. South Hadley: Bergin and Garvey.

Steinhart, Edward I.
1978   Ankole: pastoral hegemony. In *The early state*, ed. H. J. M. Claessen and P. Skalník, 131–51. The Hague: Mouton.
1985   Food production and the evolution of Ankole. In *Development and decline; The evolution of sociopolitical organization*, ed. H. J. M. Claessen, P. van de Velde, and M. E. Smith, 264–75. South Hadley: Bergin and Garvey.

Terray, Emmanuel
1975   Classes and class consciousness in the Abron kingdom of Gyaman. In *Marxist analysis and social anthropology*, ed. M. Bloch, 85–113. London: Malaby [ASA Monographs no. 2].

Toland, Judith D.
1987   Discrepancies and dissolution: breakdown of the early Inca state. In *Early state dynamics*, ed. H. J. M. Claessen and P. van de Velde, 138–53. Leiden: Brill.

Trouwborst, Albert A.
1987   From tribute to taxation. On the dynamics of the early state. In *Early state dynamics*, ed. H. J. M. Claessen and P. van de Velde, 129–137. Leiden: Brill.

Valeri, Valerio
1985   *Kingship and sacrifice; Ritual and society in ancient Hawaii.* Chicago: University of Chicago Press.

Velde, Pieter van de
1985   Early state formation in Iron Age Central Europe. In *Development and decline; The evolution of sociopolitical organization*, ed. H. J. M. Claessen, P. van de Velde, and M. E. Smith, 170–82. South Hadley: Bergin and Garvey.

Vliet, Edward Ch. L. van der
1987a   Tyranny and democracy. The evolution of politics in ancient Greece. In *Early state dynamics*, ed. H. J. M. Claessen and P. van de Velde, 70–91. Leiden: Brill.
1987b   De betekenis van redistributie en de markt voor de ontwikkeling van de staat in de Griekse polis. In *Verdelen en heersen? Redistributie en andere aspecten van het economisch bestel van en in vroege staten*, ed. M. A. van Bakel and E. Ch. L. van der Vliet, 113–37. Leiden: Instituut voor Culturele Antropologie [ICA Publ. 77].

Wee, Maarten van der
1984   *Aziatische produktiewijze en Mughal India. Een historische en teoretische kritiek.* Ph.D.thesis, Catholic University of Nijmegen.
Wilks, Ivor
1975   *Asante in the Nineteenth century.* Cambridge: Cambridge University Press.
Willems, Willem J. H.
1986   *Romans and Batavians. A regional study in the Dutch eastern river area.* Ph.D.thesis, University of Amsterdam.

1

The ABCs of Political Economy

M. Estellie Smith

Thesis and Basic Assumptions

In growing number, anthropologists are attempting to explore various aspects of the appearance and evolution of states—considerations of their origin, spread, growth and decline, essential similarity, and irreversible dynamic at the macrolevel of history. When working in the troubled context of state polities one is sometimes driven, like Leibnitz, to ask "Why is there something rather than nothing?" How is it that such polity forms emerged, took shape, and continue to be replicated, always expanding, ever more corporate, and increasingly intrusive? The question is especially poignant when one considers that state polities require (may even have created) a sector of the populace particularly vulnerable to the demands of the state that, paradoxically, its citizenry be obliged to expand their networks of interdependency while simultaneously weakening their capacity to maintain relatively self-sufficient familial and neighborly interdependencies bonded by voluntary (that is, ideationally axiomatic) consensual rules of sharing the basic necessities of life. Indeed, on not a few

31

occasions, members of that sector requested and even urged a few governing elite to take from them what some have labeled these prime directives in the quest for survival.

Are we to assume that, due to some factor such as population growth or the rise of cities, some 5000 years ago there was a dramatic watershed in human affairs, a time in which some societies made this major transformation? And that another such watershed—this time due, say, to the explosion of European colonialism or the emergence of capitalism—occurred some 500 years ago, marking the emergence of the modern state? I think it more reasonable to assume that the process was gradual and marked by steps forward and back, to the side and around—as is the case with any socioculture's "dance with time." Structure and organization became increasingly complex as populations grew, resources became both more available and more scarce, and decision making (as well as the actual and perceived necessary information for making decisions) grew more complex.[1] The next few paragraphs present an encapsulated view of that *general* historical process in order to introduce the argument that critical to the transition from nonstate to state polity, as well as to the growth and maintenance or dissolution of States, were the interdependent components of resource *accumulation*, an institutionalized structure for managing, particularly, the accumulation of those resources (the *bureaucratization* of polities), and the utilization of those resources as political and economic *capital*.

Let me first address the paradox that has attracted the attention of many and centers on the issue of the shift from egalitarian to nonegalitarian society. As a growing number of scholars agree, this is an issue best set aside.[2] On the one hand, we have the arguments of those who maintain that, for much of human history, human society was marked by egalitarian, consensual decision making—for, if this is so, what were the processes which permitted the emergence of the state in relatively short-order and which essentially rested on the loss of these characteristics for the majority of the society? On the other hand, if—as an increasing number of scholars are arguing—the whole construct of egalitarian societies is, at best dubious and, at worst, counterproductive, we have the thorny problem of the emergence of classes in the stratified polities we label "states." Agreeing with Flanagan

(1989, 262) that, ". . . the idea of egalitarian and inequalitarian societies may mask the very problem into which we wish to enquire," this paper will set this question aside and focus on one of the processes by which increasing numbers of the members of given societies became enmeshed in the system of a polity formation that increasingly deprived individuals and households of their control over the everyday stuff of existence.

Governing Systems

That which we label "the governing system" of states, whatever form it takes, is a structure that evolves from the efforts of those who seek to organize and manage units in a synergistic network or networks which, ideally (at least from the organizational perspective), is afamilial in structure.[3] The aim of the human managers of that systemic structure and organization is (again, ideally) to support (1) a durative governing structure whose full-time occupants are maintained by and occupied with the political economy of the polity as a whole and (2) satisfy the wants and needs of the population at least at the minimal level necessary for the leaders, as well as the unit, to persist through time.

It is generally agreed that human macrohistory is marked by a shift from household and family units, whose primary concern for the private welfare of their own unit is, on the whole, socioculturally recognized, accepted, and socioculturally legitimated, to larger, more interdependently complex polities with an increasing number of nonfamilial units and a growing number of decisions and activities assumed by nonkin institutions. Such associational heterogeneity seems to be required if practical needs of decision makers are to be optimally satisfied. To give some extreme examples: Families can sell, reassign, or abandon "surplus" children even when household resources are adequate for their maintenance; owners buy, sell, or move individual slaves as utility dictates; whole villages of serfs have been sold and moved depending on the economic needs of the buyer and seller; modern workers are expected to be amenable to relocation ("voluntary" or opportunistic—and sometimes over vast distances) if rational management decisions based on cost/benefit analyses demand it; and polity leaders explicitly or covertly force large populations to shift from one region to another for such reasons of state as pacification, claiming a "legitimate" presence in some disputed locale, or furthering the polity's economic growth.

This shift (for the sake of brevity let me use Durkheim's terms and refer to the change from "mechanical" to "organic" society) has been accompanied by an increased emphasis by polity decision makers on what has come to be called "political economy." This term has gone through many metamorphoses since its origin in the seventeenth century and today has a range of meanings, some sharply divergent with others and frequently dependent on the user's ideology. The following is intended to be a neutral identification, designed to examine cross-culturally what is *internally* perceived as the political economy of a specific, targeted polity. It is constituted of those polity-centered, decision-making activities of governing personnel that center around the management of resources deemed germane to the polity's macrosystemic welfare as located in the interdependency of those constituent sectors, groups, and factors that the information selected identifies as relevant to such activities and the aims intended. Some caveats briefly stated are these: (1) Decisions may be delayed, intentionally or unintentionally, but the consequences of such delays must be included; (2) polity personnel cannot always make and implement what they perceived as relevant decisions, but actions relating to attempts to address such concerns nonetheless may have consequences and should be included in an examination of a polity's political economy; (3) that decisions deemed germane to the internal workings of any of the polity's productive, distributive, saving or investment, or consumptive activities may favor as well as select one sector or group of actors is not in point as we are concerned only with what the designated polity managers determine to be optimally beneficial for the polity, given the internal and external limitations and constraints under which they perceive themselves to be operating at the time.

The conceptual realization and identification of the process may be of recent vintage, but the dynamics themselves have been recognized and taken into account by polity leaders and others for much longer.[4]

The governing system of any polity usually comes about through the efforts of a limited group of individuals acting in concert to make decisions that satisfy the subsistence expectations of those who look to them as productive decision makers. Such caretakers may minimize centrifugal tendencies of the group by: (1) providing or holding out the promise of goods or Good; (2) being viewed as possessed of particular skills or information—acquired in secular or sacred fashion; or (3) occupying such positions in lieu of opposition or a better alternative (and this is true even when such occupancy is viewed as an hereditary right since the historical record abounds with examples of those "rightful" leaders who have been removed or excluded from such positions).

Governing structures emerge—with differing degrees of explicitness and pervasiveness—in all human societies. Their existence can be underwritten by a variety of strategems, for example, pragmatic appeal to enlightened self-interest, religious rule, physical power, or natural law. Their appearance is based on a number of factors: (1) the reluctance of not a few to take responsibility for or to engage in the additional labor involved in making decisions and, contrariwise, (2) the desire of some individuals in most groups to acquire additional prestige, authority, and power among their fellows; (3) the logical sequence from (a) goal fixing to (b) determining procedures to attain the goal that leads at least some to (c) work strenuously to obtain support for implementation of their own "best solution"; (4) the differential skills and abilities of individuals that (a) set high and low levels of performance within a group (b) suggest the need for exploitive organization and distribution of resources so that, ideally, there will be improved access to resources for the group as a whole and (c) leads to exchanges among those with differential resources (for example, grain for fish, labor for technical knowledge or protection, food for honor and respect); and finally (5) the widespread cultural belief that some have traditional rights, a natural claim to rule, while others can at best earn insecure entry.

All of this said, what (aside from maximizing personal aggrandizement) are the basic components of these polity-based management processes with which leaders must be concerned? This paper argues that, in both the transition from nonstate to state, and in the growth and, even more importantly, the maintenance of the state, all polities depend on the crucial building blocks of

1. *accumulation*—establishing a store of material resources;
2. *bureaucratization*—creating regularized and durative positions of decision making; and
3. *capitalization*—investing current resources in ways that attempt to assure that they will bring a future return.[5]

Accumulation

A critical factor in the formalization (regularization, systematization, institutionalization) and relative durability[6] of a governing system is the emergence of a production, storage, and distribution program ("system" is perhaps too strong a word in some contexts) to provide the surplus[7] necessary to underwrite the activities of, as well as validate, the social personae of those who are identified by others as primarily functioning as a polity manager or caretaker. The category includes not only leaders but, more importantly, those recognized as providing the assistance and services necessary for the implementation of the primary caretakers' decisions (for example, tax/tribute collectors, record keepers, scribes, messengers and heralds; bodyguards and military aides, advisors; regional managers and ambassadors).

Some few societies even today still rely little if at all on storage; consumers produce what they need on a more or less daily, weekly, or at most seasonal basis.[8] However, beyond this most basic level of marginally located hunters and gatherers, some sort of preservation and storage technology is required if provision for future scarcity is to be made. Necessary but not sufficient for the development of such technology is public knowledge about, awareness of, and concern for, first, such periods of scarcity alternating with those of abundance and, secondly, unforeseen catastrophic events that can drastically reduce the usual or even minimal level of resources coupled with the belief that human activity can forestall catastrophe.[9]

Just as important (but neither necessary or sufficient) may be the prior introduction of claims by hieratic figures to a portion of production "for the gods" and, as well, those directly responsible for caretaking and performing necessary rituals in earthly precincts.[10] More critical, I think, is public acceptance that some individuals have special knowledge of insuring abundance and defending against the occurrence of scarcity. Members of the polity must become consensually persuaded that without such steps in times of need things would have been worse—not better but worse. The majority of members, most of the time, must accept that there are capable individuals willing to shoulder the responsibility of budgeting current production and consumptive needs so that members of the polity as a whole will have an adequate accumulation at some future time.

Budgeting is a common human activity and most of us make dozens of budgetary decisions every day. These can range from deciding that the value of a little extra sleep in the morning is greater than the cost of doing several hours of work on nothing more than a hastily gulped cup of coffee, through deciding that the benefit of working in a profession we enjoy does not compensate for the risks of low income and uncertain employment we might face if we chose it, to such decisions as the worth of "peace in our time" versus the cost of going to war "to stop facism in Europe"—or "communism in Asia." If we define a budget as the socially or individually identified and prioritized estimates of the range of socioculturally available costs and benefits over a definite period of time, "choice" can be seen as primarily grounded in whatever information that, during the crisis of decision making, is both available and selected as necessary for our calculations. The extent to which we ignore or are ignorant of potential data for evaluating short- and long-term costs and benefits is also a measure of the extent to which we increase decision-making risk—and the possibility of inappropriate (bad, wrong, short-sighted, unrealistic) budgetary decisions.

It should be noted in passing that, while I have stressed actual storage of resources such as food, water, and seed for next year's crop, there are other ways that resources can be viewed as stored; the conscious imposition of consumption constraints of a non-domesticated resource permits storage "on the hoof," "in the water (or ground)," and, as well, "in the belly" via feasts for and gifts to other humans or the gods.

Archeological data indicate that, even in paleolithic times, individual households stored material resources; thus, the shift from private to public storage, familial to social accumulation, may have been relatively easy to make. More difficult, however, are the arrangements that must be instituted for periodic dispersal of the surplus.[11]

Accumulation has upper limits. For one thing, natural forces can make unpalatable or destroy the goods (mold, spoilage, animal predators). Further, even in the absence of such forces, stored surpluses can reach a point of making the additional labor to produce it, or the need to reduce current consumption, visibly and counterproductively redundant. As accumulated goods pile up, at least some begin to wonder why continue stockpiling and even grow to resent the need to keep working to produce that which seems likely never to be consumed. Worse, accumulation represents wealth that, while attracting desired others (that is, those who add to the material and nonmaterial resource base), also tends to draw undesired others—thieves, invaders, or those viewed as parasites or "free riders." Such concerns serve as attractive arguments to quit or rebel against the regime for those who would labor less. Finally, the process of accumulation itself may encourage some members to try to exercise greater managerial control—inventing ways to dispose of the surplus internally or externally, thereby expanding their leadership activities and, in the process, enhancing their own personal utilization of the resources (for example, exotic commodities are acquired under various guises but only the elite have access to them). Thus, while there are both costs and benefits to the linked processes of accumulation and controlled, periodic dispersal, the latter especially creates an organizational problem of no small dimensions if continued production (and thus a socially acceptable rationale for the caretaking activities of the leaders) is to be ensured.

Organizing the production of a surplus, monitoring its delivery, overseeing its storage, and arranging for its dispersal—internally in time of need or (so as to get rid of truly surplus stored accumulation) as a reward, celebration, as well as externally, in exchange—all must be handled by the polity stewards. They, in turn, require the assistance of those who are knowledgeable about the detailed procedures of production, distribution, and consumption at the polity level. This creates a cadre of middle-range leaders who may be being prepared for more senior positions. Historically, sociocultures first employed part-time nonprofessionals (lieutenants or assistants to the leaders), but, in time, as some societies expanded in size, density or both, such positions evolved, first, to recruit full-time nonprofessionals, sometimes with little skill or aptitude for their work (retainers personally loyal to a particular leader or individuals required as part of their "community service" to perform such duties for a given period of time), then, finally, those full-time professional civil servants who see their primary duty as allegiance to and maintenace of the polity per se.

This thesis suggests, then, that accumulation is the basis for the governing systems and, equally important, the economy of many polities, nonstates as well as states, a necessary (perhaps even sufficient) condition for states or would-be states. If such a fund does not exist for decision makers to draw on, they can at best be situational leaders, not uncommonly able to attract and manage others when they have resources, losing such ability when there are no resources. There is usually little else to manage on a regular basis in a self-sufficient, subsistence-based community; people fend for themselves and, when times are hard, the members simply begin splitting off and moving elsewhere. In time of crisis, the population is decimated or disperses, the polity as a social entity is said to have declined or, even worse, collapsed.

A greater risk emerges, however, if, for example, the leaders see the opportunity to accumulate more and at a faster rate or if, with the advent of catastrophe, the depletion of accumulated resources threatens leaders with the loss of members and, hence, their roles as leaders. For these and other reasons, the caretakers may decide to "borrow" resources from elsewhere.

In modern economics, the national or public debt is usually defined as sums owed by governments to holders of government-issued promissory forms (bonds, notes, bills, and so forth) and requiring payment to said holders of specified amounts at specified times. Since anthropologists must adjust such definitions if they are to work in a cross-cultural, cross-temporal frame, the definition utilized here will be: The *public debt* of a polity is the liability imposed on *all* members of the society that, if honored, required the leader(s) to extract resources from polity members. It necessitates budgeting of production, distribution and consumption from time of imposition of the obligation until the obligation is repaid. Within the context of this definition we may see examples in, say, tribute imposed by conquest (and war reparations); certain "gift exchanges" between polity leaders—as when a nation pressures another to accept "free resources" in order to force the recipient to reciprocate by allowing the exploitation of its resources or the granting of special privileges to the donor's nationals; or when leaders, from ancient times to the present, acquired exotic goods, arms, or food from foreign dealers or governments with the promise to repay in kind at some future time—a promise which could only be kept if those subject to their rule contributed a higher proportion of their labor to the production of resources appropriated by the leaders. There is accumulating evidence to indicate that the latter was the case for not a few of the central European Iron Age settlements or among early city-states and expanding empires when food crises occurred and grain had to obtained from outside their spheres of control.

It is important to stress that when there is insufficient current accumulation and polity leaders are forced to enter into a relation of exchange indebtedness, two very different consequences can result. On the one hand, as the ethnographic and historical literature amply demonstrate, donors frequently receive more in return than they initially gave.[12] The debtor polity may find itself in a permanent condition of clientage that withers even existing state structures (for example, a state becomes a province or colony of another state) or, if a nonstate, becomes incapable of autonomously elaborating its structures and processes to the level where it and others recognize it as a state.[13] On the other hand, it may be that crises (especially when closely seriated) brought on by insufficient accumulation available for coping with catastrophes, such as famine, invasion, or pestilence, compelled nonstate polity leaders to initiate such indebtedness, thus initiating the process of regularized accumulation. When the debt is repaid, the managers are reluctant, for various reasons, to return to less complex administrative form, and what began as short-term or emergency measures become normative, institutionalized structures and processes. Polity heads will maintain the accumulating mechanisms, arguing the need to avoid repeating the need to become indebted to others, discovering new needs or other ways to utilize the expanded resources, and, in the process, gaining permanent increments of power, authority, and, often, more material benefits. Thus, in a twist of Marx's statement (see note 11), it is the polity leaders for whom this is the primitive accumulation form.

To summarize the discussion thus far: Accumulation and its disposal provides the wherewithal that underwrites the functioning of the majority of human polities, but especially state formations. If caretakers can provide adequate resources at previous levels and via internal accumulation only, the polity is usually identified as being in a state of balance between production and consumption—but is often viewed as stagnant and even on the brink of decline. However, such equilibrium is necessarily a temporary situation for a variety of reasons ranging from the historical circumstance of population increase to the desire of present caretakers to gain prestige (social Good) by matching, if not exceeding, the sometimes mythic performance of those who preceded them.

If successful, the attempt to accumulate a surplus—material and nonmaterial resources in excess of what is culturally defined as the current optimum supply—in order to provide for possible future scarcity, while also meeting current maintenance needs of those who govern, will, over time usually lead to an expansion of population both naturally and because such success will attract those from other groups. In the case of material resources, this can lead to even greater pressure for more surplus production, since there will be increased demand on the carrying capacity of the niche occupied.[14] This success ultimately leads to a crisis in which it becomes evident that consumption of resources is in excess of the potential for productive accumulation.

When consumption exceeds production—whether for the population as a whole or for a certain segment only, say, the religious stewards in a temple economy—caretakers can: (1) expand internal production and reduce consumption (for example, intensify effort, utilize hitherto ignored resources in the present econiche, expand technological efficiency, selectively control population growth by forced emigration or prolonged or permanent celibacy, expulsion of resident foreigners as well as barriers against newcomers, infanticide); (2) extend their accumulation range by preying on weaker polities via conquest or demands for tribute as the price for retaining some limited autonomy; (3) seek necessary resources through trade or gifts. The third option imposes obligations of reciprocity and that requirement lends itself to the formation of a public debt, which requires implementing strategies from one or both of the first two options.

Despite this (and, as I read the record; it has been several millennia since state polity leaders have been ignorant of and blind to such processes at work), the desire to maintain their positions and preserve the polity requires continuing attempts to increase accumulation—of population, goods, management procedures, and the personnel to implement them. No matter the abundance of evidence indicating that such strategies generate an ever-growing imbalance of costs relative to benefits leading to the polity's collapse, absorption by a more affluent polity, or bankruptcy and temporary dissolution into smaller polities, which, as new entities and unencumbered by past debt, can begin the state building process anew—the cycle continues.[15]

Bureaucracy

An earlier paper (Smith 1985) has dealt with the issue of identifying the variants of permanent governing positions, that is durable structural statuses filled by a succession of individuals. Two types of positions stand out: (1) leadership positions whose occupants have explicitly identified decision-making powers—elders who sit in relatively informal councils, members of polity legislative bodies, peace or war chiefs, governors, kings, premiers; and (2) the administrative and clerical functionaries who, essentially, serve at the pleasure and according to the need of these leaders to have their decisions implemented—messengers, scribes, ministers, secretaries, sheriffs, judges, record keepers. Those in the second category will, for purposes of this paper, be generically labeled "bureaucrats" though these positions vary according to the range, size, and configuration of the polity[16] and, as Weber pointed out, retainers[17] must be distinguished from bureaucratic functionaries, the latter being true civil servants who ideally place loyalty to the polity or perpetuation of the system as primary.[18] The genuine bureaucrat is frequently installed in a position that, at least at the formal level of governing, can remain relatively unaffected by changes in the leadership and, often, even changes in polity structure—Egypt before, during, and after the Ptolemies; or East European countries during the winter of 1989–90. Those who assist in implementing the decisions of the leader(s), especially in what I have labeled "Dominions" (for example, the majority of kingdoms, some chiefdoms, and even such modern states as Quadaffi's Libya or the Philippines under Marcos domination), are more accurately considered the personal retainers of those they follow; they owe their first loyalty to and consider themselves in the service of the leader(s) rather than the polity per se.[19] However, whether retainer or civil servant,[20] these are the people upon whom leaders rely to carry out their wishes.

It is so obvious it seems trivial to say that the more complex the polity, the more complex the governing system, and the more complex that system, the more information, knowledge, and experience governing personnel must have in order to keep things running smoothly. However, political observers have long realized it is far more dubious to assume that the activities and decisions of leaders contribute the most important input into governing systems. For one thing, in no governing system known have the polity leaders ever acquired their positions through promotion via *technological* competence in the minutiae of governing; they inherit, seize, are elected, or appointed to their positions. Rarely, possibly never, do they possess, nor do their roles demand, the work performance skills of the functionary's daily routine. Indeed, not uncommonly, administrative personnel, whether permanent secretary or departmental clerk, view many (perhaps all) leaders as incapable of such tasks—a perspective that magnifies their own view of the importance of their role.[21] Further, there is a significant body of evidence to indicate that, especially in very complex polity structures, functionaries have a great potential for enhancing, subverting, redirecting, and redefining leadership decisions in practice.

Whether retainer or civil servant, administrative and staff persons may be considered professional if their primary activity is attending to governing matters; many, especially in the lower positions, may perform duties in which they have neither special skill or training nor specific governing expertise. This is particularly true in very simple systems where most if not all tasks are not too far removed from ordinary daily activities, and, contrariwise, in very complex systems where a great number of minor clerks are utilized. Those both inside and external to the governing system vacillate between viewing such personnel as those who facilitate the process of bridging the gap between the governors and the governed or as gatekeepers who interfere with the governing process.

It is important to recognize that the locus of bureaucratic activity is in what I have labeled (Smith 1985) the "technical aspect" of governing. Governing is the sociocultural sector in which matters that, at least potentially, affect all polity members, the personnel of which (1) occupy linguistically marked governing positions; (2) are expected, as holders of these positions, to perform certain functions established as the normative as well as explicit, sometimes relatively narrowly defined rights and duties of the position (job descriptions) within (3) a network of such positions, usually vertically and hierarchically structured, and (4) a procedural framework of governing rules and regulations.[22]

More than others in the governing system and the socioculture at large, governing functionaries are bound by, as well as committed to, standardized procedures and rules. However, no governing system can or ever does operate with strict adherence to the letter of the law. First, standardized procedures and regulations can never be so all encompassing as to cover all contingencies; secondly, all governing personnel recognize that subtle (or not so subtle) sociocultural considerations have input that alter procedural practice, leading to greater justice or inequity—and sometimes one must have legal inequity in order to ensure justice. Too much flexibility and the populace may define the system as unpredictable and despotic, or corrupt; too rigid and attentive to "the rules" and the system becomes frustratingly unresponsive (even for the leaders) while the populace begins to invent ways to circumvent not only the functionaries but the entire process. Both extremes can lead to a dramatic deterioration in the long-term survival of both polity and its leaders. The more experienced, ambitious, and senior administrative personnel tend to learn this—as do others involved in governing.

An important part of governing expertise, then, consists of acquiring a sense of the socioculturally defined range of permissible variation to make things work, for most people, most of the time. Politics—that informal dimension of governing systems that

offers the range for negotiation, compromise, and manipulation—
is variously defined as, "the art of the possible," and "a competition for scarce public resources among those possessing differential degrees of power" (Swartz, Turner, and Tuden 1966,
7). While governing leaders—hereditary, situational, or elected—
usually acknowledge this, it is not uncommon that they are forced
to rely on functionaries to deal with the majority of cases in which
such judgements are made. This creates the paradox that those
who are supposed to be disengaged and objective in the performance of their duties are relied on to know to whom, when, where,
and how to bend, stretch, creatively interpret, select, even ignore,
the technicalities, and, often, disguise from or tactfully inform,
especially newly installed leaders, in "the way matters *really* are
handled."[23]

It is in the process of accumulation that, in most state polity
formations,[24] it becomes particularly critical for leaders to have
the support of administrative personnel who are reasonably dedicated to accurately interpreting the intent of the leaders and
competent in the performance of their duties.[25] But, in what I
have identified as *confederations, dominions, bureaucracies*, and
transitional polity types (see Smith 1985), the structural existence
and performance of such functionaries are critical.

Confederations consists of an optative amalgam of integrated,
but at least quasi-autonomous polities. Such entities frequently
have a difficult time obtaining current resources with which to
conduct confederation business, let alone accumulate future resources in, say, the event that one or more members are unable
to meet the assessments of the moment. This is probably one
reason that such polity formations are vulnerable to dissolution.[26]
Whether a military league (such as sometimes united the ancient
Greek city-states) where commitments of men and material for
defense were frequently unmet, economic unions such as the Han-
seatic League or the Zollverein, or today's multifunctional United
Nations—whose economically grounded vulnerability is well
known—these governing systems seem to face continued crises
of resource insufficiency that must be resolved by structural changes
if ineffectual functioning is not ultimately to write its doom.[27]
And, as with the U.N. or the European Community, it is common
that participants complain about the squandering of resources by

other members or the administrative sector and the concomitant drain on those of the participating polities. Meanwhile, confederation functionaries find it difficult if not impossible to plan beyond the current year because they have no accumulation fund. This decreases their efficiency as well as that of the confederation, especially since it supports the tendency of functionaries to maximize current demands and develop creative ways of storing resources.

Dominions are also vulnerable to centrifugal forces that lead either to their dissolution or, more commonly, their capture and incorporation into another domain. First, the leaders of those of any size that are genuinely autonomous must, in addition to the chief polity leaders, have local or regional leaders to oversee, especially, the extraction and forwarding of resources to the center. But it is not uncommon that these counts, dukes, subchiefs, governors, or princes have ambitions to establish their own independent domains. Such surrogates are both administrative personnel and leaders; thus, on the one hand, their first responsibility is to provide resources for their overlords, but, on the other hand (and aside from any considerations of fealty), this acts as a serious brake on their own ability to accumulate the resources that would enable them to become leaders in their own right. Further, any success at increasing resources simply may result in increased demands from the center. Secondly, and viewing the situation from the other side, these second-tier leaders *cum* functionaries represent a drain on the accumulative potential of the primary leader(s). Next, both primary and secondary leaders are always vulnerable to the suspicion that they are getting less than their legitimate share of the resources. Lastly, dominions are often based on conquest or outpost colonization, risk ventures undertaken with the support of corporate kin groups or coadventurers who expect to be rewarded with rights to resources and legal privileges if the endeavor succeeds.[28] Success, however, not only requires the distribution of such rewards but may be the only way the leader of the venture is able to maintain his domain. However, even if trustworthy,[29] such individuals are not guaranteed to be efficient functionaries; further, they rarely welcome this role. If the domain is the result of a conquest situation, there may already be functionaries in place (compare China's history of conquest), but the potential untrustworthiness of the latter also requires the creation of some sort of auditors. Leading to the creation and expansion of administrative staffs at any polity level is, on the one hand, the regional leaders' need to fulfill their commitments to the leader and their desire to do it as efficiently as possible so as to enhance their own benefits; on the other hand, those at the center must be able to audit the performance of regional and local leaders and this requires them to add such auditors (and auditors of the auditors!) to their own staff. In sum, however one looks at it, dominions require retainers or bureaucrats to assist in the process of resource extraction and accumulation; indeed, this is the basic *raison d'être* of dominion organization. However, once a challenge is issued to the leader's perception that the polity is his personal, familial domain, and constraints or checks are imposed on the leader's ultimate control over the appropriation, assignment, or allocation of the polity's resources, the dominion either begins the shift to another polity formation or becomes the domain of the successful challenger.

If, however, there develops an experienced and knowledgeable corps of governing personnel, there is a high probability that not a few bureaucrats (and even the supposedly personally loyal retainers) will begin to function in ways that are antithetical to the aims of the leader; retainers begin to alter into bureaucrats. On rare occasions, they develop their own leadership aspirations (compare the Capets); more usually, however, they create encapsulated "minidomains"—agencies, departments, ministries, and so forth. As with leaders, acquiring goods and Good (for example, prestige, knowledge, information) is, if not their primary, at least one of their most important aims; accumulation (especially of job responsibilities) offers future security. Optimizers rather than maximizers, these lower tier officials seek to have stability and regularity in the polity structure and work to minimize variation or change in leadership or even of the governing system per se. Thus, whether the changes announced by the leader(s) are designed to affect a more satisfactory state of affairs for those in command or in the lives of those ruled, functionaries often impede or sabotage implementation because of personal, ideological, or situational reasons.

The role officialdom plays in *bureaucratic* polities is well known to those who have studied the state and, relative to the polity needs for the accumulation and dispersal of resources, we need only be reminded that, the bureaucratic structure itself is a major consumer of polity resources (not always legitimately) and usually seeks to expand its intake.

Finally, during the dynamic, uncertain and sometimes prolonged *transitional* phase when the governing system is undergoing transformation from one relatively stable form to another, the polity's ability to maintain accumulated reserves, resources play a vital role—indeed, such ability (or the lack of it) may even be the reason for the changes.[30] If we have the kind of evolution that is now labeled "punctuated equilibrium" (stability interrupted by some rapid evolutionary development, a revolution or coup), the new personnel can only consolidate their regime by seizing and controlling the utilization of resources, especially those accumulated by and during the tenure of the displaced leaders. The bureaucracy of the previous regime can cooperate in locating and organizing these resources, or it can delay the process, sometimes to the ultimate collapse of the new regime. However, when a change in the formation is deliberately planned and initiated by the existing polity leaders (compare the American New Deal during the 1930s, recent changes in the polities of Eastern Europe and China, as well as the projected post-1992 European Community), the alteration is usually generated by either a desire to increase resources or the need to address a relative or absolute inadequacy of them (for example, demands grow faster than resources to meet them or resources absolutely begin to decline). In either case, the bureaucracy will expand to assist in the effort to adjust the imbalance. There is, finally, the possibility that the polity undergoes substantive change without deliberate effort by, or even in the face of resistance by, governing personnel as the result of a congeries of internal and external forces. Despite that there is little if any possibility that such personnel can exercise major management, the usual strategy is to turn to the bureaucracy for appropriate responses (compare expansion departments and numbers of officials during the periods immediately preceding the French and Russian revolutions as well as during the last days of the Austro-Hungarian empire). In any case, the role of the bureaucracy in co-opting and managing resources is important if the transition is to be completed with the polity's sovereignty intact.

One criterion for the identification of states relative to nonstates is that the former—in any of the five polity forms identified and even (perhaps especially!) when transitional—are governed by personnel who a majority of the citizenry recognize as the sole, legitimate recipients and source of a portion of the resources needed for day to day survival. To the extent that the populace— as individuals, in familial or optative association—is capable of ignoring, denying, or looking to alternatives, we see the absence of the state. In polities that, despite having institutionalized and regularized governing systems within a multicentric structure, are consensually identified as nonstates, centrally managed events are peaks or troughs in the usual round of daily affairs; marriages, internal disputes and external conflict, the raising of children, the caretaking of the sick and elderly, moral conduct, work and leisure patterns, and so forth, which are determined with little or no concern for or input from those recognized as the highest authority in the polity. They are resorted to infrequently and make their presence felt only in certain well-defined events—for example, politywide religious rituals, the ritual appearance of leader(s), broad-ranging interactions with visitors or intruders from other polities, the largely symbolic exchange of prestations. Again, to the extent that those representing the highest polity authority enter such arenas, receive demands or requests for their involvement, are reluctantly obeyed in their directives dealing with such matters, or are assumed to be the legitimate providers of such management, we designate the polity as "emergent," "formative," "primitive," "developing," or "mature" and "modern" state. And, finally, when such institutionalized management systems have existed but lose effectiveness, when civil war, invasion, and, most especially, the lack of resources to implement such management by the center leads to an inability by the center to command or demand, and alternatives to the former arrangements are substituted, we speak of the "dissolution" or "collapse" of the state.

In the shift from nonstate to state polity (especially, as seems frequently to be the case, when the final prestate or initial post-state formation is a nonstate confederation or dominion),[31] the creation of personnel to manage extraction and accumulation of resources to support long term planning is essential.[32] The more successful is resource extraction, the more inevitable is accumulation and the more durative the polity—up to a point. The increased complexity of the extraction and dispersal *cum* accumulation process both depends on and increases the need for a stable cadre of knowledgeable personnel experienced at administrating a rational system for managing the political economy of the newly emerged state.

Capital

When analyzing what they at least initially identify as "economic" data derived from outside of their own time and place, anthropologists have three choices: (1) they may utilize Western concepts (for example, those concepts and models provided by, say Adam Smith, Marx, or Keynes); (2) they may attempt to discern and translate those of the targeted socioculture; or (3) they may take existing elements from both, and recombine them in what seems to be a heuristically productive fashion. Whichever path they choose they risk being charged variously with ethnocentrism, a whiggish view of history, anachronistic error, hubris, the sin of heresy, jargon making, or just plain silliness.[33]

In trying to analyze the ways in which polities employ resources, I have selected the third route, seeing it as preferable to being trapped between the Scylla of forcing square pegs into round holes (even worse, no holes at all) or the Charybdis of being forced to admit *a priori* the impossibility of making cross-temporal, cross-cultural comparisons that will increase our understanding of sociocultural structures and processes.

Economists and political scientists (as well as modern state officials) maintain that the economic activities of polities differ from those of corporations and individuals. However, relative to the capture and flow of resources, their criteria for determining the relevant data or appropriate analytical models are firmly grounded within the narrow perimeters of Western economics. Following their model we are asked to accept that: (1) the material wealth of polities is generated by their capacity to extract *revenues* from the utilization of *productive assets*, (2) the material wealth of modern corporations is generated by their capacity to extract *revenues* from the utilization of *capital*, (3) the material wealth of households is generated by their capacity to extract *income* from wage labor, polity entitlements, rents from land, and interest from capital. This format, however, is unfortunate for two reasons: first, it prohibits us from viewing the flow of resources of polities, whether states and nonstates (and including such supranational entities as the E.E.C. and the U.N.)—their production, distribution, saving, investment, and consumption—as we would other corporate entities, for example, households, lineages, family firms, or modern multinational corporations. Such compartmentalization not only enjoins us from talking in broad terms about a polity's resource-producing resources[34] or, more specifically, such phenomena as "state capitalism," it also mystifies the activities of polity managers and polity dynamics. To try to escape this trap, *capital* and *income* are, respectively, defined as "resource-producing resources" and "new resources acquired during a fixed period."[35]

The standard tripartite division of productive components into land, labor, and capital is put to one side here since the analysis is concerned with the management of resources and, from this perspective, land and labor can be treated like other resources. Current consumption can effectively eliminate their potential for future production—as in the cases of land for strip mining, factory ship pulse fishing, ground water table depletion for tourist hotels in deserts. Further, labor energy can be consumed rather than even minimally renewed, viewed as useful only for current productivity (for example, labor captives working the ancient mines and quarries, Amerindians and Africans on New World plantations, nineteenth—and some twentieth—century factory owners, and Jews, Gypsies, and political dissidents in modern gulags or concentration camps), and labor energy can also be utilized for current recreational pleasure rather than productive purpose. Within this context we may note widespread attitudes towards the frenetic but nonproductive activities of what are pejoratively labeled the "idle rich," "jet set," or "playboys."[36]

Land and labor may also be reserved simply to guarantee their future availability—though, during the interval, they are neither productive nor do they experience any increment. Thus, we not only have wilderness areas from which all but a few scientists are excluded but, to "preserve the species," animals in wild life refuges are protected and simultaneously culled to maintain a steady-state population. As a final example, a pool of unemployed is actively promulgated in order to have a reserve surplus labor pool upon which to draw during peak production periods.

In the last instance, some are either predisposed to accept or reject my anthropologically grounded argument for defining capital and either quickly perceive that, as "resource-producing resources," land and labor power are so obviously subsumed under, rather than conflated with, capital that further elaboration and examples to shore up the proposition are unnecessary, or remain unpersuaded on this most problematic and radical part of the scheme regardless of what arguments are presented.

Now, it is true that the resources of polities differ from those of other entities if we accept the commonly held but highly questionable assumption that only polity leaders can create structures, create as well as rewrite laws, and, when necessary, exercise their primacy over legitimate force to implement their decisions. This canon does indeed privilege polities and entitle its leaders to redefine at will the game and rules of resource management, not the least of which, in state polities, is the production and control over the circulation of money.[37] Finally, alternative labels help both to anthropomorphize and mystify polity structures and processes (see note 12, on debt).

It is not "the state"—that amorphous construct we find so difficult to define—that does or does not do this or that; it is people, those who manage polities and those who manage those who manage. The decision-making processes in which these persons engage are performed within the same cognitive matrix that comes into play when private (rather than public) matters are addressed. Thus, for example, a common charge against Prime Minister Thatcher is that, true to her upbringing in the milieu of England's petty bourgeoisie, she runs the State on a cost/benefit basis with a primary concern for the books show a profit. But why should we suppose it more likely that polity managers in other places and times employed different arguments, syllogisms, or criteria to distinguish between their private versus the public good? Aristotle, for example, wrote:

It follows that one form of acquisition is naturally a part of the art of household management (*oikonomia*). It is a form of acquisition which the manager of a household must either find ready to hand, or himself provide and arrange because it ensures a supply of objects, necessary for life and *useful to the association (koinonia) of the polis or the household*, which are capable of being stored. These are the objects which may be regarded as constituting true wealth . . . (as translated and cited in Austin and Vidal-Naquet 1977, 163, my emphasis).

Such continuity in modes of decision making are probably due, in large measure, to Goldenweiser's principle of limited possibilities, which argued that the constraints within which people act *tend* to limit the range of possibilities of their action.[38] A similar argument was made by the Chinese scholar, Wang Fu-chih Wang Ch'uan-shan (1619–92) when Peking fell to the Manchus. He saw rule by these invaders as socioeconomically disastrous for the people for, he said, the barbarians were ignorant and uncaring that "cities can be fortified and maintained, that markets bring profit, that fields can be cultivated and taxes exacted." He went on to argue that the Chinese and Manchus lived differently, and their "rudimentary government system" was evidence of their native inability to meet the demands of complex imperial systems. Pastoral nomads, "content to roam around in pursuit of water and pasture . . . in accordance with seasonal demands," would never know how to manage polity resources wisely and chaos would be a constant fact of life (de Bary et al. 1960, 542–48).

Goldenweiser's principle may be applied to the issue of how individuals and groups react when confronted with resources. They have only three choices—*consume, hoard* for future consumption (save), or *utilize* the resource in the present so as to increase its future value (invest). The last option is not a modern invention: hunters and gatherers have abstained from excessive predation on wild resources, inventing socially sustained rules to inhibit the greed that would lead supernatural sources to punish them by removing such foods in seasons to come; even early Neolithic populations were aware that seeds saved for the next crop would multiply tenfold, and that economic costs exceeded benefits when stock to be slaughtered for meat were maintained beyond three years.[39]

In sum, resources and household/polity utilization of those resources are, in normal times, employed for immediate consumption, saving (future consumption with no increment in present value), or capital investment (potential future consumption of newly generated resources).

There is precedence for the general thrust of the argument being made here. Indeed, certain aspects of it are derivative of remarks made by Frankenberg (1968) in a review of various of Marshall Sahlins's economic writings (1960–65). While supporting Sahlins's attack on those anthropologists who found capitalism where it did not exist, he criticized Sahlins's apparent lack of understanding of the term "capital," maintaining that it is important to recognize that, ". . . capital precedes capitalism and in itself does not imply either entrepreneurs or a propertyless wage-earning class" (1968, 79). Frankenberg emphasized that,

> . . . when Marx said "capital is not a thing but a social relation between persons, established by the instrumentality of things" (cf. Marx, 1930, p.849) . . . what Marx was writing about specifically in *Capital* was capital with a capital C—or we might call it capitalist capital . . . . [E]ven Marx was aware of this in 1845–1846. With certain obvious amendments what [Marx and Engels] then wrote about early towns could have been by Firth of Tikopia. [Frankenberg then quotes from *The German Ideology*] "Capital in these towns was a naturally derived capital . . . Unlike modern capital which can be assessed in money and which may be indifferently invested in this thing or that, this capital was directly connected with the particular work of the owner, inseparable from it and to this extent estate capital" [Marx and Engels, 1845, 1965; p.67] (Frankenberg 1968, 79).

Frankenberg then goes on to cite a excerpt of Sahlins, the latter stating that

> . . . conspicuous consumption, however much [palatial housing, ornamentation, and luxury, finery and ceremony seem] mere self-interest, always has a more decisive social significance. It creates those invidious distinctions between rulers and ruled so conducive to a passive— hence quite economical!—acceptance of authority (Sahlins 1963, as cited by Frankenberg 1968, 79–80).

Frankenberg then notes that despite such remarks Sahlins "out-Marxes Marx in his conviction and determination that, failing capitalist class relations, there can be no other kind of class relations."

Finally, Frankenberg stresses that Sahlins "shows himself a follower of Evans-Pritchard and Fortes (1940, 8) and falls "into an error shared by Polanyi, Dalton, and others about the emergence of social classes." These scholars followed the lead of Evans-Pritchard and Fortes who flatly stated that, in most African societies,

> If wealth accumulated . . . it tends to be rapidly dissipated again and does not give rise to permanent class divisions. *Distinctions of rank, status, or occupation operate independently of differences of wealth* (as cited by Frankenberg 1968, 80 his emphasis).

While I agree with the thrust of his argument, Frankenberg seems to overlook that wealth is a culturally defined abundance of resources relative to one's cohorts and, as well, that embedded in the identification of something as "a resource" is the precondition that humans recognize it as stuff which can be or is used. Earth's atmosphere, for example, was not so categorized until this century when, first, the invention of aircraft (and particularly their use in warfare) and electronic communication media and, secondly, a growing concern with environmental pollution made us define this new resource in terms of "air space," "air time," and "clean air." Resources are whatever humans employ in the short- and long-term; other substances are (nonuseful) waste (as in "wastelands") and (postuseful) garbage.

Wealth—an abundance of resources of any kind—need not be material; in most if not all sociocultures it is also recognized as including such nonmaterial goods and Good, for example, possession of or access to information and knowledge (secular or sacred, common-sensible or esoteric); honor, dignity, and prestige; family standing or the standing of the associations to which one belongs; and protection and favoritism of, as well as access to, supernatural beings—even being "a good talker," of imposing or attractive mien, or lucky.

A decade after Frankenberg, John Weeks writing on "Fundamental economic concepts and their application to social phenomena" (1978, 21–30), stated that national economic development and growth "increases the resources available to the state for repression and control" and therefore not only a consequence but, "indeed the purpose [of economic growth], is to [strengthen and] increase the power of the state and the class that rules it . . . ." (1978, 22). Weeks and others, however, leave unanswered the question that this paper attempts to address: "Whence come the initial resources upon which state polities are founded and without which state polities flounder?"

To sum up thus far: however morphologically primitive in its initial structure, most if not all polity managers within that structure—especially state formations—must perform certain public functions which require coordination and the resources (material or nonmaterial) to underwrite the performances. The resources may be elements as diverse as practical or eschatological information, subsistence materials or luxury items for gift giving and feasting, mandatory return prestations or the ability to enlist through persuasion, wealth from the ancestors or the wealth of generations yet unborn. Resource-producing resources, that is, capital, have been and continue to be a critical component of this process *even in historical contexts that preceded the use of money-based capital in those relatively recent sociocultures that developed mercantile or industrial systems of that special systemic type we label "capitalism."*

It seems more reasonable to hypothesize that other actual or wouldbe leaders, in other times and places, faced similar structural prerequisites of polity management and growth, especially relative to resource management in what was cognitively identified as "the long-term." The rest of the paper addresses those comparabilities.

In the past as well as today, the major portion of polity revenues derive from the internal activities of its own citizenry—activities from which the state surplus value accrues. Theoretically, the more such activities occur, the greater the state's income.[40] Revenues are also derived from external sources: tariffs, tolls, licenses, or war reparations. Tending to be overlooked is the extent to which States have income-producing assets controlled as state monopolies or monopsonies—often the most lucrative of commodities. Thus, in earlier times the government of Egypt controlled foreign sales of wheat; the kings of Tyre had a monopoly over timber; Frederick II established a polity monopoly over Sicily's salt sales; and all Venetian shipping had to be conducted in state-owned vessels. Currently, the U.S.S.R. controls the sale of most of its internally generated resources, coastal nations control the sale of offshore fishing rights, and all states receive income from the sale or lease of public lands maintained and monitored by public employees (for example, timber and grazing lands). That not all of these state companies were profitable (and that some have been designed to produce profits other than those measured in monetary terms) is of little matter. Japan, for example, controls the internal marketing of rice explicitly to retain food self-sufficiency, implicitly so that the government can keep the support of the politically powerful farm sector.

Again, while defining terms like "income" and "capital" is a process surrounded with contention, it is a necessary exercise. The definitions used here are grounded in (though not wedded to) the work of modern economists but, by incorporating an anthropological perspective and utilizing comparative data that the majority of economists do not take into account, they do become more broadly applicable. Just as, in capsule form, "capital" has been defined as "resource-producing resources," so "income" is defined as "new resources acquired during a fixed period."

Capital has been identified as that portion of income which is not consumed but, through various strategies, invested, put to work, with the goal of making it productive of future returns in a sum greater than that currently held. Now, resources may be accumulated and accumulation may be labeled "wealth" but none of these are, in and of themselves, capital. For one thing, possession without utilization represents nothing more than either waste[41] or hoards, the latter accumulations of nonproductive goods (representing savings as opposed to investments). This is the analytical dilemma with which archeologists are confronted in interpreting polity formations from the material record; what are clearly community granaries, may be evidence for either an unconsumed and currently nonproductive grains produced by a cooperative agreement among commonwealth households *or* it may be the "political capital" of a managerial core whose plans may include negotiation with neighbors, supplication of or placating the supernatural, strengthening their control relative to their own members, or trade for elite luxury items.

As already stated, capital, of course, is not something new. That the term only appeared sometime in the seventeenth century shouldn't delude us into thinking that the practical utilization and consequences of capital investment only emerged then.[42] As Knight (1973) has pointed out, a number of physical phenomena (for example, inertia, friction, gravity) were noted and their dynamics allowed for or used in, say, technological invention, engineering, or architecture long before they were specifically identified or scientifically understood. Just so, the conceptual recognition of capital. Since ancient times and in most parts of the world, generosity has been deemed a valued personal characteristic, but being a wastrel and spendthrift made one an object of scorn; profligates received little if any pity when their resources were depleted. The difference between generous sharer and improvident squanderer, between good and bad household managers (distinctions which are made in a wide range of societies) consistently seems to be that good managers and generous sharers provide, first, for future needs; next, allow for current consumption (ideally at a level little if any more grand than that of neighbors and peers), and only then seeks to avoid the stigma of stinginess or greediness by openhanded liberality with whatever remains, the practical and culturally defined surplus. The prodigal, on the other hand, emphasizes current consumption needs, pays no heed to husbanding resources, and inevitably depletes the stock needed for future production—what would and should have been capital.[43]

Thus, for example, such diverse sociocultures as the early Greeks and Romans, the Chinese, and Euroamerican colonialists have elevated (and justified the imposition of) their own "civilized society" with those of, variously, tribes or co-equal states, by contrasting their own patterns of thoughtful and reasonable consumption and accumulation with those of "childish and profligate savages" or "decadent and corrupt despots." In the early Greek city-states and in Rome (even during the empire) a citizen of honorable status should never fear becoming dependent on others because the ideal citizen was a good budgeter, who could then genuinely afford to make those generous public gestures that were not just an obligation but a privilege of the affluent, a culturally approved code for announcing that one was truly favored by the gods and diligent, honorable, foresighted, and reverential to the deities.

In sum, despite not being understood or even utilized in all the current ways, the majority of sociocultures have long had an intuitive sense of capital. Hunters avoid killing (especially female) game at certain times in order to not to diminish the resource below its capacity to rebuild; farmers first set aside the seed for the next year planting, then look to the consumption level based on this year's harvest that must be set to sustain the household until the next harvest; most people in most societies view human reproduction as a process of continuously providing potential producers and caretaking insurance in years to come. So, polity decision makers work to accumulate resources (people, territory, information, power, prestige, and, most importantly perhaps, material stuff) to meet current needs and make provision for the future as perceived. However, in a further complication, as the governing system expands, the number of relevant variables to be taken into account also expands and the future extends further into the future.

The world being as it is, it might be better to say "capital is *projected* productivity." In the best of all possible worlds, income will be adequate to meet optimal consumption needs in addition to leaving adequate capital to provide future resources; phrased differently, there will be optimal capital for future income without a reduction in optimal consumption.[44] However, despite sound husbandry, many a farmer has seen the next year's fields barren; frugal, industrious families find themselves on hard times; and polities suddenly face a sea of troubles though their managers seem to have been doing everything right (Sweden's current difficulties are a case in point). It has always been the case that more economic ventures fail than succeed, whether they be wars of conquest, the entrepreneurial ventures of Athenian or Venetian patricians and bourgeoisie, third world development, or the attempts of modern, first world states to fine tune their economies. Some of this is due to the draw of the cards but not a little of it is due to the inadequacy of our attempts to model polity economies.

Conclusion

This paper has suggested that, in limning out the political economy of state polities on a temporal continuum, it is important to examine the processes by which its governing personnel accumulate the resources for capitalization of its current programs and future plans, as well as the way in which the permanent administrative staffs of polities both shaped and were shaped by the process. All state polities have a need to: (1) accumulate in order to underwrite current costs; (2) have a corps of professional, knowledgeable, and permanent bureaucrats to oversee the accumulation process; (3) capitalize in order to have the wherewithal for implementation of future programs as well as sustain its position. These are the basic components that, regardless of time, place, or sociocultural variability have, with striking homogeneity, produced both the structures of states and their dynamics.

Crucial to the argument, is the proposition that, whether for the smallest household unit or the largest empire, the capture and deployment of resources has marked human concerns for millennia. We must work to deny stylistic (often only superficial) differences derived, say, from specific historical and environmental dynamics and instead seek to isolate those individual and group activities directed to addressing, especially, panhuman, pragmatically embedded commonalities. Identifying these processes with constructs such as "income," "consumption," "saving," "capital" (only recently identified[45] but, as reflecting real world orientations, intuitively utilized and acted upon in other times and places) has, at the least, the potential of requiring critics to review certain canons of received wisdom—the debate possibly shedding new light on hitherto obscured dynamics of both state and nonstate polity structures and processes.

Since scholars tend to select the evidence that supports their arguments, and readers always interpret in view of their own data and knowledge, I have kept my citations of supporting documentation to a minimum. One's own data will either fit and support my analysis or it will not. However, there were many historical, economic, ethnographic, and archeological materials that played an important role—sometimes antithetical—in developing the stance put forth here. A few cannot go uncited though limitations of space made it impossible to cite their material: Baechler (1975), Beer (1938), Bernard (1976), Casson (1984), Champion et al (1984), Champion and Megaw (1984), Cipolla (1976), Davis (1961), Davisson and Harper (1972), Finley (1973), Höll (1983), Hopkins, (1983), Hopper (1979), Humphreys (1978), Johnson and Earle (1987), P. D. King (1972), Middleton and Tait (1958), Miller (1976), Radin (1910), de Ste. Croix, G. E. M. (1981), and Thrupp (1976).

For their willingness to engage in extended discussion, challenge, provoke, and provide insight as well as helpful sources, I am also indebted to the following scholars: C. A. Bishop, R. Carneiro, H. J. M. Claessen, J. Lewthwaite, D. Treide, and G. Ulmen. It is difficult to say what particular credits belong to them but mine is the responsibility for any flaws, weaknesses, or errors.

Notes

1. Herbert Simon's work (1979, especially pp. 7–19), on the complexities of decision making and the need for "satisficing behavior" is fundamental to the position taken here. The underlying assumptions concerning sociocultural structures owe much to the emerging work on nonlinear physics (the so-called "chaos model," see Gleick 1987) and the work going on in physics and biology concerning spontaneous self-organization—the ability of complex dynamical systems to defy the Second Law of Thermodynamics and form ordered structures over a local region.

2. Those who persist in arguing that for most of human history humans lived in egalitarian societies (notably E. Leacock and R. Lee [1982] and Woodburn [1982]) are opposed by the expanding number of ethnographers and, especially, archeologists who, like Schrirer (1984) and Soffer (1985), for example, maintain the data give evidence for hierarchy as a common feature of human society—as it is in our nearest nonhuman relatives. As Bishop (1990) has recently maintained, "Relative equality is neither indicative nor conducive of genuine equality"; and Lewthwaite has noted (1990) that, throughout human history, most people have had their decisions made for them by others, notably elder males, and "the state might at best have *usurped* the role of decision making, taken it a level further up but, since also addressing decision making at a new level of complexity, not truly taking anything away." While in general agreement, I continue to maintain that state polities *have* indulged in usurpation.

3. Brumfiel, in her thoughtful and provocative analysis of Aztec state-making (1983), points out that the fifty or more small, autonomous domains that appear to have existed within the Valley of Mexico by the end of the fourteenth century were "*not* chiefdoms (in the sense that kinship ties between ruler and ruled did not supply the

ideological basis for governance . . .)," but "if rulers were released from the constraints of the kinship ethic in dealing with commoners so, too, were the commoners in their relation with rulers. Not bound to their rulers by kinship, commoners were free to throw their support to any noble [or, one would think, non-noble as well] competitor who gained their confidence" and who, if I read Brumfiel correctly, had the resources to attract and hold what she calls "fickle" commoners (Brumfiel 1983, 269, her emphasis).

4. Not a few of the current national polities operate in ways far removed from Weber's rational bureaucratic structure or even our own descriptions or definitions of modern states. So, for example, the fortunes of the private family or household economy still exert a strong influence on the decisions of state managers today and can have significant input into the political economy of many modern states (especially dominions, see Smith 1985). For example, in Haiti, the Duvaliers, along with multiple kin—as well as their aides (and the two were not always mutually exclusive)—constructed the political economy of the state in order to privately enrich themselves. Thus, like his father, former Haitian President Jean-Claude Duvalier squeezed a huge personal fortune, estimated at hundreds of millions of dollars, from the treasury of the Western Hemisphere's poorest nation. Each government ministry had a special obligation line in the national budget that was not justified (explained) but contained funds regularly transferred to Duvalier for deposit in secret accounts abroad. Similarly masked in the official budget as legitimately circulated income and expenditures was $30,000 a month from operations at the international airport and

> from the state-controlled Minoterie d'Haiti Flour mill, where Duvalier collected $1 for every 100 pound sack of flour the mill produced, a total of $2.5 million a year . . . The State Sugar Council of the neighboring Dominican Republic said it paid Duvalier $2 million in cash [in 1986] to deliver 19,000 Haitian cane cutters to help with the annual sugar harvest. (McCullough 1986, 25)

It should not strike anyone familiar with history, politics, or economics, ancient or modern, that private families can control public offices through a sequence of generations, using public wealth and occupancy of "temple" or political positions to enrich the family (several royal families in Europe are currently benefiting in this way). This, however, does not vitiate the utility of distinguishing institutional versus private activities and examining the manner in which many individuals who claim to be sited in one or the other sphere do, in point of fact, achieve success only by utilizing the separateness of the two and skillfully crossing and recrossing the boundaries.

Finally, those who seek power, high position, and/or wealth succeed only to the extent that they can obtain entry to and have the capability to utilize existing structures effectively or create socioculturally acceptable new ones within which to achieve their goals.

It should be noted that Lamberg-Karlovsky (1988, 437–38) objects to polarization of the economy of the ancient city-state of Nippur into private and institutional (temple-palace-state) sectors on the grounds that the two sectors frequently were not mutually exclusive, claiming that

> the governor of Nippur belonged to the same family which administered the city's principal temple for five generations, directly enriching private members of the family. Rulers, temple administrators, and lower functionaries often managed public property as their own making it difficult . . . to distinguish private from public. . . . (1988, 437)

This, however, seems akin to pointing to the sweeping control exercised in Europe by the Borgia lineage through sacred and secular devices or that which the Peron, Marcus, and Pahlavi families imposed in a similar combination of church, state, and private economic forces. Other individuals and families, less spectacularly to be sure, mix the institutional and the private to the same extent— as any reading of history (not to mention current daily newspapers) will verify. We should not be surprised, then, that in Nippur the members of a particular lineage chose to maximize the family goods and Good by serving as administrators of the city's principal temple, just as certain individuals privately capitalized on linkages among the Vatican bank, Istituto per le Opere di Religione, Italy's largest private bank, Banco Ambrosiano, and the firm of Italmobiliare S.p.A; or as four generations of the Kennedy family of Massachusetts have chosen the political sphere to advance their wealth, power, and prestige. Finally, as early as 352 B.C., Demosthenes pointed out that, despite following a socioculturally-defined mode of active polity participation, "professional politicians . . . who manage public affairs have changed from beggars to rich men, and have accumulated enough to live in abundance for a long time . . ." (Austin and Vidal-Naquet 1977, 351–52). *Plus ça change, plus c'est la même chose.*

5. It is assumed here that "capital"—resource-producing resources— may exist without "capitalism," whether that is defined in terms of formal economics (as a system in which the market forces of supply and demand control prices) or in the Marxist mode (as a system in which one class, relative to other classes and especially the actual producers, controls the means of production).

6. By and large, the system persists through a series of changes in the

occupants of the positions and occupants continue to occupy positions despite changes in the structure.

7. Defined here, with a nod to Keynes, as the retained resourses of production minus consumption.

8. The unemployed, working poor, and even moderately affluent in many present day societies have (aside from the taxes and other involuntary remittances made, e.g., union dues), for several reasons, a pattern of immediate consumption of most of what they produce, relying little on storage—though they can be creative in building up social capital. So important has been this polity-directed process that I would argue that today, more than ever in human history, a significant portion of the population of many societies must depend on their polity's system of accumulation and distribution to provide for those whose self-sufficiency is constrained by personal or social conditions.

9. In some cases, people view nature or supernatural forces as rewarding or punishing humans through such cycles. Thus, any attempts to circumvent this cycle are viewed as themselves liable to bring punishment.

10. Perhaps the interconnection of feast and ritual (sacred or secular) is due to the periodic necessity to dispose of surplus accumulation.

11. Carneiro (1981) unequivocally rejects redistribution as the key to the rise of chiefdoms. He has recently argued that "... it is not redistribution which bestows real power on the chief. On the contrary, only when the chief ceases to be a redistributor and becomes a concentrator, does his power begin to grow." Carneiro goes on to point out that some "redistribution" by leaders does occur but only to "favored henchmen who have earned it by supporting him in war and other efforts to gain control of things" (Carneiro, personal communication, 1/18/90).

12. Marx pointed out that, "The national debt, i.e., the alienation [*Veräusserung*, 'alienation by sale'] of the state . . . becomes one of the most powerful levers of primitive accumulation . . . the only part of the so-called national wealth that actually enters into the collective possession of a modern nation." He goes on in a footnote to cite William Cobbett to the effect that, "in England all public institutions are designated as 'royal'; in compensation, however, there is the 'national' debt" (1977, 919). It may be noted in passing that Marx used what was for him a curiously narrow definition for the actual historical condition labeled "the public debt," identifying its institutional origin "in Genoa and Venice as early as the Middle Ages" (1977, 919).

13. The same situation can also exist, however, when a polity has no ability to attract a donor or when its members recognize the risk of such a relationship and refuse to recognize any leaders who attempt

such actions (cf., Clastre's argument in *Society against the state*, 1977).

14. That carrying capacity may also naturally deteriorate over time.

15. It is, if you will, a policy based on the philosophy expressed in *Après nous le déluge*.

16. I have identified and labeled the basic polity types as *commonwealths*, *confederations*, *dominions*, *bureaucracies*, *technocracies* — with, of course, a *transitional* formation that emerges whenever polities are in the process of shifting from one to another of the basic five (Smith 1985).

17. The staffs of modern day governing officials are of this type. Their loyalty is solely to the official they serve and should that individual leave government service they leave also — or transfer their loyality to some new master. Much of modern day governing is actually in the hands of such individuals — despite that their functioning and functions are so informal that they remain invisible to the vast majority of the citizenry, being personally selected and serving at the pleasure of their specific leader.

18. Some might assume that the polity type "bureaucracy" is marked by the presence of bureaucrats whereas these functionaries are missing in the other five types. This is not the case in the model proposed; true civil servants may be found in *all* polities to a greater or lesser extent. In bureaucracies, however, governing is dominated by the technical mode in which substantive decision making is controlled by the need to satisfy the rules and follow the pathways imposed by the bureaucracy.

19. "L'état c'est moi." Resources are assumed to belong to the rulers — though those who are magnanimous "household heads" will be generous to their dependents. This is in disagreement with the majority of scholars who take the postion, held by economist Frank Knight, that "in the seventeenth century the concept [of economics] began to be applied to the management of a 'state' — under the French name économie politique; this followed when the establishment of absolute monarchy made the state the 'estate' of the king" (1973, 2:45).

20. In addition, there is a third category which consists of young people who temporarily perform services for the leaders only so the latter may determine which shall be helped along the path to leadership. Those who fail to perform well are simply retired and replaced by other neophytes. Though still commonly employed in religious and military orders, as well as the modern corporate sector, it is rarely used in the secular governing system of complex polities and will not be discussed further.

21. This may, in point of fact, be an accurate assessment.

22. In an earlier paper (Smith 1985) I presented a model elaborating on the three basic aspectsof all governing systems: the *technical* (as

discussed here); the *formal*, which embodies the ideational, axiomatic foundations for governing in its most fundamental sense as usually expressed (and rarely implemented) in modern day constitutions; and the *informal* which allows for the range of peformance and situational flexibility that marks the day-to-day business of government functioning.

23. Lest one be tempted to charge me with a whiggish view of history, let it be noted that the earliest documents give ample evidence to support this view. Oppenheim, e.g., comments on "the intrigues and machinations of the court, reported in the royal correspondence of the Sargonids" and notes that, "The Assyrian kings . . . were always careful not to offend their high administrative officials . . . who were quite ready to revolt against a king if they did not approve of his policies" (1964, 103).

24. Only in commonwealths and technocracies (save, perhaps, for Tibet—see Smith 1985) does the significance of administrative personnel get played down—the former because, owing to the emphasis that polity governing is a community duty, there tends to be a rotation of personnel in various positions of leadership and administration with few if any having a long term involvement; the latter because, in addition to this being a logical but as yet historically unformed type, the automated reliance on governing by mechanistic formulas controls the performance of governing personnel and citizenry alike, limiting, potentially eliminating, the need for human decision making (e.g., the growing reliance in modern governments on statistics, econometrics, scenario simulations and optimal choice selection by computers. The remaining four polity types need further discussion.

25. The leaders served may be (1) gods or goddesses—as in the ancient Near East temple states or during the period of the Roman papacy's political hegemony, (2) god-kings, or (3) purely secular figures. In the first two cases, hieratic personnel are retainers of the supernatural leader but most perform secular as well as sacred activities— e.g., scribes who record contributions to, dispersals from and self-contained temple system productivity. It is no accident, I think, that in view of the prosperity that businesslike monasteries enjoyed in medieval Europe the invention of double-entry bookkeeping is attributed to an 11th century monk in a northern Italian monastery.

26. The main corrosive force, however, is structural: confederations composed of relatively coequal members usually dissolve in acrimonious bickering; those consisting of unequal partners not infrequently end up being taken over by or divided between the dominant participants and constituting the basis for another polity type.

27. And, most recently, the claimed "confederation" of the U.S.S.R.

28. For example, Edmund King (1988, 14) notes that

. . . the most important men in England immediately after the Conquest, were William's own kinsmen. Of the eight great lords who fitted about sixty or more ships for the invasion fleet of 1066, only one seems to have been unrelated to William.

29. Concern for this is the reason for and is usually signalled by regular "royal progresses" through the domain. It is an excellent way for a leader to hear and see things about such surrogates.
30. The U.K. is, with the approval and, albeit sometimes begrudging, cooperation of ministers and unions alike, privatizing its civil service. Explicitly, this is being done to free the system of bureaucratic red tape that is costly and expensive to both the government and the consumers of government service. The hidden agenda, however, seems—rather obviously—simultaneously to deal with shrinking revenues and expanding social benefit costs and actually produce income for the government by charging citizens for services hitherto expected to be "free" (*The Economist* 1990, 57–58).
31. It is important to understand that, in this model, only bureaucracies and technocracies seem to occur exclusively in state polities; commonwealths, dominions, confederations, and transitional formations can be found in both states and nonstates.
32. I am intrigued by the suggestion of D. Treide (1988) that the dual process of privatization and decentralization can be understood as the state of affairs in the initial poststate formation.
33. At the close of this paper's original reading, a colleague said, in shocked terms, "You can't define 'capital' that way!" When I asked, "Why not?" he responded, "That's not how Marx used it." At such times, one feels great sympathy with Marx's iconoclastic frustration.
34. No matter how identified for the particular polity, e.g., material wealth and autonomous control over extractive techniques, people, geography, information, polity management techniques.
35. In general, economists define personal income as the total remuneration received by a household—including wages, settlements received as a rentier or proprietor, gifts, entitlement payments (e.g., old age benefits) and, most clearly and traditionally linked to capital, dividend and interest payments.
36. And, as well, widespread attitudes towards "wasted" sexual energy (or, more specifically, male semen) that underwrites hostility towards or disdain of homosexuals and, more subliminally, some of the arguments against abortion.
37. But three points must be made. First, even today polities (or their central banks) do not have a monopoly on this; in some parts of the world private corporations pay workers with their own company scrip. For example, foreign multinational corporations in developing countries and, (as recently as the midpoint of this century) in the U.S., coal mining companies in West Virginia paid employees in

this form, thereby requiring the recipients to pay their rent (on company owned housing) and buy household food and goods (from company owned stores) with it. In times of runaway inflation this may even be preferred by the workers. Secondly, it is not uncommon that the inflation just mentioned is caused by the problematic power of the government to create its own wealth and pay its debts by simply printing more money. Lastly, the important questions of what we mean by "legitimate" are still unresolved: What is the legitimate government when internal chaos causes the government to collapse (e.g., the Inca empire or modern day Lebanon)? When does a government in exile lose its legitimacy and does that of the conquerors or revolutionary force achieve it? Legitimacy according to those ruled or the leadership recognized by other polity leaders (who may themselves disagree on what constitutes the legitimate regime)?

38. The same argument has been made relative to biological examples of convergent evolution—e.g., parallel body form in fish and marine mammals, sharks and porpoises.

39. Champion et al. (1984, 130), citing research by Renfrew (1972) and Dennell (1978) conclude that, despite a paucity of data, "If meat were a main aim, one would expect high numbers of juveniles since it is more economic to cull at this stage . . . High proportions of juveniles are a regular feature . . . suggesting a widespread concentration on meat"

40. An interesting shift has occurred in the last hundred years or so; in addition to taking on caretaking duties formerly assumed by individuals and private or religious associations, modern states have shifted from obtaining resources through a monopoly over a polity's most profitable resources (e.g., precious metals, international shipping, timber, cloth or ceramic production) to taking over or subsidizing industries and services that they, no more than the private sector, must operate at a loss (cf., railroads, utilities, steel, energy resources). Some of this is financed through taxes; much of it simply through the printing and borrowing of money. It is, of course, a deliberate decision by polity managers to trade off goods and services in exchange for a supportive (or at least acquiescent) population.

41. Waste (trash, garbage) is whatever is idiosyncratically and/or socioculturally identified as materal or nonmaterial stuff which has no perceptible utility—e.g., "he wasted his education." However, as archeology continually reminds us, "one man's trash is another man's treasure." A "wasteland" is an area with no (culturally defined) resources—cf., certain desert areas before the utility of oil was discovered and still, for many, the ecologically valuable coastal marshlands which development minded people decry as "bug infested and useless swampland."

42. Patterson (1987) makes the same point—though restricting the concept of capital to that laid out by Marx. In a review of "Merchant capital and the formation of the Inca State," he concludes (p.224) that "merchant capital did not develop . . . as a result of the peaceful unfolding of some principal of supply and demand" but instead "was an integral part of the process of empire formation . . . developed in the collision of societies based on contradictory modes of production" and this empire was not the first such state in the Andean region "to witness the development of merchant capital."

43. Two special cases must be mentioned: Leveling devices (in which the community imposes obligations to dispense current resources to the point of future indebtedness), a well known ploy to prevent one household from becoming dominant in the community; and the stratagem by which individuals (usually labeled "Big Men" or magnates) attempt to gain stature, even usurp a following, by open-handed giving. This puts them into competition with leaders who have achieved their positions by, say, genealogical succession. The latter, however (cf., much of the African ethnographic literature) can accuse such individuals of obtaining such resources through illegitimate means such as witchcraft and either fine him, thereby impoverishing him while enriching themselves, or, upon deciding that by employing supernatural devices the person has abrogated his identity as human, i.e., a community member with rights. Such a nonperson (perhaps even his entire household) can be exiled or even sold into slavery.

44. The concept of marginal utility must be added to deal adequately with consumption if we are to be able to address the issue of that difficult concept, "surplus"—especially relative to "adequate" consumption. Further, anthropologists (unlike most economists) are sensitive to the reality that some forms of consumption are more accurately categorized as investment; what may appear "wasteful consumption" may be culturally identified as "frugal investment," requiring an actual reduction in consumption if one is to properly insure future returns. I also think the question of hoarding—i.e., income that is saved, nonconsumable but also nonproductive—deserves more serious attention.

45. And, as defined by economists, economic historians, etc., consisting too often of inadequate, even ethnocentric, parameters.

References

Austin, M. M. and P. Vidal-Naquet
1977   *Economic and social history of ancient Greece.* Berkeley: University of California Press. (orig. ed. Economies et sociétés en Grèce ancienne, 1972).

Beachler, Jean
1975   *The origins of capitalism.* Oxford: Blackwell.
Bary, William T. de
1960   Translation of an essay by Wang Fu-chih, with introductory note. In *Sources of Chinese tradition*, 1:542–48. New York: Columbia University Press.
Beer, M.
1938   *Early British economics.* London: Allen and Unwin.
Bernard, Jaques
1976   Trade and finance in the Middle Ages, 900–1500. In *Fontana economic history of Europe: The Middle Ages*, ed. C. M. Cipolla. 1:274–338. New York: Harvester Press/ Barnes and Noble.
Bishop, Charles A.
1990   *Foragers and the myth of natural egalitarism.* Distinguished Lecture, North Eastern Anthropological Association. Annual Meeting 1990.
Brumfiel, Elizabeth M.
1983   Aztec state making: ecology, structure and the origin of the state. *American Anthropologist* 85:261–84.
Carneiro, Robert L.
1981   The chiefdom: Precursor of the state. In *The transition to statehood in the New World*, ed. G. D. Jones and P. R. Kautz, 37–79. Cambridge: Cambridge University Press.
Casson, Lionel
1984   *Ancient trade and society.* Detroit: Wayne State University Press.
Champion, T., C. Gamble, S. Shennan, and A. Whittle
1984   *Prehistoric Europe.* New York: Academic Press.
Champion, Timothy and J. V. S. Megaw, eds.
1984   *Settlement and society: Aspects of West European prehistory in the first millenium B.C.* New York: St. Martin's Press.
Cipolla, C. M., ed.
1976   *Fontana economic history of Europe: The Middle Ages.* Vol. I. New York: Harvester Press/Barnes and Noble.
Clastres, Pierre
1977   *Society against the state.* New York: Mole Editions, Urizen Books. (orig. ed. 1974, *La société contre l'état*).
Davis, John P.
1961   *Corporations: A study of the origin and development of great business combinations and their relation to the authority of the state.* 2 vols. New York: Putnam. (orig. ed. 1905).

Davisson, W. I. and J. E. Harper,
1972   *European economic history: The Ancient World.* Vol. I. New York: Appleton-Century-Crofts.
Dennell, R. W.
1978   *Early farming in Bulgaria from the sixth to the third millenia B.C.* Oxford: BAR Series 45.
The Economist
1990   Civil-service reform: Getting down to business. March 31:57–58.
Finley, Morris I.
1973   *The ancient economy.* Berkeley: University of California Press.
Flanagan, James G.
1989   Hierarchy in simple "egalitarian" societies. In *Annual Review of Anthropology*, 18:245–306. Palo Alto, Calif. Annual Reviews Press.
Frankenberg, R.
1968   Economic anthropology: One anthropologist's view. In *Themes in economic anthropology*, ed. R. Firth, 47–89. London: Tavistock.
Gleick, James
1987   *Chaos: Making a new science.* New York: Penguin Books.
Höll, Othmar, ed.
1983   Small states in Europe and dependence. *The Laxenburg Papers*. Vol. 6. Boulder, Colorado: Westview Press.
Hopkins, Keith
1983   Introduction. In *Trade in the ancient economy*, ed. P. Garnsey, K. Hopkins, and C. R. Whittaker, ix–xxv. Berkeley: University of California Press.
Hopper, J. R.
1979   *Trade and industry in classical Greece.* London: Thames and Hudson.
Humphreys, S. C.
1978   *Anthropology and the Greeks.* London: Routledge and Kegan Paul.
Johnson, Allen W. and Timothy Earle
1987   *The evolution of human societies: From foraging group to agrarian state.* Stanford: Stanford University Press.
King, Edmund
1988   *Medieval England, 1066–1485.* Oxford: Phaidon.
King, P. D.
1972   *Law and society in the Visigothic kingdom.* New York: Cambridge University Press.
Knight, Frank H.
1973   Economic history. In *Dictionary of the history of ideas*,

ed. P. P. Wiener, 2:44–61. New York: Charles Scribner's Sons.

Lamberg-Karlovsky, C. C.
1988   Review of M. Silver's Economic structures of the Ancient Near East. *American Antiquity* 53:437–38.

Leacock, Eleanor and Richard B. Lee, eds.
1982   *Politics and history in band societies.* New York: Cambridge University Press.

Lewthwaite, James
1990   Personal communication.

Marx, Karl
1967   Capital, transl. S. Moore and E. Aveling. Vol. 1. New York: International Publishers.
1977   Capital, transl. B. Fowkes. Vol. 1. New York: Vintage Books.

McCullough, Ed
1986   Sources of Duvalier fortune revealed. *Cape Cod Times.* April 7, p. 25. (Associated Press).

Middleton, John, and David Taite, eds.
1958   *Tribes without rulers.* London: Oxford University Press.

Miller, Edward
1976   Government economic policies and public finance, 1000–1500. In *Fontana economic history of Europe: The Middle Ages*, ed. C. M. Cipolla, 1:339–73. New York: Harvester Press/Barnes and Noble.

Oppenheim, A. Leo
1964   *Ancient Mesopotamia: Portrait of a dead civilization.* Chicago: The University of Chicago Press.

Patterson, T. C.
1987   Merchant capital and the formation of the Inca state. *Dialectical Anthropology* 12:217–29.

Radin, Max
1910   *Legislation of the Greeks and Romans on corporations.* New York: Tuttle.

Renfrew, Colin
1972   *The emergence of civilization: The Cyclades and the Aegean in the third millenium B.C.* London: Methuen.

Ste. Croix, G. E. M. de
1981   *The class struggle in the ancient Greek world.* London: Duckworth.

Schrire, Carmel, ed.
1984   *Past and present in hunter-gatherer studies.* Orlando: Academic Press.

Silver, Morris
1985   *Economic structures of the ancient Near East.* Totowa, N. J.: Barnes and Noble.

Simon, Herbert A.
1979   *Models of thought.* New Haven: Yale University Press.
Smith, M. Estellie
1985   An aspectual analysis of polity formations. In *Develop-
              ment and decline; The evolution of sociopolitical organi-
              zation,* ed. H. J. M. Claessen, P. van de Velde, and
              M. E. Smith, 97–125. South Hadley: Bergin and Garvey.
1989   The informal economy. In *Economic anthropology,* ed. S.
              Plattner, 292–317. Stanford: Stanford University Press.
Soffer, Olga
1985   Patterns of intensification as seen from the Upper Paleo-
              lithic of the Central Russian Plain. In *Prehistoric hunter-
              gatherers: The emergence of cultural complexity,* ed. T. D.
              Price and J. A. Brown, 235–73. New York: Academic
              Press.
Swartz, Marc J., Victor W. Turner, and Arthur Tuden, eds.
1966   *Political anthropology.* Chicago: Aldine.
Thrupp, Sylvia
1976   Medieval industry 1000–1500. In *Fontana economic his-
              tory of Europe: The Middle Ages,* ed. C. M. Cipolla. 1:221–
              73. New York: Harvester Press/Barnes and Noble.
Treide, Dietrich
1988   Personal communication, July 28, 1988.
Weeks, John
1978   Fundamental economic concepts and their application to
              social phenomena. In *The new economic anthropology,*
              ed. J. Clammer. New York: St. Martin's Press.
Woodburn, James
1982   Egalitarian societies. *Man* 17:431–51.

2

The Segmentary State: From the Imaginary to the Material Means of Production

Aidan Southall

The monumental and formidable achievement of Henri Claessen and Peter Skalník in their great volumes, *The Early State* (1978) and *The Study of the State* (1981), together with subsequent works by Claessen and colleagues in a still continuing series, impose a very severe obligation of serious study and digestion before other scholars can have any hope of making any significant progress in this field. While one must start the discussion from the ground of the work already done, I can hope to make no more than a beginning in building up from there.

Skalník (1983) has called for the rejection of Eurocentrist concepts, such as the state, in dealing with indigenous forms. Such a call has to be treated with the greatest gravity and respect, in these days when anthropologists are so painfully sensitive to the difficulties—for some the near impossibility—of translating adequately from one culture to another. At its most serious, this attitude results in an actual abandonment of the fieldwork enterprise, with a relapse into mere literary criticism of past works, as has happened to many prominent anthropologists in the United States (see Geertz 1988). But most of us will probably opt for living with the dilemma, not endeavoring to escape from its anguish but continuing the struggle to develop more sensitive ways of respecting the uniqueness of perception in each culture, while still searching for more effective ways to convey its richness in other media.

We should therefore be grateful to Skalník for dramatically refocusing our attention on the problem, while recognizing that, in his accounts of Nanumba, he is not able to reach very far towards this goal; first he still has to use English, with all the problems which that immediately implies, and secondly his account is still full of questionable Eurocentrist concepts such as polity, palace, chieftaincy, chief, kingmaker, regent, village, military, judicial, and many more. If Nanumba can be described without unacceptable distortion through this smokescreen of very English terms, then it cannot be beyond the realm of possibility to reformulate the concept and theory of the state in a sufficiently sensitive, cross-cultural manner as to enable some translation of other systems and situations to be made without too much violence to the original. As long as a heightened awareness of the problem is retained, some progress may be possible.

I am most unhappy about Skalník's claim that "the real contrast lies between the Euro-Asian state and the alternative sociopolitical institutions of African and other 'archaic' societies of the world" (1983, 12). This is a dangerously unscientific idea which would lead back to treating Africans as living in a primitive world entirely separate from our own. Have we not sprung from the same stock? Are there no approximate parallels between our own somewhat distant past and the rather nearer precolonial past of African societies?

I have recently been involved in a transnational, transcultural debate which is quite germane to the issue. Burton Stein adopted my concept of the "segmentary state," developed out of my interaction with the Alur and their political economy, for his historical analysis of the Cola "Empire" of medieval South India (Stein 1977), as Richard Fox also adopted it in his account of the Rajput states of North India (1977). This has caused lively debate, which still continues. Some Indian scholars—apparently like

Skalník—refuse to admit the possibility that any concept developed in the study of Africa could have any relevance for India. But none of them has produced any more convincing hypothesis. Other more open minded Indian scholars are at least prepared to consider the idea and have entered the debate.

I myself have studied "stateless," segmentary, prestate societies in Africa (1952) as well as others in which elementary aspects of state formation had already developed. It is not entirely clear from the account of Nanumba whether it approximates the segmentary, prestate model or that of the segmentary state. If it is not a state, it hardly provides any basis in itself for rejection of the notion of the state. As Krader wrote, "the society with the state is a small part of the number of societies of the human kind, and covers an extremely small time period of the entire history of humanity" (1968, 95).

Consideration of the political economy of early states is urgent, but one reason it has been neglected is that information on it is so poor. It has always been relatively neglected by historians worldwide and by political anthropologists until recently. It is dealt with very little by the contributors to Claessen and Skalník's two volumes (specifically, only by Krader). The editors' efforts at sifting theories and hypotheses and testing them against the evidence of their case studies were impressively meticulous and exhaustive, so that I think any further efforts at classification, or highest common factor definition, would be an insult to their achievement. I am now more interested in how states work, what basic similarities in their working (processes) can be found (a) at different *eras* of world history, (b) at different *stages* of their development, (c) in different climates and ecologies, and (d) in different regional *historical streams*. I am most interested in how early states seem likely to have arisen (however deficient the data may be) in relation to these four considerations. To pursue this end, the data would have to be assembled and analyzed somewhat differently than it was in these two volumes. The supreme difficulty is that the most interesting stage, from my point of view here, is the inchoate, but that is just where the data are most deficient. I would prefer to designate the inchoate form of the early state "emergent", or "incipient", as inchoate seems to convey a too negative, almost pejorative sense.

The first prerequisite is that the data and information for each of the three stages of the early state must be kept uncompromisingly distinguished. The inchoate (emergent) stage must be kept quite clearly separated from the rest. Unfortunately the contributors of the case studies did not do this. A second difficulty is that the definition of the inchoate state (Claessen and Skalník 1978, 629–33, 640) and the definition of the early state as a whole (Claessen and Skalník 1978, 640; 1981, 59) excludes consideration of what are to me the most important processes: namely, *how* centralization was achieved and, above all, how people succeeded in deceiving themselves into accepting the rise of the state around and above them, until the point was reached when they no longer had any choice and had lost the power to reject it. Here I refer to Godelier's argument that "for reasons of domination and exploitation to have arisen and reproduced themselves durably in formerly classless societies, such relations must have presented themselves as an *exchange* and as an exchange of *services*. This was how they managed to get themselves accepted . . . and to gain the consent—passive or active—of the dominated . . . . The services rendered by the dominant individuals or group must have involved, in the first place, invisible realities and forces controlling (in the thought of these societies) the reproduction of the universe and of life. . . . The monopoly of the means (to us imaginary) of reproduction of the universe and of life must have preceded the monopoly of the visible means of production" (Godelier 1978, 767). In other words, the ordinary folk of classless, prestate society encouraged the development of ritual and symbolic leadership, up to the point at which it was able to acquire *coercive* political mechanisms which made it then too late for the people to object, or escape.

I do firmly believe that this monopoly of the imaginary means of production and reproduction was the fundamental key to the emergence of the inchoate early state. Some hint of it is also recognized by Claessen and Skalník (1978, 8), when they say: "Marx discovered that the exploitation of the producers living in village communities was not based on private ownership of land, but mostly on allegiance to a deified and despotic ruler who personified the state." I must point out, however, that Marx was mistaken in his use of "despotic" here for the emergent stage, and it is unfortunate that Claessen and Skalník followed him in this. The process can be described in various ways. In one attempt, I have distinguished five logical stages (Southall 1988a, 74–77). In another way of putting it, the moment of transition to achievement of the inchoate (emergent) state was when the critically determining sanctions became political rather than ritual. At this point the monopoly of the imaginary means was transformed into the monopoly of the material means of production. I believe that all such early states were variable expressions of the Asiatic mode of production (and here I agree with Claessen and Skalník [1978, 648]) and that they were segmentary in structure. This is, of course, also Marx's distinction between the primary and secondary formations also considered by Claessen and Skalník (1978, 5, 8). But although they say their volume "will concentrate on the question of the transition between the 'primary' and 'secondary' social formation," the way they define the state effectively excludes consideration of this transition (1978, 640–41), as it says nothing about the nature of kingship, nor the internal structure of the state.[1]

In the case of the inchoate (emergent) state we need to study how high offices developed, how trade and markets first appeared, how even exceptional private ownership of land could occur, and in what sense "taxes" were "voluntary" or "tributary," rather than taking all these matters for granted. The fact that contributors did not consistently distinguish between the three phases of the early state and paid little attention to the actual process of transition to the first phase, led to some confusion in the analysis, with communal, feudal, private, personal, and "theoretical" ownership of land all mentioned as appearing together, without the causal relationships between them being explained (Claessen and Skalník 1978, 553).

In 1971 (p. 157) Service, the foremost protagonist of chiefs and chiefdoms, decided to abandon the concept, along with that of band and tribe. How did they all creep back in again? All these concepts were expressions of the failure to study the political economy empirically and logically. I have attempted to establish an alternative approach, based on political economy, in which the forms of human society which preceded the inchoate early state (an expression of the Asiatic mode of production), were first of all expressions of the foraging mode of production and later of the kinship mode of production (Southall 1988b). From the point of view of political economy, the concepts of chief, chiefship, chiefdom, chieftaincy, and so forth are unhelpful, confusing, and redundant, despite the ubiquity of their use by so many, including myself—a usage which I have discontinued for the last ten years. Leader and leadership are appropriately vague and less loaded terms, as Lewis has found (1974). Even Sahlins, strong proponent of chieftainship, uses them as synonyms: "leadership continually generates domestic surplus. The development of rank and chieftainship becomes *pari passu*, development of the productive forces" (quoted by Claessen and Skalník 1978, 15). Only if all these ambiguities and misconceptions are adequately tackled can the use of "chief" and all its derivatives be justified. However, it is more important to concentrate on achieving greater clarity on the political economy.

Most of the "chiefs" who appear in the literature were colonial creations. Some of them were divine kings who lost their status at the colonial conquest. But most of them, shorn of their colonial trappings, could adequately have been described as *big men* or local ritual leaders, notables, or *primi inter pares*. Some writers simply use "chief" for subordinate local rulers under a suzerain. I use "suzerainty" to mark ritual hegemony in distinction to political sovereignty and define the segmentary state as one in which the spheres of ritual suzerainty and political sovereignty do not coincide. The former extends widely, towards a flexible, changing periphery. The latter is confined to the central, core domain (Southall 1988a, 52).

I think the Claessen-Skalník analysis could be taken further if more complex discriminations could be made. We need analyses, and analyses of political economies, not just for the early state, nor even separately for inchoate, typical, and transitional early states, but each of these three categories has to be distinguished for my four points listed above: era, stage, ecology, and historical stream.

I will try to illustrate this by a few concrete instances. Fried's distinction (1967) between pristine and secondary forms, though often not so clear cut in concrete instances, must not be ignored. What appears to our present knowledge as the earliest states in

major regions assume tremendous importance. The accounts of
Egypt and China (Claessen and Skalník 1978, 191–234) were
therefore greatly to be welcomed. But they are somewhat dis-
appointing, because neither writer consistently distinguishes inchoate from later situations, and doubtless because of the paucity
of data, they tend to veer away from the earliest period, which
is the most significant, yet the worst documented.

The examples of undisputedly pristine states are so few that it
seems impossible to do without reference to Sumeria, which may
have been the earliest of all. In America, the Aztecs and the
Incas can tell us little about the *earliest* American states, because
they were the very last before the Spanish conquest. Burger (1989,
69) has recently shown that the coastal people in Peru began
constructing large scale, monumental architecture five thousand
years ago.

The same point applies to other contributions. For example,
the ancient city-states of the Yoruba, especially Ile-Ife, constitute
one of the most important cases of pristine state formation in
Africa. Unfortunately we know very little about the conditions
of the political economy in which they emerged. Clearly, it is an
account of the Yoruba city-state in its earliest discernible form
which would be the most significant, yet Kochakova concentrates
on the nineteenth century, and focuses on the Oyo empire rather
than on the earlier forms (Kochakova, in Claessen and Skalník
1978, 495–510). We have accounts of Ankole (in Claessen and
Skalník 1978, 131–50), Rwanda (in Claessen and Skalník 1981,
15–34), and Nyoro (in Claessen and Skalník 1981, 353–70) in
East Africa. It is now clear that the Ankole and Rwanda states
are both secondary and late expressions compared to Nyoro, and
the power and centralization of both was misleadingly exagger-
ated to fulfil colonial administrative needs (Chrétien 1985; Morris
1957; Newbury n.d.). It is therefore hard to classify Ankole as a
pristine early state (Claessen and Skalník 1978, 620). The so-
called Kitara Empire of the Nyoro, which existed before non-
African influences reached the area early in the nineteenth century, appears to conform to my idea of the segmentary state
(Southall 1988a, 56).

I follow Stein (1977), in believing that very few preindustrial
states were truly unitary or truly centralized. Kathleen Gough's

field studies add confirmation to Stein's view (Gough 1981). The term "centralization" is used in a variable and sometimes inappropriate sense. By politically centralized state, I mean not only that the institutions of power are significantly gathered at the center, but that they do, in fact, exercise ultimate authority throughout the territory of the state, whose boundaries must therefore be clearly and convincingly defined. In Vansina's account of the Kuba state, the best account of any African state from this point of view (Vansina 1978a, 1978b, 1962), he stresses centralization and the development of bureaucracy, making plain that these were developing all the time from the early seventeenth to the late nineteenth century. A certain ambiguity remains, as is perhaps inevitable. In 1962 he refers to the Kuba as among the *less* centralized aristocratic kingdoms: "all the chiefs are still descendants of the aboriginal rulers and the kingdom is little more than a protectorate from the nucleus over the outlying provinces" (1962, 333). "The state consisted of a core with about 43% of the population and perhaps 40% of the land in the center, with satellite chiefdoms east and west. The core consisted of the single Bushoong chiefdom [province?] of which the king was chief [hereditary ruler?]. It was by far the largest in the country and the Bushoong dominated the state" (1978b, 360). "The other ethnic units were not united at all and consequently formed a large cloud of *satellite* chiefdoms around the core" (1978a, 6). Surely a king is a king and not a chief, and king of a kingdom, not a chiefdom. We should pay more respect to the terms which the people themselves use. The Alur express the matter simply and clearly. The king is *rwoth*, and subordinate kings in the segmentary system would also be called *rwoth* in their own localities, though in the larger scheme of things they are *nyathi rwoth* (child of king, as are the king's sons, or quite properly "kinglets"). By extension, all the men of a lineage descended from a king are called *rwodhi* (plural). It seems to me that with this core and periphery structure, the Kuba kingdom presents the essential characteristics of my segmentary state and this would have been especially true of the earlier period. Later on, the core became unusually large, and dominant, in relation to the periphery. In 1962 Vansina rejected my concept of segmentary but in 1978 accepted it: "unlike kingdoms that have been and can be described as segmentary, the Kuba state was so conceived that no office at any level was a miniature replica of any other, as happens when authority is delegated undivided"—and here he refers to the Alur (1978a, 131). But, in fact, the most important of all the royal symbols of office *was* repeated in replica for "in each chiefdom the eagle feather chief dominated the hierarchy. The king was the eagle feather chief of the Bushoong and therefore was at the top of their hierarchy" (1978a, 133). The same satellite simile was used by Tambiah in delineating the Thai "galactic" state, which seems to conform with all the criteria of the segmentary state (Tambiah 1976). The term "despotic," also used by Vansina in his classification (1962) seems to be a misconception, except in so far as it could apply to some segmentary states *in the core domain.*

Another excellent account of the development of an African kingdom through time, giving full weight to the political economy, is that of Willis on the Fipa (Willis 1981). Referring to the segmentary state he says: "the available evidence strongly suggests that the first form of unitary political organization, to emerge in Ufipa was of this type" (1981, 13) noting that this is true of the neighboring Mambwe also, and that "it is remarkable how readily the mythical concepts and relations translate into key Marxist concepts" (1981, 37).

Fried's concept of the pristine state (1967, 1975) may have been too rigidly exclusionary, but there can be little doubt that states which developed late in time and under manifold foreign influences cannot tell us much about *early* state formation, however much they tell us about other political processes. The earliest possible available account of an African segmentary state, is that of the Kongo, a pristine kingdom in the fifteenth century.[2]

Kasja Ekholm (1972) has given the most comprehending account of its origins and emergence. In 1491, the Portuguese baptised the king and six high dignitaries, at their impatient and importunate request, with the queen, the king's son, and other notables a month later (Ekholm 1972, 146–47). Soon these royal converts were burning and destroying the gods and temples of the country. In a succession battle for the throne in 1506, the Christian candidate defeated the forces of those defending the traditional beliefs and institutions of the Kongo kingdom (1972,

150). Twenty-four years after its discovery, the pristine state of Kongo had ceased to be.

Yet, when the Portuguese arrived, the Kongo inhabitants were quite convinced that Kongo was unique among all kingdoms (just as, *mutatis mutandis*, the Colas and the Chinese were). "Kongo was the only kingdom which God had personally created. Its people were the richest, the most intelligent and in general the best in the world . . . Try as the whites would to maintain that there were even greater kings in other parts of the world, with armies, cities and palaces, it made no impression. These claims were simply dismissed on the grounds that foreign kings were not Kongolese kings; there was only one Kongo and it was only there one could find 'la noblesse, les riches, les plaisirs" (Ekholm 1972, 1). Kongo was thus a "World Kingdom" in the sense that both Cola and China were. The sudden change and conversion apparently had to do with the Kongolese "inability to differentiate between their own white ancestors and people of flesh and blood whose skin happened to be lighter than their's" (1972, 147). In this case the Kongolese were victims of the same tragic mistake which destroyed the Inca, the Aztec, and the Hawaiians. Another aspect was that "the traditional religion did not function in unequivocal support of those in political power" (1972, 151). It appears that every heir to the throne had to murder a brother or sister's son to qualify, and to steal the souls of young girls by the power of witchcraft (1972, 168). There is also a tradition that the founder of the kingdom killed his father's pregnant sister, which made his father furious but was held worthy of esteem by others (1972, 165). There were terrifying and dangerous implications of becoming king which could have motivated the seemingly desperate grasping at a new religion. A similarly sudden switch occurred when missionaries reached the Merina kingdom in Madagascar (Southall 1979).

Foreign accounts that purport to describe the Kongo state and political system after 1506 cannot, without very careful sifting, tell us what the Kongo kingdom was like before the Portuguese interference. Failing to recognize this fundamental differentiation, many later accounts of the sixteenth, seventeenth, and eighteenth centuries, as well as numerous recent accounts derived from them, convey the categorical impression that Kongo was an absolute, centralized state. This is the same confusion and illusion which I have tried to dispel in Africa and Stein has endeavored to do in Asia. There are many now familiar misunderstandings— such as that Kongo was a *despotic* kingdom with "absolute power in practice and in theory" (Vansina 1962, 332), for Dapper had written that its ruler had absolute power over his subjects—in *1686*! By this time the king was used as a pawn in the organization of the slave trade by the Portuguese and was backed by their military power. The king "owned both the land and its inhabitants" (Ekholm 1972, 14) but, as we know now, all ritual divine kings by definition made this claim, which was true only in a mystical sense. The Europeans thought Kongo was the same type of feudal kingdom as their's back home, because they were determined to use it and exploit it as if it was, so they described a hierarchy of higher and lower *vassals* with *dukes, marquises*, and *counts* (Ekholm 1972, 12). Most of this was never true in any period, least of all before the Portuguese interference.

Ekholm quotes the conclusions of Suret-Canale and Cathérine Coquéry-Vidrovitch that the central power of the first tropical African states was based on its monopoly of external long distance trade, in apparent agreement, (1972, 101–2), but after further consideration concludes *"what the king controlled was not, in the first place, external trade, but prestige objects, both domestic and (later) European, which made up the articles of trade"* (1972, 103). Clearly, in pre-European times it was the king's monopoly of the supply of domestic prestige goods on which his economic and hence political power was based.

The *nzimbu* (*olivancillaria*) shell "was Kongo's prestige article number one" (1972, 117). *Nzimbu* was "legal tender." No one would sell anything for either gold or silver, but only for *nzimbu*. Throughout most of the sixteenth century they refused to sell slaves for anything other than *nzimbu*. It was required for initiation, marriage, prestation to the central of local rulers, and for buying even higher status in the all pervasive secret society, to which, "in principle, all adult men belong" (1972, 115). This "society" must have made up the real power within the state and aimed at total domination of the society (1972, 116). Every ruler had to be a witch (*ndoki*). The *ndoki* left his own body while sleeping and "ate" people (their inner persons), or turned into a leopard or other wild animal. When someone wished to join the *ndoki* society he (or she) had to give the souls of relatives in payment for initiation (1972, 176). Exactly as with the Alur, the king had two opposing images. "He was both the virile, brutal conqueror, and the legitimate, and sacred chief" (1972, 176). But his sacrality was of the same nature as witchcraft and "without this extraordinary faculty he would have been defenseless, totally lacking in power and prestige" (1972, 177). The power of many African rulers was based on a mystical force equivalent to witchcraft.

The *nzimbu* "money" was found "here and there up and down the coast and in certain rivers", but the most valuable were fished up by women round the far away island of Loanda. It was probably the ubiquitious working of the social and the prestige system, through kinship, marriage alliance, and the secret society, which resulted in the flow of *nzimbu* into the king's hands, rather than any politically imposed monopoly.

The basic social unit in Kongo was the local matrilineage, or group of such, which might be differently ranked, integrated within the village under the leadership of the head of the dominant matrilineage. Within every household and extended family the dominant figure was the senior mother's brother, who had extraordinary powers, including the ultimate right to sell his sister's sons into slavery. Young men treated their mother's brothers with profound deference. They labored for them and had to rely upon them and other kin entirely for the prestige goods which alone would enable them to marry and become adult and to enter the "graduated society" and increase their social status. Through the relationship of matrilineage to matrilineage, and thereby of village to village, and through the framework of the fearsome "graduated society" throughout the whole realm, all available surplus was channeled into prestige goods, which being used at every level to buy increased status from those already above, tended inevitably to flow to the top, ultimately to the king (since peripheral leaders had to secure confirmation in office by supplying adequate prestige goods to the king). From the king, the flow was reversed in splendid largesse to his people, at least those at the center and those most prominent, according to the fashion of all such prestige systems.

The Kongo kingdom was thus held together not at all by despotism or absolute power, which was totally unavailable, but by allegiance to the supernatural services of the king and the peripheral rulers, some of them his close kin. It was supported by a common culture and a common kinship system, a system of unbalanced reciprocity whereby prestige goods flowed up to the king and down to his favorites. It was further reinforced by the dread authority of the pervasive secret society in which all aimed at preeminence, and by the kinship authority system which was transmitted, by segmentary stages, from the most distant rural family to the royal family itself. For the ambivalent fear and respect of the sister's son to his mother's brother in the most humble family was even more strongly operative in the royal family, as well as at all levels in between.

It seems clear that the Kongo kingdom cannot have been anything other than a segmentary state, in which the direct political power of the king was extremely limited, but his ritual and mystical suzerainty spread extremely wide, transmitted through the complementary opposition of territorial segments at several subsidiary levels. But this segmentary system was extremely large by African standards, a fact which renders even more absurd the idea of its having been unitary, centralized, and despotic. Its territory was some 600 kilometers long and 500 wide, with a possible population of several million (Ekholm 1972, 11). These figures are so large as to prompt a certain caution, but they are interesting in putting the Kongo almost within the same range of territorial size as the Cola empire, despite its lower level of specialization, production, and technology. It may have been an emergent form of the Asiatic mode of production.

Once we give serious attention to the Asiatic mode of production, it becomes imperative to consider its relationship to the feudal mode of production as well, since, apart from the "unique" ancient mode of production, these are the only two modes of production applicable to state societies in the precapitalist era. This ancient mode of production developed only in the Greco-Roman world, which started Europe on its distinctive path, and which, with the fall of Rome, led to the European version of feudalism and so to the birth of capitalism. In no other region of the world, outside Greece and Rome (noting the unusual reversal of sequence in ancient Israel) did state systems appear capable of developing to the point at which they could dispense with kingship. This extraordinary innovation (of the democratic city-state), could only be maintained by small polities. It could not cope with the Roman Empire in its large scale phase, although the form of it was studiously maintained and never appeared again in human history until the emergence of the medieval communes.

As long as the concept of the Asiatic mode of production was banned under Stalin, all the societies which might have been considered expressions of it had to be classed as "feudal." It is now possible to consider the matter more openly on its merits. There are two complex, competing processes, which I characterize schematically as *centralization* and *decentralization*, which are bound to occur at least in all large precapitalist state societies where power is unequally distributed. Each process is concerned with control of both power and wealth and property, above all land. It is the situations and circumstances which lead (*en longue durée*) to decentralization and accomodation to it, which precipitate systems of the *feudal* type and it is situations which allow certain processes to occur in the direction of centralization, which will take the form of the *Asiatic* mode of production. But there are two very distinct aspects of the latter, which largely correspond to a more elementary and a more developed form. In the elementary form, the centralization is achieved primarily at the ritual or even mystical level. This is the situation in which the suzerain *reigns* over a large number of communities each of which retain a high degree of political and economic autonomy, as in Marx's classical formulation (Marx 1973, 473).

If such a system develops to the point at which the ruling class is able gradually to transform ritual controls into political controls, as is clearly to its advantage, then the system moves toward the achievement of a truly centralized, unitary state. This has in fact been rather rare in history, and classical China is the most notable case. The development of an effective bureaucracy is one of the few ways of achieving it. But at different periods, China exemplifies both centralizing and decentralizing processes. The Shang dynasty probably exemplified the Asiatic mode of production in its ritually centralized and fairly small scale elementary form. The Chou dynasty, which followed the breakdown of the Shang, is usually described as feudal (Wheatly 1971, 118–19) and seemingly with good reason. In the strong periods of the Ch'in, Han, and T'ang dynasties a more and more effective bureaucracy was trained and institutionalized, enabling China to develop toward a politically centralized state, which remained the objective of the mandarins and ruling class as a whole. But there were always contradictory forces at work. Mandarins who, in their public and official capacity, furthered the interests of the politically centralized state also privately wished to secure control of landed estates, both for their own retirement and for the strengthening of their families and lineages. In periods when the central government was weakened by defeat, rebellion, internal dissension, bankruptcy, or whatever cause, notables all over the empire took advantage of the opportunity to seize control of land for themselves and to gain control of a labor force to work it as well. The economic drive to secure productive land had its political and military counterpart in warlordism. In this political economy it is the grabbing of land, to secure control of productive forces and so increase personal and family wealth, which is the driving force. The political structure of feudalism is the minimal accomodation of competing interests which enables these goals to be effectively pursued and gives to the leader at the top of the hierarchy the semblance of sovereignty and legitimacy without actual control of the territory.

The feudal mode of production in Europe was, in effect, systematized, institutionalized warlordism. This decentralized situation arose from the collapse of the Roman Empire, the territorial takeover by the Germanic immigrants, and the attempts of their leaders to establish polities in emulation of Rome, but without the political or economic resources to achieve this. Occasional circumstances favored a higher degree of centralization, as when William of Normandy, a feudal lord from northwestern France, conquered England and endeavored to establish a very centralized administration, as indicated by the meticulous details of the Domesday Book. In a similar way, and on a much greater scale, China in its strongest periods aimed, without ever fully succeeding, at a comprehensive allocation of cultivable land to every single man, woman, and child in agrarian families throughout the empire in each succeeding generation.

While purist historians regard European feudalism as absolutely *sui generis*, there is widespread agreement that the Japanese political economy was an expression of the feudal mode of production, more or less centralized or decentralized at different periods. These concepts and processes can only be demonstrated and explained by diachronic analysis. We have to overcome the idea that comparison requires synchrony.

Returning to Skalník's point about the difference between Africa and Eurasia, it is true that, outside Pharaonic Egypt and the Sudan, with Ethiopia and the later Muslim states of North Africa, very few African societies were able to achieve statehood until a late period, and usually even then under direct or indirect external influences. The thirteenth and fourteenth century kingdom of Zimbabwe, with its access to important mineral resources and to distant coastal trade, may have been a state expressing the Asiatic mode of production in its early, ritually centralized form (Huffman 1981, 1982 and n.d.). The Kongo kingdom when the Portuguese reached it in the sixteenth century, which seems to have been free of any influences from outside Africa, seems also to have been a state expressing the early form of the Asiatic mode of production (Ekholm 1972). The same may have been true of Benin and Ile-Ife. I conclude that the *range of polities* in Africa and Eurasia is very different, for obvious historical reasons, yet the ranges *overlap* and neither is *sui generis*.

I feel that the proliferation of different modes of production applied to African societies by various writers ("African," tributary, lineage, and so forth) has been confusing and counterproductive. I see aboriginal African political economies as expressing the foraging mode of production (Southall 1988b), where hunting and gathering economies of "immediate return" survived, and the kinship mode of production in most other cases. Most of the African societies which developed forms of the state did so very recently under the direct or indirect influence of European (and in some regions Arab) penetration.

I do not in the least wish to imply that the problems are solved, nor to pretend that they can be adequately addressed in such an abbreviated account. I called the Alur polities segmentary states to draw attention to the problem. Skalník's Nanun may also be a segmentary state in this sense, but it is not quite clear to me exactly what authority, power, and sanctions the *bimbilla naa* and his entourage had. I was so impressed by the gulf of scale separating the Alur polity I studied from Burton Stein's Cola polity that I felt it appropriate to distinguish them categorically (despite the segmentary structure of both) by regarding the Cola empire as an expression of the Asiatic mode of production and the Alur as an expression of the kinship mode of production. That is to say, although I called it a segmentary state, it was *hardly* a state, hardly a two class society, and it could not prevent secession. But the facts are not beyond question, slight changes of emphasis here and there could swing the argument and a decision could be made either way. Very many African societies present a similar problem. I think it is permissible to refer to kings and kingdoms in these cases, terms which are appropriately flexible, rather than chiefs and chiefdoms, in order to avoid discriminating against them simply because they are not Western, although politically they were not fully states. Nothing is solved by introducing the concept of chiefdom and pretending there is a clear-cut categorical distinction where there is none. I prefer to retain the dynamic appearance of becoming, of a certain degree of intermediacy and ambiguity. But I do not wish to imply any evolutionary imperative, or that all systems must develop into states—although one has to admit that there has been a certain trend, in that states have increasingly enveloped the world.

Jean-Claude Muller provides an interesting treatment of this problem, which his ethnographic data insistently raises (Muller 1981, 1988). The Rukuba have twenty-four "sacred kings" each heading a village of about 500 people. Muller vacillates somewhat in referring to them as kings or chiefs. Nor is the description of the Rukuba as a "tribe" particularly convincing. Although he tries to eschew the assumption of inevitable development from small and simple to larger and more elaborate forms (1981, 245–46), he nevertheless becomes involved in "plausible transitions" (1981, 246–47). The important point he makes is that "divine" or "sacred" kings have been found in very large states and in tiny groups which lack all the characteristics of a state—even more striking in the case of the Rukuba, if one remembers that the great Masters of the Fishing Spear among the segmentary Dinka (Lienhardt 1961) displayed many of the essential features of divine kings. After all, the paradigmatic divine king in *The Golden Bough* reigned over a highly nebulous territory. The sacred kings of the Rukuba have a primeval look, but we do not really know their history. The peoples of the Jos Plateau seem to have taken refuge there from the marauding horsemen of the plains who terrorized many of the Plateau peoples with brutal slave raids. One can easily image the radical political changes which might have taken place.

The systems which precede feudalism, as we know from European history, have some similarities with the small scale systems which morphologically seem to represent less developed expressions of the Asiatic mode of production. Painter (1983, 1) describes the dominant form in western Europe from the seventh to the tenth century as "Germanic" monarchy. From early times the Germanic peoples chose "chieftains" to lead them in war. (Thus "war leaders" is appropriate; "chieftain" is gratuitous). If war was prolonged they tended to become permanent and bolstered their position with mythical traditions of divine origin (Painter, ibid.). They had a small group of close followers as bodyguards and incipient officials (Weber's administrative staff) bound by oath. As war leaders they had the right to call every man to military service. There was no tax and the king relied mainly on lands reserved for him to obtain economic resources. Government was very limited and the people administered their own justice. Royal officials were mere supervisors. The king's chief peace time occupation was securing supplies of wine and concubines. This sounds so like the conventional portrait of the African chief surrounded by beer and wives! But we need to know more about the prestations offered to the Germanic king and the rituals performed by him as a descendant of the gods. The implications of cognatic kinship for the organization of the Germanic political economy have not been adequately worked out, but it is clear that the local community retained control of the land and had free access to the means of production, as in Marx's account of the emergence of the Asiatic mode of production (Marx 1973, 472–74).

The more developed form of Germanic monarchy arose from contact with the Christian church as a handy instrument of administration and sacral legitimacy and through it with the Byzantine version of Hellenistic kingship (Painter 1983, 2). The feudal system arose out of the "almost incredible confusion" which followed Charlemagne's death for a century and a half, when "the various parts of the state could defend themselves only through the development of a feudal hierarchy" (Painter 1983, 8). This process was essentially one of land grabbing, together with the political rights and privileges which went with it. Expressions of the feudal mode of production always seem to have arisen from situations of breakdown such as this, as with periods of chaos between Chinese dynasties, or the breakdown of Japan's seventh century attempt to emulate the bureaucratic state of T'ang China.

Although Wittfogel's hydraulic theory is rightly discredited (in the sense of a directly causative theory of state formation), I wonder whether there might not be a different kind of factor at work in ecologies where the water resources are a very large scale factor, even though it may be only a series of interconnected and cooperative local communities which are struggling to cope with them. It is possible that the formidable, awe-inspiring and sometimes unpredictable quality of water resources which the cultivators of local communities had to deal with in the valleys of the Tigris and Euphrates, Indus and Ganges, or the Yellow River in China, as well as the impressive regularity of the annual Nile flooding in Egypt, called forth a gradual development of the symbolic expression of responsibility for these indispensable natural resources on the part of the community leaders—a valued public service, as Godelier (1978) suggests. This factor would seem to be less potent in the case of the temperate climate and relatively reliable rainfall of western Europe.

Of all the "progressive" modes of production distinguished by Marx, it is notorious that the Asiatic mode has raised intractable problems which are quite different from those which might beset any of the other modes. This is related to the fact that Marxist theory is based on the idea of dialectical contradictions leading to transition and transformation, whereas the Asiatic mode of production conveys the impression that it might have developed gradually out of prestate and preclass forms of human society. Zagarell (1986) has tried to address this by detailing the potential contradictions involved in the development of kin-based societies and argued for a "revolutionary" break.

If we could refine the formulation of the Asiatic mode of production to reconcile this disharmony, we should also be able to understand the essential nature of the early state more clearly. Many problems remain, which require more time and space to work out, but reformulation rather than abandonment is required.

Notes

1. Several of the problems mentioned here have been addressed by us in later publications (editors note).
2. See in this volume the chapter by Tymowski on the mid-fifteenth century West African Wolof state (editors note).

References

Burger, Richard L.
1989   Long before the Inca. *Natural History* February: 66–73.
Claessen, Henri J. M. and Peter Skalník, eds.
1978   *The early state*. The Hague: Mouton.
1981   *The study of the state*. The Hague: Mouton.
Chrétien, J.-P.
1985   Hutu et Tutsi au Rwanda et au Burundi. In *Au coeur de l'ethnie*, ed. J.-L. Amselle and E. Mbokolo, 129–65. Paris: Editions de la Découverte.
Ekholm, Kasja
1972   *Power and prestige: The rise and fall of the Kongo kingdom*. Uppsala: Skriv Service AB.
Fox, R. J.
1971   *King, clan, raja and rule: State—hinterland relations in pre-industrial India*. Berkeley: University of California Press.
1977   *Urban anthropology: Cities in their cultural setting*. Englewood Cliffs: Prentice Hall.
Fox, R. J., ed.
1970   *Urban India: Society, space and image*. Durham: Duke University Press.
1977   *Realm and region in traditional India*. Durham: Duke University Press.
Fried, Morton
1967   *The evolution of political society*. New York: Random House.
1975   *The notion of tribe*. Menlo Park: Cummings.
Geertz, Clifford
1988   *Works and lives: The anthropologist as author*. Stanford: Stanford University Press.

Godelier, Maurice
1978   Infrastructure, society and history. *Current Anthropology*
               19:763–71.
Gough, Kathleen
1981   *Rural society in Southeast India.* Cambridge: Cambridge
               University Press.
Huffman, T. N.
1981   Snakes and birds: Expressive space at Great Zimbabwe.
               African Studies 40:131–50.
1982   Archaeology and ethnohistory of the African Iron Age.
               Annual Review of Anthropology 11:133–50.
N.d.   Great Zimbabwe and the politics of space. In *The indig-
               enous African town*, ed. M. Posnansky and D. Broken-
               shaw. Los Angeles: Heinemann. In press.
Krader, Lawrence
1968   *Formation of the state.* Englewood Cliffs: Prentice Hall.
Lewis, Herbert S.
1974   *Leaders and followers: Some anthropological perspectives.*
               Addison-Wesley Module in Anthropology No. 50.
Lienhardt, Godfrey
1961   *Divinity and experience: The religion of the Dinka.* Oxford:
               Clarendon.
Marx, Karl
1973   *Grundrisse. Foundations of the Critique of Political Econ-
               omy.* Translated by M. Nicolaus. New York: Random
               House/Vintage.
Morris, H. F.
1957   The making of Ankole. *Uganda Journal* 21:1–15.
Muller, Jean-Claude
1981   "Divine kingship" in chiefdoms and states. A single ide-
               ological model. In *The study of the state*, ed. H. J. M.
               Claessen and P. Skalník, 239–50. The Hague: Mouton.
1988   Teaching political ideology through initiation ceremonies.
               The Rukuba case (Central Nigeria). Paper presented at
               12th ICAES, Zagreb, Yougoslavia.
Newbury, Cathérine
n.d.   The cohesion of oppression: Clientship and ethnicity in
               colonial Kinyaga (Rwanda). Part 2, Statebuilding in pre-
               colonial and colonial Rwanda. N.p.
Painter, S.
1983   *French chivalry. Chivalric ideas and practices in medieval
               France.* Ithaca: Cornell University Press. (orig. ed. 1940).
Service, Elman R.
1971   *Cultural evolutionism. Theory in practice.* New York: Holt,
               Rinehart and Winston.

Skalník, Peter
1983   Questioning the concept of the state in indigenous Africa. *Social Dynamics* 9:11–28.
Southall, Aidan W.
1952   Lineage formation among the Luo. International Africa Institute, *Memorandum* 31. London: Oxford University Press.
1979   White strangers and their religion in East Africa and Madagascar. In *Strangers in East African societies*, ed. W. A. Shack and E. P. Skinner, 211–26. Berkeley: University of California Press.
1988a   The segmentary state in Africa and Asia. *Comparative Studies in Society and History* 30:52–82.
1988b   Mode of production theory: The Foraging mode of production and the Kinship mode of production. *Dialectical Anthropology* 12:165–92.
Stein, Burton
1977   The segmentary state in South Indian history. In *Realm and region in traditional India*, ed. R. J. Fox, 3–51. Durham: Duke University Press.
1980   *Peasant state and society in medieval South India.* Delhi: Oxford University Press.
Tambiah, S. J.
1976   *World conqueror and world renouncer.* Cambridge: Cambridge University Press.
Vansina, Jan
1962   A comparison of African kingdoms. *Africa* 22:324–35.
1978a   *The children of Woot. A history of the Kuba peoples.* Madison: University of Wisconsin Press.
1978b   The Kuba state. In *The early state*, ed. H. J. M. Claessen and P. Skalník, 359–80. The Hague: Mouton.
Wheatly, P.
1971   *The pivot of the four quarters; A preliminary enquiry into the origins and character of the ancient Chinese city.* Chicago: Aldine.
Willis, R.
1981   *A state in the making. Myth, history, and social transformation in pre-colonial Ufipa.* Bloomington: Indiana University Press.
Zagarell, A.
1986   Structural discontinuity: A critical factor in the emergence of primary and secondary states. *Dialectical Anthropology* 10:155–77.

3

The Political Economy of the Interlacustrine States in East Africa

Albert A. Trouwborst

The interlacustrine area of East Africa derives its name from being bounded by the big lakes of Tanganyika, Victoria, Kivu, and a few smaller ones. As a cultural area it is well known in the ethnographic literature. In this essay the discussion will be limited to some of the early states which formerly existed in the area like Buganda, Bunyoro, Ankole, Rwanda, and Burundi.

Though these states showed many similarities they also differed in some important respects. For instance a big, strong, centralized kingdom like Buganda existed next to a much less developed state like Ankole or the very small states of the Soga, whom some anthropologists would not even call states (Cohen 1981, 92).

The main point I want to discuss here is whether the various states in this area could indeed be said to possess a political economy and to what extent their economies were administered and controlled from the center. In trying to find an answer to the problems involved, I continually had to keep in mind that the interlacustrine states were preliterate and that the use of money or of another generalized means of exchange was unknown. Their income consisted of different kinds of tribute in kind and of corvée labor.

The situation in which these states found themselves at the end of the nineteenth century was very similar to the one described by Southall (1988, 63) for the Alur, as follows: "the combination of foot transportation, hilly terrain, a highly localized economy, no markets, and quite limited exchange meant minimal communication between the different components of the segmentary polity, apart from those quite close to one another." Whether his conclusion "So that a centralized unitary political organization was out of the question" would apply also to the economy of the interlacustrine states will be the subject of the discussion in the following pages.

The King at the Center: the Income of the State

It is well known that the interlacustrine states, in terms of generally accepted anthropological classifications, belonged to the category of centralized political systems. The question however is, what exactly do we mean when we speak of "centralized"? In an economic sense one might say that the king acted as the centre of distribution to which goods and services flowed and from which these were handed out again to various officials, clients, and the population in general. However, this is of course a way of speaking: redistribution was not a matter of a physical flow of goods to the geographical centre of the country. Much of the tribute and corvée labour remained at local levels, partly at the royal domains distributed all over the country, partly at the courts of chiefs and subchiefs. Sometimes, it is true, tribute collection was done by centrally appointed officials (Karugire 1971, 114), but often local collectors at the level of districts or subdistricts did the job. No such thing as a central accounting office or exchequer of the state existed. We must also realize that the flow of goods addressed to the "state" was not accumulated in one single centre. Neither was there a central organization to have an overall view of the quantity of tribute collected. This is quite understandable in view of the fact, already mentioned, that bookkeeping was unknown and that tribute was delivered in kind and could more easily be delivered locally than to one central locality. In the same way it was easier to have the corvée labourers come to the various palaces, royal domains, and chiefly kraals dispersed over the country than to concentrate them in one or a few places.

Royal control over what happened in the districts also was minimal. The governors of the districts, to a large extent, relegated to themselves the collection of tribute. The king let them do this freely, as long as they handed part of their income to him. Another sort of income, which did not imply internal control from the centre, was formed by the tribute delivered by subjugated areas. All the king demanded in those cases was a tribute in recognition of his suzerainty without his exerting any influence on the state of affairs within the areas concerned (Steinhart 1977, 19–20). The same applied to clients of the kings and chiefs, who were installed on estates and lived from the gifts and the labor provided by the inhabitants.

For all these reasons it is difficult to maintain without qualification that the political economy of the interlacustrine states had a centralized character and could be considered as a centrally administered whole.

On the other hand, I do not want to underestimate the economic importance of the royal institution either. Though there was no question of a precise estimate of the income of the king, the fact that tribute often was collected in his name and was partly brought to his domains and residences underlined and confirmed his wealth. These domains and other places where tribute was brought were sometimes very extensive and represented considerable economic assets. The royal grain stores could be enormous constructions, some of which even had their own names (Nsanze 1980, 27). Moreover, the presence of royal domains and of suppliers of specialized kinds of tribute in various parts of the country, to a certain extent, also established his authority in the periphery of the state. The king surely was the richest man of the country, and the control of his possessions alone already gave him much power. Besides, his income did not depend exclusively on the redistribution circuit: further sources of income consisted of raids and commerce.

Of these two activities, however, commerce does not seem to have played a very important role in the state formation in the interlacustrine area; wars and military raids on the other hand did. In Buganda according to Wrigley (1964, 18) "predation" constituted "the real basis of their economy" and not food production. Most of the material rewards given by the king to his favourites "came as a result of participation in wars and raids" (Fallers 1964, 110). In the other interlacustrine states wars and raids also were a very common phenomenon and certainly constituted an important source of income for the state, though probably not always to the same extent as in the case of Buganda. Wrigley has described this state "as essentially a military machine designed for the exploitation of its weaker neighbours" (Wrigley 1964, 19), but I do not think that this would apply to the same extent to all the other kingdoms in the area.

In the case of Buganda we are told that each chief had its own following "whose primary loyalty was to him rather than to the state" (Wrigley 1964, 20). The chief led this following to the war and was himself expected to entertain them with food and beer (Wrigley, ibid.). It is true that in times of war the king relied on the assistance of his chiefs, but these chiefs fought their own wars also, were even supposed to do so, and used at least part of the booty to their own profit (Botte 1982). Karugire (1971, 188) tells us that Nkole traditions made a distinction between wars and raids. Wars were national affairs authorized by the king, raids were "private adventures by the individual chiefs and their followers" for which no permission of the king was needed, although the booty had to be brought to him.

As a final conclusion, I feel safe to say that the king, though militarily maybe more powerful than any other force in the state, could not always effectively control his chiefs, who sometimes even rebelled against him. The institution of a national army, based on a monopoly for the use of armed violence did not exist in the interlacustrine area. Nevertheless the income derived by the king from booty was considerable. Quite understandable therefore that the lust for plunder was a main motive for warfare in the region.

The King at the Center: Expenditures

With reference to the expenditures of the interlacustrine states, we see the same kind of decentralization as we established in the foregoing section. Here the main reason is that no large national constructions or public works existed which necessitated the central investment of funds. It is true that the royal capitals and domains and those of the chiefs sometimes consisted of quite impressive buildings and that the king, his family, and household demonstrated wealth in the form of ivory and shell ornaments and that they possessed large herds of cattle.

However, a far greater part of the income of the state, furnished by way of tribute, corvée labour, fines, and confiscations, was used in support of the private needs of the king, his family, his officials, and his personnel or was redistributed to his subjects.

The income of the state, to the extent that one might call it that, was therefore spent in personal terms. There was a direct personal link between the "taxpayer" on the one hand and the state and its officials on the other hand. It will be clear that this implied that expenditure also had a decentralized character.

On the other hand, symbolically the king stood at the center of the system. National ceremonies were celebrated in which the king was the central ritual figure and to which representatives from all parts of the country brought all kinds of gifts with them. These ceremonies were held to guarantee the well-being and the fertility of the whole nation, but also had a festive character. The population was regaled with beer and meat, and many gifts were redistributed. One should keep in mind, however, that not every one who rendered prestations to the king received gifts in return (see also Claessen 1987, 68). Redistribution was selective. What was received by the king and other authorities was used to reward favorites or people from whom important services were expected in the future. Other people received nothing, especially people with a low status.

Claessen has rightly stressed the importance of redistribution in terms of the reinforcement of the legitimacy of government. He has in that context shown the way in which prestige-giving goods were used by the authorities to mobilize support. This certainly applies to the interlacustrine area where a following formed by the distribution of rewards was "a key-stone of political life" (Cohen 1977, 79. See also Trouwborst 1956, 86ff.).

As to the question of whether these aspects of the redistribution economy contributed to the centralization of the state, I want to point out first that the wealth of the king and the prestige attached to him attracted many people from all over the country. The king and other highly placed personalities would also have many clients personally attached to them, even in territories under the authority of chiefs. This implied that the royal court had a network of relationships reaching into the periphery of the state. Its "aura of luxury and prestige" (Southall 1988, 60) diffused far and wide.

The above mentioned public ceremonies, some annually, some incidentally, like those at the intronisation or the death of the kings, drew vast numbers of people to the royal courts and were the occasion for large scale distributions of food and beer that are still remembered with pleasure (Nsanze 1980, 25). However, on the local level most people only entertained economic relations with their local chiefs on whom they depended for support in their daily affairs.

My conclusion therefore is that as regards expenditures also, redistribution had a very decentralized character. It was true that the king stood at the center of the state, but this was true basically only in a symbolic sense.

Kingship and Management

It is sometimes suggested that the states in the interlacustrine area performed managerial functions. Mair, for instance, declares that the *katikiro*, "prime minister" of Buganda was "very definitively an administrative official; he took the lead in the organization of public works and the collection of taxes and also in the planning of wars" (Mair 1962, 146). It appears that the *katikiro* equally "was reponsible for the construction of the royal palace" and "for the roads of access to it" (ibid.).

In the case of Burundi also, it is told that the state had a "managerial function." This is described, however, mainly in terms of the way the agricultural calendar was regulated through the annual national sowing ceremony called *umuganuro* (Mworoha 1987, 174). Another example given by this author was that in the case of epidemic cattle diseases those cattle that had stayed alive were sent to the king to reconstitute his herds. In that way the survival of the cattle population was guaranteed (Mworoha, ibid.; for a similar example from Rwanda see Vidal 1974, 72).

These few examples give an indication of the limited extent of the intervention of the royal court of Burundi in the economy of the country. Mworoha himself remarks that the influence of the state in the production was only marginal. The same impression can be gained from the case of Ankole where the chiefs did have "very little to administer" (Karugire 1971). And even when Maquet (1954) talks about the administrative structure of the state of Rwanda, this refers mainly to the organization of the collection of tribute by the various armies. I think therefore that Buganda again was an exception. Its system of public roads, for instance, was certainly unique in the region before the coming of the Europeans (Mair 1962, 146). However, even in the case of Buganda, so it seems to me, the managerial role of the state was a limited one and was mainly restricted to military affairs. This was, by the way, not unimportant as one considers the judgment of Wrigley, already cited, according to which the main income from the state was derived from the plunder of war.

How limited the control of the state was in the case of Ankole is stressed by several authors. This state consisted, according to Steinhart (1978, 144–45), of two economies, the pastoral and agricultural ones, which were largely autonomous and self-sufficient. As regards the agricultural economy of the Iru (agricultural) part of the population, the situation is described as one where the daily life and communal decision making remained mostly in the hands of the agricultural elite itself "unbothered and unconcerned with the larger affairs of state cherished by the Hima [pastoral] elite" (see also Doornbos 1978, 30ff.) I would not go so far as to suggest that the same was true for the other interlacustrine states, but I am of the opinion that the economic integration everywhere in the region was weakly developed.

Symbolic Aspects of the Political Economy

As we saw, the conditions for the collection of tribute were not at all conducive to the centralization of the state. Symbolically however, royalty constituted the center and the unifying force of the state. Even though not all subjects of the state stood in a direct relationship with their sovereign, they all recognized that he was the supreme giver of everything they owned and that he was the one who was responsible for their well-being. Officials, especially ritual functionaries in various parts of the country, entertained relations with the court and were required to contribute to and participate in the national celebrations. The very circumstance mentioned in the first part of this essay, that is, that prestations to the state were rendered in kind, facilitated their symbolic elaboration.

To give a complete account of all the kinds of relations—most of them implying the exchange of prestations and gifts—would require a tremendously long list. Besides the services of all kinds of religious functionaries: diviners, sorcerers, rainmakers, priests, drummakers, keepers of the royal graves, and so forth, many secular functionaries like ministers, military commanders, advisors, and judges were employed. At lower levels worked people like herdsmen, milkers, cultivators, cooks, butchers, watchmen, maids of honour, nursemaids, and so on. In terms of goods, agricultural produce in the form of grain, milk, honey, and beer were delivered to the royal domains, but also industrial products like barkcloth, milk pots, salt, iron, weapons, and hoes. In Burundi, according to tradition, each of these prestations was delivered on the basis of agreements in the past between certain lineages and the king. For instance, being milkers or herdsmen in the service of the king might be the privilege of a very small number of lineages. These were said to have rendered special services to the king in the days of the origin of the state and were accordingly rewarded by being given prestigious functions.

As a result, a highly refined and many-stranded system of prestations and remunerations had developed, adapted to all kinds of personal, local, economic, and political circumstances. The system expressed thereby, in a symbolic way, the great diversity of ties between the various groups of rulers and ruled.

A final word must be said about the eventual existence of a public moral concerning the prestations to be delivered to the state. Such a notion was absent, partly because of the nonexistence of public works and other public facilities for the population. The prestations can best be seen as a matter of personal reciprocal relationships between the ruler and the ruled. In these states no citizens, but clients, were to be found.

Conclusion

The early states in the interlacustrine area certainly did not know a uniform and well-integrated public administration of the economy. The basis of the economy was provided by a network of relationships, which assured the rulers of a living and gave the population some material but especially spiritual rewards. A political economy in the sense of a public administration of the interests of the state and its subjects scarcely existed.

I can therefore to a great extent adopt the position of Southall, when he concludes, on the basis of his analysis of some African and Asian segmentary states, that these constituted "essentially moral systems" where the kings had mainly a ritual authority, political authority being restricted to the central domain of the kingdom. I conclude in conformity with Southall's statement that in the interlacustrine states also "polity and economy were not effectively integrated because no effective or regular system of administration extended from the centre" (Southall 1988, 68; 74ff.). This may remind us of what was said about the integration of the political economy of the interlacustrine states.

However, I would like to qualify these conclusions by pointing out, as I did in the foregoing sections, that, after all, the king did send his representatives to the preripheral regions, that he did have residences and domains in many parts of the country, and that even in the outlying districts many people were linked to the royal courts to tributary relationships.

Stressing the ritual aspect of kingship should not make one forget that ritual cannot do without economics. The public national ceremonies for instance, required an enormous organization and constituted a formidable economic effort.

I furthermore think that the economic effects of the military exploits of the interlacustrine states did have a profound influence, though very often in a negative way, on the economies of the whole region. Vast flows of cattle, and not to forget wives, were directed to the courts of the victorious kings and provided wealth to many capitals and domains, though the victims suffered.

One can say therefore that though the kings did not succeed in really exercising an effective control on the economy as a whole, they were successful in keeping in motion vast amounts of goods and services which helped them to defend their economic, political, and ritual position as central figures in the state.

References

Botte, R.
1982   La guerre interne au Burundi. In *Guerres de lignages et guerres d'états en Afrique*, textes rassemblés par Jean Bazin et Emmanuel Terray, 269–314. Paris: Editions des Archives Contemporaines.

Claessen, H. J. M.
1987   Redistributie en andere zaken—de economie van de Vroege Staat. In *Verdelen en heersen? Redistributie en andere aspecten van het economische bestel in en van Vroege Staten*, onder redactie van M.A. van Bakel en E. Ch. L. van der Vliet, 39–74. ICA Publication 77. Leiden: ICA.

Cohen, D. W.
1977   *Womunafu's Bunafu. A Study of Authority in a Nineteenth-Century African Community*. Princeton, New Jersey: Princeton University Press.

Cohen, R.
1981   Evolution, Fission and the Early State. In *The Study of the State*. ed. H. J. M. Claessen and P. Skalnik, 87–115. The Hague: Mouton.

Doornbos, M. R.
1978   *Not all the King's Men. Inequality as a Political Instrument in Ankole, Uganda*. The Hague: Mouton

Fallers, L. A.
1964   Social Stratification in Traditional Buganda. In *The King's Men. Leadership and Status in Buganda on the Eve of Independence*, ed. L. A. Fallers, 64–116. London: Oxford University Press.

Karugire, S. R.
1971   *A History of the Kingdom of Nkore in Western Uganda to 1896*. Oxford: Claredon Press.

Mair, L.
1962   *Primitive Government*. Harmondsworth: Penguin Books.

Maquet, J. J.
1954   *Le système des relations sociales dans le Ruanda ancien*. Annales du Musée royal du Congo Belge, Tervuren.

Mworoha, E.
1987   *Histoire du Burundi. Des origines à la fin du xixe siècle*. Paris: Hatier.

Nsanze, E.
1980   *Un domaine royal au Burundi, Mbuye env. 1850–1945.*
            Paris: Société Française d'Outre-Mer.
Southall, A. W.
1988   The Segmentary State in Africa and Asia. *Comparative
            Studies in Society and History.* 30:52–82.
Steinhart, E. J.
1977   *Conflict and Collaboration. The Kingdom of Western
            Uganda, 1890–1907.* Princeton: Princeton University Press.
Steinhart, E. J.
1978   Ankole: Pastoral Hegemony. In *The Early State,* ed.
            H. J. M. Claessen and P. Skalník, 131–50. The Hague:
            Mouton.
Trouwborst, A. A.
1956   *Vee als voorwerp van rijkdom in Oost Afrika.* Den Haag:
            Excelsior.
Vidal, C.
1974   Economie de la société féodale rwandaise. *Cahiers d'Etudes
            Africaines,* 53, no. 14: 52–74.
Wrigley, P.
1964   The Changing Economic Structure of Buganda. In *The
            King's Men. Leadership and Status in Buganda on the Eve
            of Independence,* ed. L. A. Fallers, 16–63. London: Ox-
            ford University Press.

4

Paradise Regained: Myth and Reality in the Political Economy of the Early State

Ronald Cohen

Recent and widely read interpretations of early states in the western Sudan have described their precolonial political and economic inequality, with its highly stratified social life, as a delicately evolved precapitalist formation. Despotic statehood, although admittedly present, is envisioned as having been wondrously civil and constitutional. The inequalities associated with early states are said to have been controlled and functionally ameliorated by traditional processes of sensitive, almost utopian, redistribution woven into the political economy of these Islamic emirates. Or so we are told. In this paper I wish first to examine the myth of precapitalist eden—functionalist inequality—and explain it. Then secondly, to take a closer look at the reported, observed, and remembered reality—the early Sudanic state as a power center that both protected, redistributed, *and* simultaneously preyed on, persecuted, and quite impersonally destroyed those near or even within its borders for the sake of maintaining power or enriching its treasury and the coffers of its leaders.

My thesis is simple. The political economy of the early state was many things, but above all it was fearsome and destructive. Equilibrating forces flourished, and widely distributed benefits were indeed part of ordinary life. But—and this is my point— only in circumstances in which hierarchical loyalty and obedience were required for the stability of the state and its power vis-a-vis its neighbors and its periphery. One of the primary characteristics of such states was the capacity for, and the ready delivery of— terror.

The Myth of Precapitalist Eden

Among a particular genre of Africanist scholars, the precolonial early state was marked primarily by harmonious and humane social and political life. The inequalities so obvious to early travellers, the colonial officials, and others who first viewed these emirates after conquest are interpreted by these observers as superficial orderings that mask a benign and mutually beneficial set of relations. Although not condoned, the early state's highly developed stratification is seen as part of the inevitable outcome of regional history. Its evolution within the Islamic world is therefore viewed as "natural." In effect, local and regional events have sifted and winnowed development outcomes over time allowing for utilitarian results—helpful to the greatest number, harmful to the least.

The clearest and most fulsome presentation of this point of view has been constructed by Watts (1983, 82–147). The basic assumption is the well-known approach of the "moral economy"—"the social provision of minimum income in the face of high risk" (1983, 89)—imbedded into the reciprocity and redistribution of precapitalist "class" relations. In this theory, the risk is due to the inevitability of periods of elongated drought in the savanna that sometimes run several years in a row, producing famine conditions for the bulk of the population. Examining the evidence, Watts (1983, 100) concludes that rainfall patterns have been relatively stable over the last millenium, some periods wetter, some dryer, but all alike in the inevitability of drought conditions arriving unpredictably for any one year as part of normal expectations.

The provisioning fostered by the so-called moral economy of the early state has two dimensions. The horizontal dimension is of less concern here, first because it is present in both state and nonstate systems, and secondly it refers primarily to obligatory sharing and gift-giving among kin and community members. Having a clearly acknowledged higher rank, or wishing to have one, also involves giving more than one receives, thus building unequal wealth exchange into reciprocal (often ceremonial) exchanges. A chief may receive a chicken from a peasant household at his daughter's wedding and give a brace of three or four when the peasant's household performs a similar rite de passage. However, one point is less well-known and should be stressed. Granted that peasant households do distribute food and other forms of subsistence resources, for example, labor, on a reciprocal basis, these norms are so strong and potentially impoverishing that people fear such obligations may weaken their own household capacity to survive. Villagers with greater wealth often avoid situations where obligatory sharing and claims on generosity may be made directly by the needy. And within households counter measures have evolved. Thus granaries are of two types in the area. One a large above ground variety, another below ground and secret. The latter serves the purpose of being a store of food outside public awareness and therefore beyond the reach of the moral economy except as it touches intrahousehold obligations. Besides ceremonials, village life is an arena in which people may ask, and generosity may demand, that those who have must share with those who do not. Household heads are deeply concerned about this communal obligation especially during times of drought, when calls on supplies from others in one's network of friends and relations easily produce quick depletion of household stores. Prudent men therefore always put some of their stored crops below ground in secret stores away from the possible and legitimate claims of kin and neighbors during the inevitable onset of moderate to severe shortages.[1] Although people know that such stores exist, it is impolite and insulting to suggest to a potential donor that he is hoarding food when his neighbors are short or lacking in food stores.

The other form is hierarchical—really a kind of redistributive benificence that conditions and supports the myth of "merrie

Africa." Raynault (1975, 12) speaks of local leaders and dignitaries in the Hausa state of Maradi who, during times of droughts and possible famine, "were expected to open their granaries—filled in large measure by the labor power or rents collected from the peasantry—and to provide assistance to the local inhabitants." Watts (1983, 123) refers to this extension of household reciprocity into the realm of hierarchical responsibility as "shock absorbers for the peasantry" which "provided the social context of famine occurrence and constituted the admittedly brittle strands of an indigenous relief program" (Watts 1983, 124). Unfortunately, the notion that such systems are "brittle" is not expanded or explained.

The model is again the household, an organized social, economic, and political unit under the authority of the head who managed its adaptation using whatever skill and power he could obtain through traditional, that is, constitutional, means and by applying political resources and skills. And the nucleus of this cell was the patron-client relation. The subordinate delivered loyalty, obedience, and labor; the superior protected his client both politically and economically. Household heads did (and still do) this for their members and related subordinate households. And political leaders were enjoined by constitutional principles of legitimacy to behave on a wider scale in this same way towards those over whom they had authority. As with households, the wealth accumulated by political leaders was countered by an obligation to redistribute to those under the rule of the monarch (Raynault 1976, 88). The king's capital city was not simply a locus of power but also a granary for the welfare of the realm from which largesse, especially in times of stress, was sent to the needy and the loyal (Nicolas 1969, 197).

Village-state relations were similar. According to Watts (1983, 135–36) if the rulers ignored or violated the needs of the common people their "hegemony . . . was vacuous." Using force was "impractical" or operated through patron-client relations. The labor needs of households and political leaders and the differential access to wealth meant that people sought protection in exchange for loyalty and labor at the hands of benign superiors. If seriously over-exploited, the peasants had recourse to banditry, and during hard times tax exemptions were granted throughout the area.

Written records of these royal privileges have survived (Palmer 1936, 13–53) which tell of tax exemptions given in perpetuity to lineage groups for services, for shorter periods because of economic hardship, and for dangerous location at the borders, especially against desert raiders (Cohen 1971a and b). In the Sokoto Caliphate, Last (1978, 26) writes of the low degree of exploitation and control that was possible in this widely dispersed and theologically inspired Islamic state. And another writer goes further and suggests that the Hausa state of Damagaram extracted extra taxes especially at times of drought from those who could pay in order to help the needy (cited in Watts 1983). As the Kanuri say, "The Emir is father of all the people"—meaning he sustains and protects his subjects especially the needy in times of great shortages. More pointedly the Hausa say "The Emir never ran short of food" (Watts 1983, 139).

The diagram given in figure 4.1 is adapted from Watts (1983, 141), although changed significantly to reflect my own interpretations of these same materials. They indicate economic resources circulated in the form of gifts, taxes, and prestations. The entire system—regional in its general outlines—is too complex to describe in detail but was widespread throughout the area. What is important is the conclusion reached by everyone working on the economic history of these Sudanic kingdoms that (1) labor was short, (2) slave labor and clientage and even corvée labor were used by households and by the political hierarchy, and (3) that the economic receipts of households were distributed horizontally through reciprocal ceremonial exchanges as:

1. charity to those less fortunate especially religious practitioners,
2. stored, consumed, and sold by households,
3. returned by the political hierarchy as relief of the peasantry when the inevitable shortages resulting from drought occurred in this area of semiarid rain-fed agriculture.

The Real in the Ideal

It is clear that Watts (1983) understands the idealized redistributive nature of this model of these despotic states and that "the moral economy was . . . not always moral." (1983, 146). Using

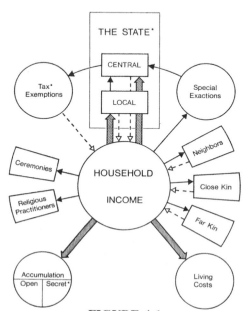

FIGURE 4.1
Household relations and the state in precolonial Borno*

  * Compare this with the functionalist models of Watts (1983;141) which
    describe how the state reciprocates and gives back its revenues to
    the households in periods of shortages.
** Tax exemptions can be granted during hard times, or for special
    services rendered to the state. Times of shortage increase the amount
    of household accumulation that is held in secret. The state may and
    may not redistribute food and other resources during hard times
    depending upon its needs for warfare, foreign debts, and the resource
    needs of the capital city based nobility. To simplify matters household
    income—from farm and off-farm activity minus income of household
    members kept for themselves, is omitted.

the class paradigm, he describes without explanation or comment
how local folk wisdom includes the remembrance that it was common people not the rulers who suffered during famine. And that
ordinarily the state "must have . . . assisted in the reproduction

of inequality." (1983, 146). But as with most other writers on this topic, he fails to specify any regularity of shortfall between the ideal model of a benificient state and the reality of day to day operations. The implication is strong that exceptions were the unusual and random results of unskilled leadership.

Nothing could be further from the actual facts. Ideally just and redistributive, in reality the governments of these early states had to face constant political and economic threats to their survival. In particular they had to support a very expensive court nobility in the capital city and to equip on a regular, usually annual, basis, large military forces (up to ten thousand or more for Bornu, less for smaller states, but still in the thousands according to Smaldone [1976], and Reyna [1990], and constantly settle foreign debts. All this in addition to the needs of the moral economy for widespread redistribution, without which loyalty and subordination tended to shrivel, stimulating rivals both within and beyond the borders to immediately stir and support revolts. Not only was the moral economy not always moral, it was *systematically* at variance with its ideals as part and parcel of its very nature and the conditions of survival for these early states.

Finally, it is important to note that this gap in the record is the basis for an even more fundamental distortion which echoes the efforts of African scholars to envision a functionalist and utopian picture of the precolonial emirates. In this conception they are seen as highly evolved Islamic states operating an integrated polity under the benign care of a monarch who administered a quasi theocracy in the interest of the people, with moral-judicial guidance and advice from Islamic scholars. But all of this was broken up and destroyed by colonial conquest which is seen as having brutalized these ancient states (see Usman and Alkali 1983). While much of these images and events are valid, the avoidance of any serious consideration of precolonial despotic government and the correlated political-economic realities engenders a structuralist logic. That is to say, a capacity to abstract similar functionalist and benign patterns of power and authority in which a mythic history of patron-client relations is created whose moral imperatives compensated for inequality and the economic risks of life in the Sahel. Using this interpretation, contemporary scholars have created an image of history in which an ideal model of a just and kind state—not a flesh and blood state—was contacted and altered for the worse by the international and satanic forces of the colonial instrusion. Bad as it was, such a paradigm makes colonialism even worse, once it is depicted as having crushed a constitutional state whose evolution produced a moral economy adapted to overcome the constant threat of drought and famine, while caring for the basic needs of the peasantry.[2]

But it makes it less real. Besides, the colonial expansion into Africa was heinous enough. Exaggeration is unnecessary, especially if it distorts our understanding of how the early state actually operated and what happened to it once colonial conquest made possible the dominance of European officials over these ancient monarchies.

Why all this distorted interpretation should become "normal science" provides more insight into intellectual history than to the understanding of early states. And it is not terribly complex, simply a matter of fad and fashion running through a particular strand of scholarship. From this point of view (see also Usman 1983), the most determinative, the most powerful force in the history of these societies has been the inequality of the world capitalist system and the exploitation and degradation characteristic of this world order and its expression within colonialism. Here the judgements and personal distaste these writers, African and expatriate, feel for Western capitalist and colonialist nations creates a readiness to see precolonial societies as innocent victims. This enhances the egregiousness of colonialism by providing an Eden-like construction of precolonial contexts.

Such distortions can become scholarly traditions. They assume early Sahelian states were based on stratification that was ameliorated by Islamic traditions of justice and charity. This theologically based constitutionalism supported the adaptation of these fragile hegemonies to periodic droughts using complex systems of redistribution to ensure the survival of the peasantry. And this in turn made it possible for rulers like household heads responsible for those under their charge to claim sufficient legitimacy to maintain the inequity of state power. This idealized conception is part of the widespread folk image and traditions of the Sudanic states, especially among descendants of the ruling groups. It also fits the theoretical and paradigmatic needs of those who wish to see the

African predicament as primarily the result of external forces derived from states of the capitalist world core, whose imperialist exploitation and expansion is theorized to be the most explanatory and most destructive source in Africa's long history. Within this paradigm of the early state as a utopian achievement, its history and development are made into idealized constructions of political and economic virtue. This makes colonialism all the more villainous. For that which was overcome and destroyed was in effect an extraordinary achievement, sifted and winnowed through time by countless African leaders and peoples. But, and this is their point, all of this was brought to a sad end at the hands of colonial barbarism. That this thesis is partly true is no excuse for swallowing its distortions along with its validity.

Sudanic Power: The Underside of the Myth of Merrie Africa

It is important to clarify my position on the model of the precolonial utopian state claimed as the product of evolution and the moral economy. There is little doubt that many, if not most of the elements described by scholars concerning its redistributive norms (moral economy, in modern jargon) and its justice are valid features of the early state in the western Sudan (Cohen 1987, 1971a and b). These states did create loyalties, did provide welfare benefits and adjudicative services, and they protected citizens against the depradations of hostile forces outside the kingdom. While this was developing they fostered an ideology of superiority about statehood itself, "the place with a bad king is better than one with no king at all" is an old Kanuri saying describing this evaluation. And all the while, the state was a force for creating state-based ethnicity. Talleyrand was right when he said that the only thing one cannot do with a sword is sit on it. States without benefits—real and imagined—are contradictions in terms. But this is far from the whole picture. These Sudanic states were dependent upon coercive, often brutal forms of suppression and exploitation that created the insecurity upon which hierarchy and its benefits depended. To be in a violent land without protectors—without connection to counterforce—meant being a victim or a candidate for flight to hinterlands.

The state structures were consistent across the entire region.

State power and authority emanated from a walled citadel wherein dwelt the monarch and his court of nobles, religious practitioners, and the craftsmen and traders who serviced the governmental aristocrats both slave and free. Outside the capital town were the villages, chieftaincies, tributary states, nomads, and foreign powers who competed in the region with one another for control over the countryside and its peoples. Traders moved back and forth, as did religious practitioners, nomads, spies, and of course armies and raiding parties looking to wage war and obtain plunder. The hinterland outside the capital was often populated with peoples of somewhat different cultures, Chadic speakers in the central area, and Central Saharans in the east towards Darfur. In the Chad basin the Kanuri came as intrusive conquerors from the Sahara. Other states, Hausa, Bagirmi, and the smaller ones to the south, were local groups who had evolved statehood in reaction to the power and domination of the larger Islamic ones, taking up Islam as well at some point in their development. Villages, nucleated chieftaincies, and pastoral nomadic groups of Fulani and Arab descent were attached as units or divided up into named clan-based segments, and attached to the major states as fief-holdings under clients of the nobles who lived permanently in the capital. As states survived, the emergent culture of the citadel became the upper class tradition, while local or "little traditions" survived and altered and assimilated elements of the "great tradition" of the capital, making for an emergent statewide ethnicity identified with the ruling group and its traditions and contacts outside the region.

To support a capital city of the size of Bornu's pre-nineteenth century capital at Ngazargamo on the Yo River—a circular walled city, one mile in diameter with many towns and villages nearby dependent upon it for markets and protection—took enormous resources. Kano is even larger. And the smaller states had capital towns that boasted as much as ten to fifty thousand residents. Ngazargamo and Kano were most likely over 100,000 as long ago as the 1820s when they were first described by European travellers (Ngazargamo as a set of newly burnt ruins). Major capitals boasted large palace compounds, households of nobles, and traders all of whom had troops of retainers and their polygynous families. The leading men, including a specialized military nobility, had troops of soldiers under arms who formed the basis of a small standing army. This was expanded manyfold at times of large military campaigns, generally held annually, but with many smaller sallies during the year, especially during the dry season. All of this, plus the foreign trade for luxury goods and for armaments, meant that the capital city required a constant inflow of goods and services— foodstuffs, servants, slaves, craftsmen, religious practitioners— from the hinterland. Watts (1983) describes this, defensively, as "rent" while another writer on the area calls it more aptly, "predatory accumulation" (Reyna 1990).

How was the capital provisioned both for subsistence and its sumptuary goods and services? Taxation was regularized through the fief holding system, a harvest and cattle tax, as well as a general tax named a religious tithe (*zakat*), but given directly to the monarch (as Commander of the Faithful) through intermediaries who collected it nationally rather than through the fief system. In addition, a prolific number of special gifts were sent up the hierarchy, for lower offices, for adjudication services, for market fees, for almost any specialized functions in the economy that were regulated from the court. In Kanuri the suffix 'ram' attached to an entity or an activity means the tax (real, remembered, or potential) attached to it, and it can be used for almost anything unless tax exemptions (treating goods or activities as "haram," taboo, like the pig) have been pronounced or given to a household in writing for perpetuity. Those collecting fees took some for themselves and passed on the rest to their superiors, usually in preset proportions. The greater the exaction, the greater the return for the hierarchy of officials involved in collection. On the other hand, overzealous collections could indeed send people off to settle elsewhere, either autonomously in wild hilly areas to the south, or under the protection of other local chiefs and nobles who promised them less oppressive taxation in return for loyalty, military levies, and political support when factional disputes arose in the state. More to the point, in scarce times, times of elongated warfare, or other situations to be described below, widespread and bloody coercion could be visited on the countryside creating famine and want even when the rains were sufficient.

Tributes were sent by nearby societies, left to rule themselves, often with a resident consul to represent the interests of the central power whose conquest had reduced the principality to the status of captive. The tributary could carry on its own public life, but every year had to send massive amounts of movable wealth to the capital city of its conqueror. Bornu had such relations with Zinder, with Kanem, and the border states to the west. Tributes could run to thousands of units of grain, thousands of cattle, goats, and sheep as well as horses and camels, and the local craft goods, especially armaments. Failure to deliver meant war and destruction. On the other hand the tributary was in a state of constant intrigue with the enemies of its regional imperial master. More than any other single factor, this particular form of foreign relations kept the interstate environment in a constant state of tension and potential warfare. Any weakness on the part of the conqueror meant an almost instant shrinkage of its sphere of influence and its capacity to garner in wealth from the surrounding peripheries (Cohen 1971a). It is important here as with all taxation to understand that it is moot and difficult to show that such tributes were a form of "surplus." They were exactions based on unequal power. Whether or not they impoverished those obliged to pay depended upon the negotiating abilities and record of loyalty and obedience of the subordinates, not on the supplies available. Supply was an issue in the negotiations, but not necessarily the governing factor unless good relations had been established beforehand.

Extra income for the capital came from a number of sources. Any superior could declare an *nzia* (called *dubu* among the Hausa) or have it declared for him by loyal and enthusiastic subordinates. Anyone beholden to the honored one must bring money, and goods, raw or processed, cattle, clothes, jewellery, or whatever and it was collected in the household of the superior at a huge feast. The piles of goods on rugs proclaimed the popularity and *duno* or strength of the leader. Failure to accumulate a large amount was shameful and could lead to punishing exactions by subordinates. The monarch in Bornu was also accustomed to giving special taxing rights to young nobles who wished to set up house in the capital on their own, or who had given him special and excellent aid in war. The noble could then take a band of armed followers, go to the designated area, and demand or take by force as much as he could garner for himself and his followers (*budji collata*—to roll up [possessions] in mats) or, if some mercy was involved, he would take half of all the goods (*budji reta*) to be found in the area—food, clothing, slaves, or enslave the people if they were not Muslim, leaving those in the area devastated, with nothing or at best with half of their own capital to face the future. Fiefs or village clusters could be divided up and redistributed to nobles who had distinguished themselves. On such occasions the new lord of the area would either appear in person or send out his subordinates to demand gifts in recognition of his newly obtained feudal rights over the villages. Failure to do so was considered to be recalcitrance and rebelliousness. Reyna (personal communication) notes that in Bagirmi, to the east of Bornu, sudden or regular need for exactions by the monarch or his favorites was often, not always, directed to areas where it was felt there was sufficient surpluses in real terms, so that those in dire straights were left to recoup. Besides, they made less profitable victims.

Rebelliousness was the major reason for war and plunder. Tributary states in the region, small ethnic groups nearby, and subdued and incorporated villages were variously able to resist the power of the center to enforce annual and informal exactions. The farther from the center, the closer they were to nearby major powers who might protect them, or who might support a particular heir to the local chiefship against one who was loyal to the center, then the more likely a local area might try to avoid sending tributes, or claim hardship when tax collectors arrived. Or even refuse to cooperate at tax time. This was the most consistent problem of these early states. Those villages close to the capital physically, or those related by clanship and close ties going back in time were generally loyal. Those who were of different ethnic backgrounds, of previously autonomous history, or who had historic ties to other large states in the region were constantly poised to rebel. Any sign of weakness or of inattention to the application of coercive exactions by the center provided a temptation to local leaders to thumb their noses at the capital and the payments of tributes, taxes, and gifts. Tijani's (1980) study of Ngala in eastern Bornu shows an incorporated semiautonomous ethnic group within the Bornu state constantly seeking independence, alliance with Bornu's enemies the Bagirmi, to the east of Bornu, and constantly facing violent and merciless reincorporation by the Bornu government intent on maintaining its control over this segment of the state.

And there was always the problem of foreign debt. Rulers of the emirate kingdoms, as well as many of the nobles in the capital and the trading groups, engaged in foreign trade with other emirates, most especially across the Sahara. This brought sumptuary goods into the savanna from as far away as Venice and Turkey; guns, clothes, jewellery, perfumes, mirrors, swords, chain mail, dates, camels, horses, and many other imports were paid for in exports of leather goods, korans (beautifully written and housed in embossed leather boxes), and in slaves, especially women, children, and above all costly, profitable eunuchs. The latter were "manufactured" (surgically) in the savanna and shipped to the greater Islamic world where there was a constant demand for them as harem keepers and most importantly as subaltern officials. In the early state, eunuchs were bureaucratic agents in government who had no issue and therefore gave superiors the right of appointment with no worries over the development of patrimonial rights which eventually proliferate into a serious and self-perpetuating nobility who form segmenting interest groups with demands for power and influence among competing royal candidates. Fiefholding nobles, even those made to live in the capital with dispersed fiefs, ultimately form a power center which, if ever unified, leads to opposition to the monarch and support for a rival claimant. In this sense Magna Carta can be said to be the result of a lack of totally loyal nonpatrimonial royal functionaries, in a word—eunuchs. In Bornu, an ex-slave dealer whose father had manufactured eunuchs discussed the trade in detail. Before the colonial conquest, his father he noted coolly, regularly castrated 40 to 50 adult men captured in government led raids in order to obtain one survivor for sale or use as a eunuch. This was why the price was so high, he explained.

A ruler in serious debt to the North Africa trade had to obtain revenues quickly or face a cutoff in his imports. If the situation became serious, the ruler had to mount a war campaign and raid for revenues even if it meant plundering his own subjects. Richardson's (1854) eye witness account of the Emir of Zinder in debt to North African traders and mounting a war campaign on rebellious subjects within his own state, near the border with Kano, is the most graphic account we have of such revenue collection using force of arms against one's own subjects for debt repayments. However I was told of many such raids in nineteenth century Bornu especially against villages near the southern and western borders of the state which often tried to avoid tax obligations. If recalcitrance did not provide enough villages to plunder, then accusations of pre-Islamic practices could be used as evidence that the villages in question were practicing apostasy and should be cleansed of their pagan ways so that true religion might be reestablished. Sokoto accused Bornu of such practices in the early nineteenth century before attacking and destroying its capital for what were clearly political rather than religious or economic reasons (Ibn Fartua 1967).

The actual practice of retribution was coolly and impersonally bloody. The word "cool" is used locally to describe how a proper soldier, especially a leader, usually on horseback, behaved during battle. As Reyna (1990) points out, warriors were trained to enter battle and face death, mete out carnage amongst the enemy with no show of emotion. The same was true of Bornu according to stories of battle behavior and instructions I received on how to comport myself in horsed showings of soldiery. A serious face, no smiling, simply an intent on killing, burning, and destroying and carrying away anything in sight. As Reyna notes it was not particularly heroic, rather it was simply normal, mostly economically oriented plunder.

A Kanuri titled aristocrat in a rural village (in the 1950s) calmly lit a match and burned down a peasant hut which quickly spread to several others. A crowd gathered and a bucket brigade put out the fire. The noble told me the next day, that he had asked the peasant for something and been refused. He burned the house, he said to teach the *kirdi* (pagan) a lesson. In the days before the white man had ruined the country, he said, he would have had the man killed immediately for such impudence. Others told me later that the noble had been drinking and asked that the household head's wife be made over to him for sexual services for the night. The peasant refused, told his wife to leave, and his huts were burnt. Everyone agreed it was wrong and evil. But, no one mentioned punishment. He is one of the important people, titled.

Nothing can be done, they said. Although this was an odd, abnormal event. The fact that it could occur at all, that the arson would go unpunished, and that the arsonist would coolly brag of it being a light retribution compared to what might have happened in the past is what is significant about the event. The impersonality of the noble's reactions was notable. The household head was a non-Muslim, a *kirdi* or pagan, a nonperson with rights limited by his unbeliever status. However, when asked if he would do the same to a Muslim, the noble shrugged and said one should not do such things, *"Amma wu kuntuwo, sandi talaa,"* [But I am noble, they are common peasants]. In other words the rank differences between ruler and ruled means I have the right to do as I please. Checked with others, this logic of the idea was denied, but a few noted that such cruelty and worse was practiced in "the old days," that is, in precolonial times.

The question of slavery and the nature of the state is complex. Undoubtedly slavery was widespread. Travellers in the nineteenth century speak of ordinary households owning several slaves each.[3] Ruling households in the capital had up to several dozen slave men, women, and eunuchs. One of the privileges of the titled nobility was the establishment of slave villages (*karliyari*, literally the place of the slaves). In Bornu, towns still bear the name. These were places where slaves captured in raids could be interned, sometimes in chains under armed guard, until they became used to their status, to work on farms for the nobles granaries in the capital city. A share of the crop was kept by the slaves for their own subsistence and they were a human bank account of resources of servants, concubines, and the soldiery of the noble.

Raiding for slaves on *razzia* was watched by the travellers and carefully described (Denham and Clapperton 1826; Barth 1857; Nachtigal 1971; see also Smaldone 1977; and Reyna 1990). Towns on the borders of the state, or recalcitrant fiefs, or tributaries would be set upon by large armies. Towns ranged from five hundred up to tens of thousands. The army sizes varied from three or four thousand to over ten thousand armed men in cavalry, muskets, spears, and bows and arrows (Smaldone 1977; Reyna 1990). The settlement was attacked, sometimes put to siege, the men most often killed on the spot, the women and children taken as slaves. Sieges involved burning crops, and the village itself, then taking any and all movable property for booty to be divided amongst the soldiers and their leaders with some reserved for the monarch on their return. Some towns on the periphery developed watches to warn of incoming raids so people could flee. Others were more trusting. Still others made treaty arrangements (*amana*) to be left to peace if they led the raiders to other settlements where the unsuspecting could be plundered.

Finally there is the issue of redistribution of grain during drought times. Given the manifold means of amassing large granaries in the capital, it is certain that some of it was redistributed to loyal followers during times of extreme shortage. I was told of this by members of noble families who spoke proudly of the noblesse oblige of their ancestors. On the other hand, Barth (1857) notes that wealthy nobles in the nineteenth century capital of Kuka kept their storehouses full from tributes, slave settlements under their ownership, and raids. During times of shortage they waited for the prices to go up then sold on the local urban market using the drought induced shortages to enrich themselves because their political position allowed for large stores that could be used for market speculation.

It is important in this analysis to note that I have not used the term "surplus" to describe the portion of the early state's productive capacity going to the ruling group in the capital and to local chiefs. There is no evidence that people's contribution to the upkeep of the capital, often as not forced out of them, was a surplus. Clearly villagers knew that some of their crops and herds had to be given to the political leadership and possibly they prepared for it in their cropping and other economic strategies. Possibly. But, except for Reyna's data that exactions skipped over more impoverished areas, there is no evidence in the historical record to support this claim. Furthermore exactions were often in the form of punishments, as they were normally in terms of the size of the crop and the animal population in each household. Proportionate taxation can be planned for, to some extent. But the needs of the rulers, the possibility of the fief changing hands, of conquest by a neighboring state all meant that devastating exactions could be made at any time for political reasons well beyond the capacities of country people to know or prepare for in advance. The best strategy under such conditions of insecurity was to find, hopefully, a firm and powerful protector amongst the rulers who could speak for his towns, protect them when necessary, and even provide for them if times were hard. No wonder then that loyalty and obedience, patron-client, hierarchical relations were so highly developed. They were for ordinary people, quite literally matters of life and death, and even then, as we have seen, nothing but death and taxes—often comingled—was certain.

Conclusion

The early state in the Sudan has been depicted in recent literature as a benign redistributive system of inequality in which the power of the state was used as a form of adaptation to periodic droughts. There is evidence to support the conclusion that this was an ideal sometimes practiced but often abrogated because of the needs of the ruling groups for wealth to sustain themselves in the capital citadel in a more luxurious life-style, to pay for foreign debts, and most importantly to pay for the costs of war, the major survival mechanism of the early state. Those who were close to the capital, those who were devoted and loyal were protected. Those who sought autonomy, or were unfortunate enough to be at some remove from the capital in physical distance or sociocultural terms were the objects of extreme exploitation and unpredictable plunder. Paradoxically, such insecurity is the root determinant of hierarchy. When power and authority provide licence for plunder and state terror, it is adaptive, indeed necessary, for peasants to obtain protection when and if it is available. The early state was certainly a workable solution to competition for power among polities in a region. But to see it as a benign form of generosity and justice among happy loyal peasants living in a "moral economy" is to hide from its dark side, the side above all others, upon which its success depended.

Notes

1. This point is important because Watts (1983) uses a colonial survey from the 1950s, the wettest decade of the twentieth century to document the fact that 94 percent of Bornu and Bauchi households report having no food stores in July, proof that colonialism's destruction of

the moral economy deepened the universal hunger during the growing season. The survey could not have turned up any evidence of hidden underground stores whose existence is always a household secret. I lived in the area during the 1950s and did my own surveys and household visits. A few indigent households were without food in the so-called hungry period, but the abundant rains of the period provided sufficient stores for most normal farmers. The fact that colonial surveys were connected in peoples minds with taxation, and were undoubtedly based solely, on above ground stores explains the difference between my observations and those reported by Watts (1983).

2. The rainfall data for the savanna and southern Sahara shows that droughts were indeed common throughout the last millenium. Watts (1983) suggests that the insecurity was rather stable, that in fact things were no different before and after colonial rule began. As far as I can tell this is not so. Nicholson's research (1982; 1987) has shown that the twentieth century is the driest in the last five hundred years. However, from the point of view of anticolonialism as theory, the claim can be made that this is not so, that rainfall is a constant. Then deteriorating circumstances in the real world can be blamed on externally induced colonialism. Until very recently this has been the style of third world scholarship, along with many outside Africa who use condemnation as a form of explanation. Colonialism was in many respects an outrage, but it did not change rainfall patterns.

3. See Barth's (1857, vol 2) chapter on Kuka in which he describes the households of the ruling group in Bornu, especially that of Abba Gana the Waziri or chief minister of the monarch's court. After the first capital of Ngazargamo was sacked for the second time in the first decade of the nineteenth century, it was moved closer to Lake Chad. Kuka was the settlement of the Kanemi's, who replaced the earlier rulers as a second dynasty.

References

Barth, Heinrich
1857   *Travels and discoveries in North and Central Africa.* London: Longman, Brown, Green, Longmans, and Roberts.
Cohen, Ronald
1971a   Incorporation in Bornu. In *From tribe to nation in Africa*, ed. R. Cohen and J. Middleton. Pittsburgh: Intext.
1971b   From empire to colony. In *Colonialism in Africa 1870–1960*, ed. V. Turner. Vol. 3, *Profiles of change.* Cambridge: Cambridge University Press.
1987   *The Kanuri of Bornu.* Prospect Heights, Ill.: Waveland.

Denham, D. and Capt. Clapperton
1826   *Narrative of travels and discoveries in Northern and Central
            Africa*. London: Murray.
Ibn Fartua
1967   *The Kanem Wars of Mai Idris Alooma*. Trans. H. R. Pal-
            mer. Vol. 1, *Sudanese memoirs*. London: Cass.
Last, D. M.
1967   *The Sokoto caliphate*. London: Longmans.
Nachtigal, Gustav
1971   *Sahara and Sudan*. Trans. A. B. G. Fisher and H. J. Fisher,
            with R. S. O'Fahey. London: Hurst.
Nicholas, G.
1969   Fondements magico-religieux du pouvoir politique au sein
            de la principauté Hausa du Gobir. *Journal de la Société
            des Africanistes* 39:199–231.
Nicholson, S. E.
1982   *The Sahel: A climatic perspective*. Paris: Organization for
            Economic Development and Cooperation.
1987   Climate drought and famine in Africa. In *Food in Sub-
            Saharan Africa*, ed. A. Hansen and D. E. McMillan. Boul-
            der: Lynne Riener.
Palmer, H. R.
1936   *Bornu, Sahara, and Sudan*. Lagos: Government Printer.
Raynault, C.
1975   Le cas de la région du Maradi, Niger. In *Sècheresse et
            famine du Sahel*, ed. J. Copans. Vol. 1. Paris: Maspero.
1976   Transformation du système de production et inégalité
            économique: le cas d'un village Haoussa (Niger). *Cana-
            dian Journal of African Studies* 10:273–306.
Reyna, S. P.
1990   *Wars without end: The political economy of a pre-colonial
            state*. Hanover: University Press of New England.
Richardson, J.
1854   *Narrative of a mission to Central Africa*. London: Chap-
            man and Hall.
Smaldone, J. P.
1977   *Warfare in the Sokoto caliphate*. Cambride: Cambridge
            University Press.
Tijani, K.
1980   *Political and administrative development in pre-colonial
            Bornu*. Unpublished Ph.D. dissertation. Ahmadu Bello
            University, Zaria.
Usman, Y. B.
1986   *Nigeria against the I.M.F.: The home market strategy*. Ka-
            duna: Vanguard.

Usman, Y. B. and M. N. Alkali, eds.
1983   *Studies in the history of pre-colonial Bornu.* Zaria: National Publication Center.
Watts, M.
1983   *Silent violence.* Berkeley: University of California Press.

5

Wolof Economy and Political Organization: The West African Coast in the Mid-Fifteenth Century

Michal Tymowski

In the years 1455 and 1456, the young Venetian merchant Alvise da Ca da Mosto travelled twice to the West African coast. He himself gave his reasons for undertaking these expeditions, which were hazardous but remunerative, and described their circumstances. En route from Venice to Flanders, his galleys touched land in Portugal, where the envoys of Infante Henry the Navigator, and later the Infante himself, encouraged the young Venetian to take part in an expedition to Africa, which, they insisted, was bound to bring quite considerable profit (Ca da Mosto 1978, 476–77). "I was young, well fitted to sustain all hardships, desirous of seeing the world and things never before seen by our nation", wrote Ca da Mosto, "and hoped to draw from it honour and profit" (Ca da Mosto 1937, 5; 1978, 477). Thus the Venetian was prompted by curiosity and a desire to be rich. Especially the former motive is important for our purpose. The voyage gave rise to a description of the West African coast from the point of view of a man eager to see and understand as much as possible of a world previously unknown to him. There are good grounds for believing that his description is reliable. Ca da Mosto wrote his memoirs between 1463 and 1469, when in his thirties, when his impressions of the expedition were still fresh in his mind. His work was first published in Venice in 1507, and then repeatedly reissued in the sixteenth century, both in the Italian language and in numerous translations (Ca da Mosto 1937, xliii–xliv; Ca da Mosto 1978, 466). Giovanni Battista Ramusio's edition of 1550 enjoyed the greatest popularity and served as basis for Marica Milanesi's edition of 1978, which I have used for this article. Quotations in English come from G. R. Crone's edition of 1937, published in the Hakluyt Society series.

Ca da Mosto was not the first European to proceed southward to Cabo Verde from the mouth of the river Senegal. The Portuguese had visited the mouth of the Senegal and had likewise been to Cabo Verde before him: Dinis Dias was there in 1445 or 1446 (Boxer 1969; Malowist 1976). Actually, Ca da Mosto is regarded as the discoverer of the Cape Verde Islands (Ca da Mosto 1937, xxxvi–xlii; Ca da Mosto 1978, 465). The Portuguese voyages have been described by chroniclers such as Gomes Eanes de Zurara (1960), Diogo Gomes (1959), and Joao de Barros (1945). Ca da Mosto's description is that of a traveller and an eyewitness (Brulez 1968, 312); moreover, his text includes a considerable amount of detailed information, all of which accounts for its exceptional value as a source of information on the economic and political situation on the West African coast around the mid-fifteenth century.

Ca da Mosto's description contains the first written mention of the Wolof people and its political organization. The writer uses the name "Gilofi", (Ca da Mosto 1978, 495). There is no doubt about the identification of the people concerned, on account of both the name and geographical information. Evidence on the basis of written sources from the sixteenth to the eighteenth century, and oral traditions gathered in the nineteenth and twentieth centuries indicates that the Wolof formed several states in the past: Djoloff, Walo, Cayor, and Baol. In the fifteenth century, the inland state of Djoloff was the most powerful. Walo, situated at the mouth of the Senegal, and Cayor, located south of Walo, were subdued by Djoloff. In the sixteenth century Djoloff's dominance over the coastal states ended (Brigaud 1962; Monteil 1966, 1967; Barry 1972; Suret Canale and Barry 1976; Curtin 1975). The titles of the Wolof rulers and dignitaries are known to us from the oral tradition. In Djoloff, the sovereign was styled *burba*, in Walo *brak*, and in Cayor *damel* (Gaden 1912; Rousseau 1929, 1931, 1933; Wade 1964). These titles may also be instrumental in the interpretations of Ca da Mosto's description. Oral traditions also include information on the economy and the forms of its exploitation by the state organizations of the Wolof. Yet, these present a picture of a situation prevailing after several centuries of contact with Europeans, as a result of economic and political pressure exerted on the Wolof from the outside. The character and the broad range of the transformations taking place in the sixteenth to the nineteenth century are well covered in the literature (Brulez 1968; Curtin 1975). Because of this, Ca da Mosto's description not only is the first record to include a mention of the Wolof people, but also is valuable because of its character as a source of comprehensive information on the Wolof economy and sociopolitical organization in a period preceding the transformations caused by the contacts of these people with Europeans.

Economy

The Wolof were an agricultural people. They prepared land by lighting bush fires and tilled it with the use of hoes with iron edges. They grew millet, beans, vegetables, some rice, and cotton. They produced palm wine, and supplemented their diet by fruit gathering, the production of vegetable oil, and fishing. They bred cows: milk is mentioned as one of their beverages (Ca da Mosto 1978, 505; Mauny 1961, 230–75). They were not short of salt, which was in great demand in the rest of Africa, as they obtained this by evaporating ocean water. They imported iron from the banks of the river Gambia, probably from the Mande peoples (Ca da Mosto 1978, 498–99), and horses from the Arabs and the Berbers in the north, paying for these commodities with slaves. Horses were very expensive, and consequently were a symbol of wealth and power. Gold was also imported in small quantities (Ca da Mosto 1978, 500, 511). External trade was extremely important to those in power. The fact that there was external trading does not necessarily imply that there was a surplus of goods, since the Wolof mostly exchanged slaves for the imported goods (Karpinski 1968, 83). Rather the existence of external trade testifies to the occurrence of social divisions on the basis of power, war, and the capture of people (Ca da Mosto 1978, 496). On the other hand, the existence of economic surpluses is evidenced by the operation of markets. Ca da Mosto visited a market which was held twice weekly. The commodities brought for sale here included cotton, cotton thread and cloth, vegetables, oil, millet, wooden bowls, palm leaf mats, and, occasionally, weapons. Ca da Mosto also saw some gold being offered for sale, though in small quantities. At the market visited by him, goods were sold by barter; money was not used. People came to the market from within a distance of four to five miles (6 to 7.5 km), "for those who dwelt farther off attended other markets" (Ca da Mosto 1937, 48–49; 1978, 510–11). This suggests that local exchange was regular and that economic surpluses were steady. The fact that the goods brought to the market included craftmen's products is another piece of evidence for this. Yet, the surpluses must have been quite limited. Ca da Mosto writes that the people at the market "were exceedingly poor." Elsewhere he observes that they are "unwilling to exert themselves to sow more than will barely support them throughout the year. Few trouble to raise supplies for the market" (Ca da Mosto 1937, 42; 1978, 506). The limited extent of the surpluses is also confirmed by the absence of towns or of even a single urban centre. Markets were held in fields, near villages. Those in power had to take the poverty of their subjects into account in the exercise of their rule and in the levying of tribute and other impositions. They could therefore exploit their subjects only to a limited degree.

Political Organization

Ca da Mosto described two Wolof rulers. One of them, Zuchalin, ruled an area south of the mouth of the river Senegal, and was referred to as "re di Senega", king of Senega (Ca da Mosto 1978, 495; 1937, 29). Ca da Mosto may have been talking here of the ruler of the kingdom of Walo. According to the Venetian traveller, the ruler was not a hereditary sovereign, but was selected as such by the local lords. His kingdom was small and his people poor. The king "has no fixed income: save that each year the lords of the country in order to stand well with him, present him with horses . . . forage, beasts such as cows and goats, vegetables, millet and the like" (Ca da Mosto 1937, 30). These gifts were not sufficient to keep him, so that he supplemented his income by means of regular raids, as a result of which he came by slaves, whom he sold in exchange for horses or settled on land (Ca da Mosto 1978, 496).

The mode of settlement and supervision of these captives was linked to the polygamy of the ruler. He had many wives and kept eight to ten per village. Each of them had a house, land, beasts, and slaves to cultivate the land at her disposal. The ruler travelled up and down the country all the time, and lived in one village after another, where his wives provided for him and his attendants. Food was not abundant and, as Ca da Mosto observed, the people in the king's retinue "are always hungry" (Ca da Mosto 1937, 30–31; 1978, 496–97). Lesser chiefs acted along similar lines.

Ca da Mosto refers to the other ruler as "Budomel", which is assumed to be a corruption of Bor-damel, the name of the ruler of the kingdom of Cayor, whose rulers bore the title *damel* (Rousseau 1933; Monteil 1966, 74; Suret Canale and Barry 1976, 473). Ca da Mosto met Budomel personally, talked to him and had dealings with him. He, moreover, travelled inland, all of which makes his testimony especially valuable. Budomel was likewise an elective ruler. Ca da Mosto does not call him "king of Senega", like Zuchalin, but "signore," lord, and the area over which he ruled as "paese di Budomel," the country of Budomel, while he also uses the expression "terra di Budomel" (Ca da Mosto 1978, 499; 1937, 35). We also learn that Budomel "was lord only of a part of this realm." We may surmise that this implies that even in the mid-fifteenth century, Cayor was still dependent on Djoloff. Ca da Mosto also observes that Budomel and other local rulers "are not lords by virtue of treasure or money, for they possess neither, nor do they expend any money; but on account of ceremonies and the following of people they may truly be called lords" (Ca da Mosto 1937, 37; 1978, 502). Ca da Mosto points out the typical West African custom of dropping on the ground in front of the ruler and sprinkling one's head with sand. In another passage he speaks of the role of the ruler's retinue as a symbol of his power. He says that even though Budomel's means were limited, his power was quite remarkable, and he inspired much awe in his subjects (Ca da Mosto 1978, 503–4).

Budomel's train was not large. For the meeting with Ca da Mosto, he rode at the head of about fifteen horsemen and one hundred and fifty footmen, even though the occasion was important and Budomel wanted to display his status. Usually his train included some two hundred followers, who came and went. The system of providing for this ruler's train was the same as in the case of Zuchalin: Budomel's wives, who lived in various villages, sent him food (Ca da Mosto 1978, 505). Ca da Mosto stayed at one of these villages, in which there were forty to fifty huts, and where nine of Budomel's wives lived. Each had five to six girls in attendance, probably slaves. From time to time, Budomel would visit one of the villages, where he consumed part of the crop and met his wives (Ca da Mosto 1978, 502).

Like Zucholin, Budomel had no towns in his state, but only villages (Ca da Mosto 1978, 502). Probably none of these was his sole fixed residence. The ruler travelled through his country and received his subjects wherever he was currently residing. But he may have had a chief residence where he stayed more frequently than elsewhere. This surmise is based on the description of Budomel's village, which the traveller called "casa sua". At the entrance of his house there were seven courtyards, to which visiting subjects were admitted according to their social rank (Ca da Mosto 1978, 503). The ruler usually saw them for a short while only. Only dignitaries, military leaders, and foreign merchants, Muslim (Arabs, Berbers) and Christian, were admitted to his presence (Ca da Mosto 1978, 503, 505).

We know little of the "lords" mentioned several times by Ca da Mosto, except that they elected the ruler and were obliged to present gifts in his favour, and that their style of left was reminiscent of the ruler's. We also know that differences in social hierarchy were observed during the subjects' meetings with the ruler. We are told about one of the officials, Bisboror, that he was Budomel's nephew (*nipote*), the chief of one of the villages in which Budomel lived (Ca da Mosto 1978, 501, 507). It appears that family links were important in the adminstration of the state, and not just in the case of the villages of the ruler's wives and of slave villages. Other persons could similarly raise their social status as a result of a kinship tie with the ruler.

Political Economy

On the basis of the information we have, we may attempt a description of what the ruler and the ruling group did to ensure an inflow of income. The Wolof at this time had only just laid the foundations of a system of tribute and duties that was to encompass the entire population. At this stage, the system involved gifts in the form of agricultural and farming products or imported horses. The difference between a fully developed system of tribute and a system of customary gifts lies, in my opinion, in the scope of the services rendered, which is limited in the case of the gifts. We may surmise that this resulted from weakness of the economy, in which there were only small surpluses, and an inability to increase the fiscal pressure on the subjects. The system of the presentation of gifts may be viewed as one integrating all the subjects—through the mediation of local lords that is, chiefs of villages or great families—into the organizational framework of the state revenues. It was, therefore, a widespread system; on the other hand, it was subtly adjusted to the limited potential of the economy.

The traveller states outright that the gifts were not sufficient to support the ruler. Therefore it was necessary to think up other forms and systems on which the sovereign and the ruling group could build the political economy. These systems differed from that of gift giving in that they involved only part of the population or select sectors of the economy.

Regrettably, we have no information on market fees. *Ex silentio* conclusions can never be reliable, but it is not precluded that Ca da Mosto failed to notice whether any fees were collected at the market visited by him. Neither did he observe any form of interference by the authorities at the market, which is rather intriguing. He may have left out of his account what he found natural, and described only what he found exotic. Hence it cannot be definitely stated whether or not market fees were collected.

The largest, and more importantly, stable part of the ruler's income came from slave villages administered by his wives. Ca da Mosto's description indicates that food from these villages constituted the basis of the ruler's and his warriors' livelihood. But even this method did not provide sufficient food since, as we know, members of the retinue were pinched with hunger. In the circumstances, raids and plunder were a necessity. Booty in the form of agricultural products and domesticated animals permitted the ruler to make up for the deficiencies and satisfy the needs of his train. Slaves were the most important prize. Their settlement on land led to the creation and development of the slave villages mentioned above. Thus the slave village system could not have worked without raids and the capture of people.

External trade was another form of activity supplementing the scant resources from gifts, slave villages, and raids. It was a source of commodities unobtainable in the framework of the local economy, the most important of which were horses, a symbol of wealth and prestige. These were purchased from Arabs and Berbers at a price of nine to fourteen slaves per horse (Ca da Mosto 1978, 511). Since the establishment of relations with Europeans, horses could also be purchased from them. Because slaves were exchanged for horses, raids as the source of booty and people were also the source of the main trade commodity. Conversely, horses made raids aimed at the capture of people more effective. The exchange of slaves for horses, made possible by raids, became a distinct economic and governmental activity, largely independent of the internal economy. What was important was a supply of food for the army, but this derived only in part from exploitation of the local economy and in part from plunder. We know nothing of the conditions and mechanisms of external trade involving other commodities, such as iron, imported from the banks of the river Gambia, and gold in small quantities. We may only surmise that slaves, and perhaps also salt, were exchanged for these goods.

Interpretation

Thus the economic foundations of the nascent Wolof state and the modes of securing the necessary income for the sovereign and the ruling group varied. Perhaps the restriction of tribute—or rather taxation?—to customary gifts resulted not only from weaknesses of the economy but also from the nature of government, which was elective and therefore to some degree dependent on and controlled by the social factor. In this situation, the sovereign and the ruling group evolved distinct, profit oriented activities. Slave villages were, in fact, economic enclaves. Raids and foreign trade were aspects of economic, political, and military activity that were largely independent of the local community and the traditional economy.

The three modes of assuring additional sources of revenue were strictly interrelated. None could be developed without the other two. On the other hand, all were weakly connected with, and independent of, the remainder of the economy. It looks as if a distinct area or enclave of economic activity at the disposal of the ruling group and the sovereign was created in the framework of the early state organization. The population, living in traditional extended family and village communities, was not involved in it and was not subjected to strong pressures of state taxation.

It would be difficult to indicate a similar separation between a state and a nonstate sector on the political plane. Extra income independent of the local economy strengthened the ruler's position with regard to all of his subjects. The ruler was the lord of the population at large, set apart by his prestige, ceremonies, and retinue. The nascent state organization evolved new institutions or transformed existing ones. Apart from the sovereign's distinct authority, these included his court and his retinue. These institutions functioned within the framework of the entire community, embracing all subjects rather than parts of the population. The evolution of the sovereign's kinship system reached a scale unknown in prestate times. His family included relations exercizing the functions of local chiefs, probably also military commanders. They were active within the context of the entire society. The ruler's wives, who administered slave villages, were active within a specific sector of the economy aimed at providing extra revenue for the ruler.

Another important factor, aside from the creation of new, distinct spheres of activity, was the shifting of part of the costs of the state apparatus to foreign populations outside its territory.

This was achieved through raids, which can be considered against the background of the role of wars in the history of West Africa in general (Bazin and Terray 1982). The outcome of such raids varied. The simplest type was that involving the plundering and exploitation of neighbors. As a result, the difference in development between a protected, better populated state territory and the ravaged neighbouring territories increased. In this particular case, depopulated and devastated areas were not incorporated into the state territory. Another variant may also have been possible: the raided areas were gradually incorporated into the state territory in such a way that, rather than being plundered, the population of such an invaded area was in time made to pay tribute. Yet another variant entailed the attacked community's effective defence and creation of its own state organization. This usually did not put an end to the raids and wars.

Summary

The type of political organization evolved by the Wolof, as described in the mid-fifteenth century by Ca da Mosto, indicates that, despite limited scope of the economy and small surpluses, a state could come into being and build the foundations of an economy through: (1) the creation of enclaves, controlled and exploited by ruling groups within the frame work of the entire economy; (2) shifting part of the burden in connection with the creation of the state outside its territory, either through external trade or by means of raids on neighbours. Both types of activity undertaken by the ruling group were strictly interrelated. Both enabled the restriction of fiscal pressure on the local population living in traditional communities.

References

Barros, Joao de
1945   *Asia de Joao de Barros. Dos feitos os Portugueses fizeram no descobrimentos e conquista dos mares e terras do Oriente. Primeira decada.* Ed. Hernani Cidado. Lisbon: Manuel Murias.
Barry, Boubacar
1972   *Le royaume du Waalo. Le Sénégal avant la conquête.* Paris: Maspero.

Bazin, Jean and Emmanuel Terray, eds.
1982   *Guerre de lignages et guerre d'états en Afrique.* Paris: Édi-
          tions des Archives Contemporaines.

Boxer, C. R.
1969   *The Portuguese seaborne empire 1415–1825.* London: Ox-
          ford University Press.

Brigaud, Felix
1962   Histoire traditionelle du Sénégal. *Études sénégalaises* 9:24–
          56.

Brulez, W.
1968   Les voyages de Cadamosto et le commerce guinéen au 15e
          siècle. *Bulletin de l'Institut Belge de Rome.* 39:311–26.

Ca da Mosto, Alvise
1937   *The voyages of Cadamosto and other documents on West-
          ern Africa in the second half of the 15th century.* Ed. G.
          R. Crone. London: Hakluyt Society.
1978   Le navigazioni di Alvise Ca'da Mosto e Pietro di Sintra.
          In *Navigazioni e viaggi*, Giovanni Battista Ramusio, ed.
          M. Milanesi. 1:461–542. Torino: Einaudi.

Curtin, Philip D.
1975   *Economic changes in precolonial Africa. Senegambia in
          the era of the slave trade.* Madison: University of Wisconsin
          Press.

Gaden, Henri
1912   Légendes et coutumes sénégalaises (Cahiers de Yoro Dyao).
          Revue d'Ethnographie et de Sociologie 3/4:1–31.

Gomes, Diogo
1959   *De la première découverte de la Guinée, récit par Diogo
          Gomes, fin du 15e siècle*, ed. Th. Monod, R. Mauny, and
          G. Duval. Bissau: Centro de Estudios da Guiné Portu-
          guesa.

Karpinski, Rafal
1968   Considérations sur les échanges de caractère local et ex-
          térieur de la Sénégambie dans la deuxième moitié du 15e
          et au début du 16e siècle. *Africana Bulletin* 8:65–83.

Mauny, Raymond
1961   *Tableau géographique de l'Ouest africain au Moyen Age.*
          Dakar: Institut Français d'Afrique noir.

Monteil, Vincent
1966   *Esquisses sénégalaises (Walo, Kayor, Dyolof, Mourides.
          Un visionaire).* Dakar: Université de Dakar. Institut Fran-
          çais d'Afrique noir.
1967   The Wolof kingdom of Kayor. In *West African kingdoms
          in the nineteenth century*, ed. C. Daryll Forde and P. M.
          Kaberry, 260–81. London: I.A.I. and Oxford University
          Press.

Rousseau, R.
1929–33   Le Sénégal d'autrefois. Étude sur le Oualo; Cahiers de
               Yoro Dyae. *Bulletin du Comité d'Études historiques et
               scientifiques de l'AOF.* Vols. 12, 14, 16.
Suret Canale, Jean and Boubacar Barry
1976   The Western Atlantic Coast to 1800. In *History of West
               Africa*, ed. J.F.A. Ajayi and M.Crowder, 1:456–511. Lon-
               don: Longman.
Wade, Ahmadou
1964   Chronique du Walo sénégalais (1186–1855) published and
               edited by V. Monteil. *Bulletin de l'IFAN*, Series B, Vol.
               26, no. 3/4, 440–98. Dakar: Institut Français d'Afrique
               noir.
Zurara, Gomes Eanes
1960   *Chronique de Guinée*, ed. L. Bourdon. Dakar: Institut
               Français d'Afrique noir.

6

Early State Economics: Cahokia, Capital of the Ramey State

Patricia J. O'Brien

Cahokia is the largest archaeological site north of the Rio Grande and the largest Middle Mississippian site in the United States. At its height it covered 8.4 km², had over 100 earthen mounds, and may have had a population of 25,000 people or more. For these reasons it has a special role in relation to theories concerning the cultural development of native North Americans, but the site also has wider theoretical significance.

To some (Fowler 1974; Mochon 1972; O'Brien 1972a; Porter 1969) it is evidence that the American Indian achieved either an "urban" or a "protourban" condition. To others (Ford 1974; Hines 1977; 1978; Peebles and Kus 1977), this and other Middle Mississippian sites indicate that pre-Columbian cultural development in this land peaked at a "chiefdom" level. To two other scholars, Sears (1968) and Gibbon (1974) Middle Mississippian at this site represents an elaboration of political development at a "state" level. Such diversity of opinion about a single archaeological site or about a single cultural tradition is reflective not simply of disagreements on data interpretation but of deeper theoretical issues and perspectives.

First, these disagreements are obviously definitional: how does one define "urban", the "city", the "state", and the "chiefdom"? Second, how does one operationalize the correlates of a definition? That is, what evidence, be it archaeological, ethnographic, or historical, can be considered indicative of a specific definition? Third, how adequate or useful are the concepts of "chiefdom" and "state"? And fourth, how powerful is the cultural evolutionary paradigm of bands-tribes-chiefdoms-states upon which it is based?

The reason these issues are of particular merit lies in the fact that, although there is a very large literature on the nature of the state and how it arose within the fields anthropology, history, political science, and sociology, the examples employed in almost all those studies are fundamentally historical in nature. That is, they are based upon written records.

The earliest state in the world apparently arose in ancient Sumer in the Near East, but our historical documents from the Sumerian city-states deal with completely transformed systems. Since the beginnings of the state are to be found in prehistory, we must recognize that it is ultimately the archaeological record which must be the source of our understanding of how ths change occurred. Haas (1982) has explicitly recognized this by the title of his book: *The Evolution of the Prehistoric State*. Still, in facing this issue he too had to not only define what he meant by the state, but had to outline the correlates of his definition(s).

Cahokia's great merit is to be found in two facts; (1) that it was a social system which was in the throes of "state transformation," and (2) the archaeological data on that transformation are reasonably available. In the ancient Sumerian cities, and in other ancient cultures, the archaeological evidence of change is deeply buried—under tens of meters of urban debris, so that an archaeologist or other scholar often has only the contents of a ten meter square pit upon which to base theories of culture change. At Cahokia one has to dig only a meter or so below the ground to uncover the data which is essential for such developments. Therefore Cahokia's nature and that of other Middle Mississippian communities is significant.

For the purpose of this paper it will be accepted that Cahokia is the capital of the "Ramey" state, and as an example of a very early state its economic system is important and will be examined here. The political arguments of its statehood will not be presented here because they have been outlined elsewhere (O'Brien, n.d.).

The size of Cahokia, about 25,000 at its peak (Gregg 1975b, 134), and the size and number of its nearby communities (Metro or East St. Louis, St. Louis, Mitchell, and Pulcher) within the American Bottom locality make it apparent that the area would have been rapidly depleted of some of its most basic resources (wood and resident game, for example). At the same time it completely lacked other necessary resources (salt, chert, sandstone, and so forth) except as they occurred in small quantities within the area. Moreover, in spite of all the different site surveys within the locality, archaeologists have not located sufficient numbers of farmsteads to supply the necessary quantities of foodstuff (corn, sunflower and squash) needed to support the farmers and occupants of those civic-ceremonial centers (Woods and Lopinot 1989). Therefore the delineation of Cahokia's hinterland (figure 6.1) and its more farflung economic ties is important (figure 6.2). This will be done by examining Cahokia's (1) subsistence base and labor force, (2) its trading network, and (3) evidence, if any, of tribute.

Subsistence and Labor Specialization

Subsistence at Cahokia and other sites in the American Bottom, its basic economy, was built upon agricultural production stressing corn and squash cultivars. Domesticates like sunflower, maygrass, marsh elder, and the bottle gourd were grown but were less important (Johannessen 1984). This system is characterized by a series of individual farmsteads, some of which have been documented as having raised fields (Fowler 1969; Riley and Freimuth 1979), as well as other specialized agricultural sites (Gregg 1975a), whose produce fed the occupants of the surrounding larger communities as well as the farmers themselves.

The widespread nature of this system of farmsteads, throughout the Middle Mississippian universe, has been documented by Con-

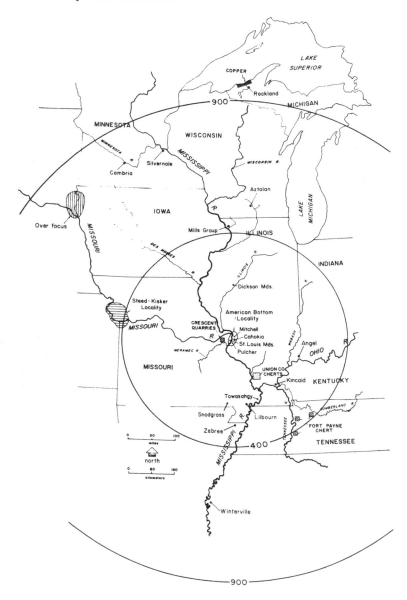

FIGURE 6.1
The American Bottom locality showing the location of major temple
mound sites within it: Cahokia, Mitchell, Metro (East St. Louis), St. Louis
and Pulcher groups.

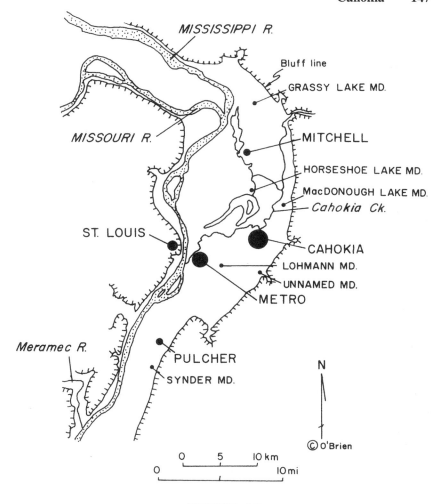

FIGURE 6.2
Map of the heart of the Mississippi River drainage showing the location of Middle Mississippian or Cahokia influenced sites; the 400 and 900 km radii of the trade network is indicated.

ner (1985), Mehrer (1988), O'Brien (1978), Smith (1978a and b), and Wagner (1986), while one of the earliest Mississippian farmsteads ever analyzed was Hatchery West, about 75 km due east of Cahokia (Binford et al. 1970). Unfortunately, its full import was not recognized in the late 1960s. In addition, Lewis (1982) discusses the very small agricultural hamlets in this system. Other plant resources used extensively were nuts: hickory and walnut almost exclusively; seeds: erect knotweed, goosefoot, wild sunflower, wild marsh elder, and pigweed; and fruits and berries: grape, wild plum, chokecherry, persimmon, paw paw, blackberry, and black haw (Johannessen 1984).

Protein resources were based on small mammal hunting, especially of white-tailed deer, and extensive exploitation of waterfowl, fish, reptiles, amphibians, and mollusca from the nearby Mississippi River and numerous streams and oxbow lakes (Kelly 1979). Dog was also consumed. Lewis (1974) and Smith (1975) document this same pattern for other Middle Mississippian communities. These animals were procured at specialized hunting, fishing, fowling, and mollusca collection stations. Additionally, the pelts of small furbearers and deerskin would have been used for clothing. The presence of spindle whorls point to cloth production.

Thus fundamentally, Cahokia with its elite and commoners was supported by farmers in its hinterland who lived on farmsteads which were linked to agricultural hamlets and villages that in turn were tied to one-temple-mound communities also specializing in agricultural production. These farmers undoubtedly hunted and fished for their own consumption, but likely some of these foodstuffs were taken to large centers like Cahokia. Additionally, it is quite likely that some of the inhabitants of Cahokia and the other towns had productive gardens, and hunted and fished for recreation, to supplement their own protein resources, to exchange with neighbors, and also to use as barter in the trading centers (markets?) of those large communities.

The rest of the economy was based on a labor force (excluding the farmers) of skilled and unskilled workers. The unskilled workers without doubt built the hundreds of earthen mounds found throughout the American Bottom as well as the ceremonial structures and the residences of the elites. Also, they were probably the miners who dug the cherts at quarries, the galena, and the copper.

The specialists included potters (Griffith 1981; O'Brien 1972b; Porter 1976, 1983; Stimmell and Helmann 1981), shell bead manufacturers (Harn [1971, 36] reports two bead manufacturing areas:

one at the Merrill Tract 15B in Cahokia and the other at the Wilshire site (Ms-v-342) at Granite City, Illinois, Yerkes [1983] documents these activities extensively at Cahokia itself), and metalworkers (Cushing 1894; Watson 1950). The artistry of flint knappers and lapidists imply their existence. The activities of weavers are documented on textile impressed ceramics (Holmes 1896) and garments rendered in art. Feather working is implied through art also.

Some of these individuals produced commodities used by large numbers of the populace while others made "prestige" items or "gifts" used mainly by the ruling elite. Some of the products of these crafts were the result of part-time cottage industries (Prentice 1983).

The raw materials for this system were obtained at specialized extraction sites involved in the mining of copper, flint, galena, special clays, and other exotic stones as well as lumber, salt, and conch and rapine bird trophy procurement (Bell 1953; Foster and Whitney 1850; Hoxie 1980; Ives 1975; Keslin 1964; Lewis 1889; Muller 1984; Walthall 1981). These sites are found distributed over a 900 km radius from Cahokia (see figure 6.2).

Trade

While most of these materials are within a 450 km radius of the American Bottom some come from over 900 km away. All these people were involved in the production of items used by the ruling elite, but many of these items were also used by the local rural population. Whether this system was a "redistributive" type or a more elaborate "market" type is the subject of different opinions. Nevertheless it is the most complex and sophisticated economic system north of Mexico and is qualitatively different from the more ancient Hopewellian economy of a thousand years earlier. For our purposes, we will ask the question: what kinds of commodities were traded in the Cahokia exchange system and how were they acquired?

Evidence of a class of traders among the descendents of the Middle Mississippians is reported historically and is summarized in Myer's (1928, 738) monumental study of Indian trails in the southeastern United States. He notes that, in general, traders had a low status. Because those local cultures (Cherokee, Natchez, and so forth) were bearers of the Middle Mississippian tradition into the earliest historic period, one may infer that such a class of low status traders probably existed in immediate prehistoric times. Archeological evidence supporting this is suggested by Hudson (1976, 88–89) who notes that the "long-nose god" masks which were found in Middle Mississippian sites, including Cahokia, may belong to traders. He argues thus because historically the Aztec traders, *pochteca*, worshipped *Yacatecuhtli* who is portrayed with a long nose.

The importance of this type of ethnohistoric evidence points up the problem of locating archaeological data acceptable to establish a class of traders, and of trade itself.

The problems of trade and of identifying it archaeologically are outlined by Crawford (1973) in her discussion of the problem of invisible imports and exports in third millennium B.C. in Mesopotamia. She points out that historical records show the importing and exporting of specific highly perishable materials: garments and cloth of wool and cotton, grain, fish, beasts, oils, fats, wood, and so forth. All these materials are documented in the literature of later Mesopotamian times as imports, but there are practically no archaeological traces of them.

Swanton (1946, 737–42), in his study of the Indians of the Southeast, points out that historically the following items were traded: fruit, *kunti* flour, mockingbirds, pet squirrels, root of *Angelica*, medicinal shrubs like *Ilex vomitoria*, cloaks, corn, peas, beans, deer skins, furs (wildcat, black fox, beaver, otter), deer and bear meat, baskets and mats, oil in jugs, dried or smoked fish, canoes, wooden platters, and salt. All these items are perishable. Also traded were flint, shark's teeth, marine shell, pottery (bowls and dishes), tobacco pipes, copper, pearls, and ivory-billed woodpecker bills. These items would be generally imperishable, and, in fact, are found in the archaeological record.

Thus, the ethnohistoric record establishes (1) the presence of a class of traders, (2) that trade was extensive, and (3) that as in the Near East many items would not survive in the archaeological record. It should be mentioned here that we have archaeological data on a great many of the imperishable goods mentioned in the historic record at Cahokia and other sites, as will be established in the following discussion.

Chipped stone artifacts at Cahokia are manufactured from three cherts: Crescent, Mill Creek, and Illinois Novaculite; unfortunately no detailed information quantifying these cherts has been published. In 1974 while examining Illinois State Museum ceramics from Tract 15B at Cahokia, I was struck by the small numbers of chipped stone tools in the collection (excluding the chert debris). Because of an interest in trade and resources, I quantified chert types based on finished artifacts and utilized flakes. I discovered (by weight) that 42.5% of the finished artifacts (FA) were made of Mill Creek chert compared to only 0.01% of the utilized flakes (UF); 52.2% FA were Crescent chert to 84.2% UF; 2.5% FA were Illinois Novaculite to 11.6% UF; and 2.8% FA were of unknown cherts to .03% UF. Thus, over 40% of the finished artifacts were made of foreign cherts while almost 85 percent of the utilized flakes came from the Cahokia controlled Crescent quarries.

Quantification of these materials is also available from the nearby Mitchell site just to the north of Cahokia in the American Bottom. Porter (1974, 881–85) reports 15.6% of the chert was Mill Creek, 1% was Illinois Novaculite (called Koalin), 0.9% was Dongola, and 0.3% was "Root beer chert." The rest, 82.2%, was from the Crescent quarries. Also in the American Bottom is the Horseshoe Lake site (Gregg 1975a, 271), a small one-temple-mound agricultural community, where about 7% of the chert was Mill Creek and the rest (93%), Crescent chert. At the Range site, a farmstead near Cahokia, 2.4% of the chert was Mill Creek and the rest local cherts (Mehrer 1982, 106–12).

This pattern of imported chert utilization is not unique to Cahokia and the American Bottom sites. Perazio (1981, 85), at the Orendorf site in the central Illinois River valley, about 230 km north of Cahokia, reports use of a local chert called Avon as well as Burlington (Crescent) cherts from the lower part of the Illinois valley, Dongola and Kaolin (Illinois Novaculite) cherts from Union County, and possibly Harrison County, Indiana hornstone and Lamoine chert, but no Mill Creek cherts. He also says the chert debris is predominantly local, but that the chert percentages are reversed for the finished artifacts suggesting higher grade materials were preferred for them.

Southard (1973) reports a similar import pattern at the site of Towosahgy in southeastern Missouri, where 36.4% of the chert was Mill Creek, 5% Illinois Novaculite, 9% Fort Payne, 33.6% local cobble, and 15.9% unknown. Imported chert—Mill Creek and Dover (Fort Payne) "in their natural state as large slabs"— was found in the nearby Powers phase sites in southeastern Missouri and was used in hoe and knife manufacture (Price and Griffin 1979, 18–19). As early as 1953, Bell (1953, 300) noted the foreign cherts at the Kincaid site on the Ohio River in southeastern Illinois, for he reported 25% Dover (Fort Payne) chert, 8% Mill Creek, 5% Illinois Novaculite, 10% local gravels and 52% unknown cherts at the site.

While we might expect some imported cherts at large sites, it is interesting to note that even an isolated farmstead like the Bonnie Creek site on a tributary of the Big Muddy River in southern Illinois, over a 175 km from Cahokia, got 17% of its chert from the Crescent quarries area. This clearly suggests, since cherts are mundane materials, an economic integration of Middle Mississippian nonelites incompatible with a chiefdom model. It also makes one wonder, "what is given in exchange?" Food stuffs, produced by the farming family, is the logical answer, but is archaeologically invisible.

The Crescent quarries are located in Missouri about 48 km due west from Cahokia. The area around them has been surveyed by Ives (1975), and no temple mounds or other village sites are located beside them (see figures 6.1–6.2). They would seem to belong to Cahokia's hinterland. The distance to Cahokia via the Meramec River and up the Mississippi is about 64 km. An overland portage and passage down the Missouri River constitutes a trip of about 97 km.

Mill Creek chert, Illinois Novaculite, and Dongola are only found in Union County in southern Illinois. While no significant recent work has been done on sites in the area (see Phillips 1900), a cluster of temple mound communities is present. Minimally, they suggest a local hierarchy directing the exploitation of these resources. The approximate distance from the Union County quarry areas (near the mouth of the Big Muddy River) would be roughly

177 km on a straight line. The distance via the Mississippi River would be closer to 225 or 240 km. Additionally, Dover or Fort Payne chert comes from Perry, Humphry, Stewart, and Cheatham Counties in western Tennessee which is even further away. What is significant about these data is the fact that something as mundane as chert was imported in "quantity" by Middle Mississippian communities of different sizes.

Other mundane manufacturing materials were also imported, for Porter (1974, 922) notes that the heavy, iron-cemented sandstones used for abrading tools (all of which were made of such stone) at the Mitchell site also came from Jackson and Union Counties in southern Illinois. This sandstone was used at Cahokia's Tract 15B for over half the abrading tools. How widespread this practice of sandstone importation was is difficult to assess because resource studies of these materials have not been made at other sites.

Other nonperishable materials traded between Cahokia and other Mississippi sites are ceramics. Cahokia trade ceramics, especially the ceremonial ware: Ramey Incised, has been found at Steed-Kisker sites in the Kansas City area, at Dickson Mound's locality sites on the Illinois River, in the Apple River sites in Jo Davies County, Illinois (Bennett 1945, 1952), at Aztalan in southern Wisconsin, from a mound on Chambers Island in Green Bay, Wisconsin (Gillman 1874, 374–75), far to the north in the copper mining district of Keweenaw Point along southern Lake Superior (James B. Griffin, personal communication), and to the south at the Winterville site in Mississippi (Brain 1969, 307).

More exotic and ceremonial materials traded to Cahokia included copper, galena, conch, *olivella* shell, sharks' teeth, and mica. Geological data on prehistoric copper mining has been known since at least as early as A.D. 1850 through the report of Foster and Whitney (1850, 158–63). In addition to describing extensive Indian mining operations, they also reported on a pyramidal temple mound near the town of Rockland (Foster and Whitney 1850, 161). Unfortunately, we have almost no data on the nature of that site. Further data on copper exploitation is to be found in the work of Cremin (1980, 7–16) and his associates (Dorothy 1980, 39–90; Hoxie 1980, 25–38) who report on the Sand Point site (20BG14) on the Keweenaw Peninsula. The site is only about

55 km northeast of Rockland and has a "moderately sized copper workshop" (Hoxie 1980, 32). Ceramics resembling those from Aztalan and Cahokia have been reported and may be trade vessels (Dorothy 1980, 69).

The presence of the temple mound in the area can reasonably be considered evidence of a permanent Middle Mississippian intrusion into the area and is not what one would expect if only small expeditions were entering the area to exploit the copper mines. The Ramey symbolism on the pottery from Sand Point could mean the local people simply liked the pottery or it could be reflective of an acceptance of the religious ideology associated with that symbolism: Hall's (1972) "rain-fertility-continuity of life" elements or Howard's (1968) green corn ceremonialism, while the temple mound itself is associated with a mortuary complex outlined by Brown (1976) with its attendent ancestor worship. By the way, Lewis (1889) reported burials were found under that mound when it was excavated by local people in the last century.

Walthall (1981, 41–42) in his major study of prehistoric galena utilization reports the bulk of Mississippian galena is derived from the Southeastern Missouri Potosi deposits and suggests "Cahokia was a major Mississippian export center for galena." Also a large deposit of mica from the western North Carolina was found in Mound 72, and mica was mined and traded from that region (Ferguson 1978, 211–17). The importation of conch, sharks' teeth, *olivella*, and *marginella* from the Gulf Coast has been extensive documented (Titterington 1938, 15; Yerkes 1983, 512), but unfortunately no quantification of its volume is possible at this time.

One can see from this list that many of the imperishable items traded in the historic period were traded in the prehistoric. Of most interest is the bulk trading of chert and sandstone, both primary materials used in tool manufacture.

If we examine the problem of invisible trade at Cahokia, we may make some interesting inferences. At Cahokia we find spindle whorls; these are centrally perforated ceramic disks usually made of potsherds and reflect textile production. Spindle whorls are common at Cahokia, but none have been found in the Kansas City area at the Steed-Kisker sites. By contrast there are practically no end scrapers at Cahokia, a common tool for processing animal hides and ubiquitous on the Plains with its great bison herds. Endscrapers are common at the Steed-Kisker sites, and they are also found in very high incidence at the Dickson Mounds site on the Illinois River (Harn 1975, 425). The latter site has been suggested as a center for processing and exchanging bison hides and bringing them to Cahokia (Lawrence Conrad, personal communication).

Given Midwestern weather conditions, textiles and hides for clothing would be essential, and our common sense and a few artifacts indicate that textiles and hides could have been an important commodity, but that they would have been an *invisible* one. Another invisible trade item would have been meat (dried deer and bison, as jerky or pemmican). Interestingly, McAdams (1880, 35–36) reported finding buffalo teeth at Cahokia in the nineteenth century so there is some archaeological proof of this assertion. A third invisible (or almost invisible) commodity would be fish, dried or smoked, but it too is partially documented in Kelly's (1979, 8) faunal lists, for she reports sturgeon and pike, northern cold water fish, at American Bottom sites surrounding Cahokia. A fourth partly invisible commodity would have been salt. It is not completely invisible because the salt pans used in its manufacture are distinctive and have been recovered in the ceramic assemblages at Cahokia (O'Brien 1972). Cahokia's nearest salt source is on the Meramec River near the Crescent quarries, but the main salt processing area in the eastern United States is in the Cumberland region of Tennessee which includes the Great Salt Spring north of the Ohio River in southeastern Illinois (Muller 1984). Finally, corn, seeds, and squash, to name only a few foods, would have been invisible trade too.

Pertinent to the source of sturgeon, and probably pike, are comments made by Schoolcraft (1821, 171–78) in 1820. He reported visiting the Keweenaw Point copper mining area on the shores of southern Lake Superior where, on the Portage River, he saw a fishweir from which the Indians had taken enough fish in a few hours to feed a regiment. He said the Indians had used it from time immemorial (Schoolcraft 1821, 174). This weir was only 50 km from the Rockland mound site and only about 10 km from the Sand Point site.

The few American Bottom farmstead sites (known to date) would not have been able to supply the foodstuffs for the maximum of 30,000 people estimated for Cahokia, nor for the minimum of 5,000 over its 500 years history (Gregg 1975b). Cahokia, in just the 100 years of its fluorescence, would have destroyed all the local wood resources for construction and fuel, and the American Bottom area also had to supply the Mitchell, Dupo, Metro, and St. Louis mound groups.

Wood is a highly perishable material, but floated wood charcoal has been recovered from the Mitchell site and identified as bald cypress and spruce. Spruce comes from the woods to the north in Wisconsin and Minnesota (Porter 1974, 133–37), while bald cypress comes from southern Illinois, southeastern Missouri and eastern Arkansas. Wood, of course, is a primary building material and is needed as fuel for cooking and heat.

Specific Middle Mississippian communities specialized in the manufacture of salt which they extracted from saline springs throughout the southeastern United States (Keslin 1964). At Cahokia salt pans are found, and salt processing sites—including a temple-mound site—are found near the mouth of the Meramec River on the west bank of the Mississippi River. Those sites are south of Cahokia by about 32 km, but even they would not have been large enough to supply the whole of the American Bottom, especially since there is evidence it was used in pottery manufacture (Stimmell and Helmann 1981; Stimmell, Helmann, and Hancock 1982) as well as being eaten. Probably salt (with chert) came from Tennessee and Cumberland River drainage which has numerous saline springs. Salt pans litter the Mississippian sites there.

Thus, one can see that the trading system of Cahokia and Middle Mississipians in general involved the importation of both mundane materials in bulk as well as exotic materials, and that it necessitated the creation of specialized extraction sites associated with the exploitation of specific resources: chert, lumber, salt, copper, and so forth. In the literature on trade there is an emphasis on the movement of mundane commodities in large sophisticated market economies. These are the vital industrial materials of which Childe speaks (1950, 16). The bulk trading of mundane items occurs throughout the Middle Mississippian world, and it is obvious that Cahokia functioned as a center for such a network at its peak.

Also potentially associated with trade in state systems are "ports of trade." Polanyi (1968) observes that what he calls "port of trade" did not become evident in the north Syrian coast until the second millennium B.C., and that such ports of trade have been found among the kingdoms of Whydah and Dahomey of West Africa, among the Aztec-Maya area in Mexico, in the Indian Ocean, in Madras, Calcutta, Rangoon, Burma, Colombo, as well as in China. The port of trade, he contends, is a universal aspect of overseas trade and precedes the establishment of international markets. He points out that ports of trade are (1) usually found in coastal or riverine locales, (2) are usually equipped with warehouses and storage, as well as a population skilled in portage and handling of wares, and (3) the trade normally is politically neutral with its neutrality safeguarded by formal agreements between hinterland powers or by consensus of the overseas trading powers involved.

First, strategically, Cahokia is ideally situated to be a port of trade because it is so near the juncture of Missouri, Mississippi, and Illinois Rivers (figure 6.2), and the evidence just reviewed indicates large trading exchanges were functioning. Additionally, as figure 6.1 shows, two American Bottom sites several kilometers west of Cahokia, the St. Louis and Metro or East St. Louis mound groups, are across from each other on the west and east sides of the Mississippi River in a position to completely control all river traffic.

Second, a correlate of storage and warehousing, archeologically speaking, is the presence of such facilities, and at Cahokia we have some clues concerning them. The first clue comes not from Cahokia itself, but from the Mitchell site, a companion Mississippian site located just to the north of Cahokia on Long Lake in the American Bottom. Porter (1974) shows that this site had a single occupation of short duration and its basic function was to be a port of trade. Porter believes that the excavated plaza areas was a market place where people gathered and exchanged goods. If his agrument is correct, it would perhaps hold for other Mississippian towns as they all have central plazas.

A more fascinating piece of data on plazas comes from Tract 15B at Cahokia itself. There in a secondary plaza (the main central plaza is south of Monks Mound) located between four mounds about 500 meters west of Monks Mound, a large structure called a bastion compound, was excavated (Wittry and Vogel 1962, 16, 28). The bastions were about 10 feet in diameter and were separated by about 18 foot intervals. The structure was probably about 180 feet square at least, and was located in the center of this plaza.

Although the entrance is guarded by a double bastion, giving it a fort-like appearance, it is difficult to conceive of it as being a jail for evidence of daily living is nearly absent. One interpretation of it is that it may have been a trading center; another that it is a storage center of some kind. Whether storing ceremonial paraphernalia or military paraphernalia (hence in that sense functioning as an arsenal), or whether it functioned as storage for trading materials cannot be ascertained on the present evidence.

Unfortunately very little archaeological debris was found within it. Still the structure could have functioned as a market with the merchants storing their materials within the "bastions" and laying them out as is done in bazaars in the Near East today, then locking and closing the facility in the evening. Such a routine would not be incompatible with the way market places were run within ports of trade in the sense that the buyer would come and purchase his goods in a small enclosed area under a manager who would maintain law and order and set value equivalencies. The problem with such interpretations is testing them vigorously using only concrete archaeological data (excluding the structure itself).

This is an especially acute problem at Cahokia (as it may be in other centers) because the Cahokians seem to have gone in for some massive garbage collection. Chmurny (1973) in his analysis of the barrow pit under Mound 51 has definitely shown that the pit (which was originally the dirt source for building Monks Mound), was rapidly filled with garbage and other debris, suggesting that the Cahokians were systematically collecting their garbage and filling in the areas they had excavated to get dirt for temple mounds. This practice hinders the establishment of functional patterns at Cahokia, especially when practically no artifact material is recovered from the different structures.

Ironically though, if this compound was functioning as a market, we would, in fact, not expect to find a great deal of material because it would be kept clean. The traders themselves would remove their materials after the market meetings or fairs were ended. They would take home what they did not sell and would return with it and more when the market reopened.

Thus, it is possible that Cahokia functioned as a "port of trade", via structures like the compound, and if that is the case we have evidence of warehousing and storage. A population skilled in portage and handling wares (that is, traders and the bearers) cannot be documented, except if one accepted the long-nose god masks as evidence of this group. Still, the physical capacities of the people who carried the earth to build mounds would be no different than that needed to carry loads of trade goods. Indeed, using De Peso's (1980, 20–21) modified information on overland foot travel and inland boat travel distances for the Mesoamerican world economy, we find the average distances covered by those traders to be 484 km. When these data are combined with early Near Eastern information on lengths of trade routes the average is raised to 550 km or 22 days of travel (De Peso 1980, 20–21). If these data are applied to Cahokia's trading network, we find that the sites of Wisconsin, northern Michigan, southeastern Minnesota, eastern South Dakota, western Missouri, and northern Illinois are within the trading sphere of the site (distances of 400 to 900 km are involved; see figure 6.2).

Finally, whether Cahokia possessed a more sophisticated true market economy of the sort that Polanyi attributes to the overseas trading system of the Ancient Greeks cannot be established at present. Still, given Cahokia's apparent ideological dominance throughout the heart of America as reflected in what have been called "Old Village" influences in the past, especially via ceramic design motifs, it was probably *not* politically neutral. This latter issue will be examined next.

Tribute

The third aspect of the economics of the early state is tribute. The concept of tribute has a number of meanings, but fundamentally it involves a reoccurring payment of a sum of money or other valuable goods by one people to the ruler of another people. It is different from taxes because taxes are paid by citizens to their government. For this reason tribute involves questions of political dominance and subordination. Those who receive tribute have power over those who give it. Tribute can be expressed by payment in money, in goods, in services, in human lives, or in any combination thereof (see Trouwborst 1987, 129–37). Mair (1977, 96–97), quoting Maquet, observes that a function of tribute was to "provide the ruling class with consumption goods," and "to maintain it in power."

Archaeological evidence of tribute, in a setting where coinage was not used and written records were lacking, presents difficulties. It could potentially be identified by the presence of exotic materials or artifacts, made from exotics which only occur in one region, appearing in another, although one would have to be able to rule out trade as their source. Or, in the case of a shipment of "dancing girls," the tribute paying populace might be physically distinct enough to be identified as intrusive in the dominant population. Regardless of the nature of tribute though, it implies dominance and force in the relationship and the most logical manner in which it is expressed in the archaeological record will be in warfare. Therefore we will seek evidence of Cahokia dominating other populations, their lands, and resources within a warlike setting.

In the 1930s and 1940s it had been recognized by archaeologists working in different regions of the Midwest that archaeological complexes were present that had strong Cahokian similarities, the phrase "Old Village" and "Trappist" (for two broad chronological periods at Cahokia) were commonly employed to express these relationships. Cahokia was seen as the source of these traits, and explanations for them ranged from simple "influences" to "direct colonization" depending on the number and character of the similarities.

Fortified towns like Dickson Mounds in central Illinois (Harn 1975), Aztalan in southern Wisconsin (Bennett 1952) and the Mills Group on the Apple River in northwestern Illinois (Bennett 1945) are all temple mound communities of varying size. Each is considered representative of a direct migration out of Cahokia because there is no evidence of a local Mississippian evolution. Indeed, the indigenous cultural complexes are called Late Woodland. Each site is north of Cahokia. Figure 6.3 shows the geographic distribution of those sites as well as other one-temple-mound communities whose character is not as well known. These

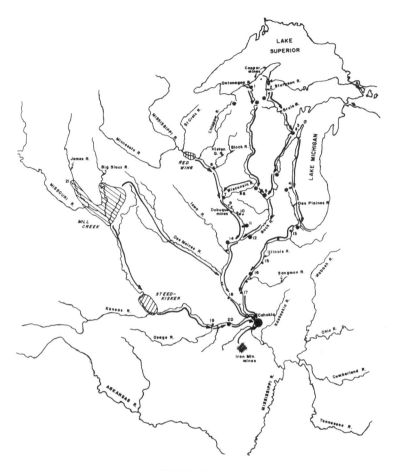

FIGURE 6.3
**Map of the movement of resources and trade goods between Cahokia
and northern and western Mississippian sites and complexes (arrows
mark the routes, asterisks the portage points. Note 1 identifies the sites
and resources).**

Note: The names of the sites in figure 6.3 are as follows: Rockland (1),
Sand Point site (2), Chamber Island site (3), N. Milwaukee (4), Aztalan
(5), Gottshall Pictograph site (6), Prairie du Chien (7), Trempealeau
(8), Edwards site (9), Mills Group (10), Thomson "Mounds" (11), Spring
Hill "Mounds" (12), Mt. Joliet (13), Muscatine Island mounds (14),
Kingston (15), Dickson Mounds (16), LaGrange mound (17), Ashburn
mound (18), Cote Sans Dessein mound (19), Berger mounds (20), and
the Mitchell, S.D. site (21). Also marked are the location of the Hixton
quarry, the Dubuque galena mines, the Iron Mtn. or Potosi hematite-
galena mines, and the "Sturgeon" river.

latter sites were destroyed at the end of the nineteenth century as the modern United States developed, so in a few cases we do not know if they were originally fortified or were tied to Cahokia, but we do know they are culturally intrusive. Each site is strategically situated to monitor river traffic on either the Mississippi and/or its tributaries. Each site is associated with an important resource.

First, the largest site, Aztalan, is stragetically situated in the center of the distribution of a series of sites in the northernmost reaches of Cahokia's polity. Aztalan, though located on the Crawfish River southeast of Madison, Wisconsin, is surrounded by one-temple-mound sites. East of it is a site in northern edges of the City of Milwaukee, along the ancient Green Bay Trail. Northeast of it, at the entrance to Green Bay, is a site on Chambers Island controlling transport through the bay and south towards the Des Plaines River or on to Aztalan. Far to the north is the Rockland site, on the Ontonagan River, which is positioned to monitor the transport of fish and copper from Keweenaw Point south, over the upper Wisconsin River via the Crawfish to Aztalan and down the Rock River to Cahokia. An alternative route was southwest over the Black River to Trempealeau and south down the Mississippi River past the galena mines north and south of Dubuque, Iowa, or south-southeast over the Wisconsin River to the site at Prairie du Chien just north of Dubuque, Iowa in the vicinity of galena mining operations.

Aztalan has been suggested (Porter 1969, 161) as the major "frontier" town in the north, especially for the important copper trade of upper Michigan; we could add, for fish, furs, and lumber too. A Mississippian presence in the form of a small pyramidal mound site was reported as early as 1850 on the Ontonagon River near Rockland, Michigan (Foster and Whitney 1850, 160–62), situated roughly in the center of a 50 km long area of aboriginal copper mining activity. That mound was visited by Lewis (1889) who discovered that the local population had excavated into it. Burials were reported at its base. Unfortunately, we have no pottery associated with it for precise cultural assignment, although James B. Griffin (personal communication) reports Cahokia pottery from the general region as noted earlier. On the Illinois River the Dickson Mounds site has been suggested as a resource area for animal products (Lawrence Conrad, personal communication), especially meat and bison hides from the Prairie-Plains periphery to the west.

Too little work has been done on the Apple River sites to enable us to totally understand their role in this system, but the nearby Upper Mississippi Valley galena mines were significant. Also there are other sites further north in the Red Wing area of southeastern Minnesota, along the Mississippi and Minnesota rivers, that reflect "Old Village influences," but they are not temple-mound towns (Gibbon 1974, 129–30). Again the exact relationships of these sites to Cahokia are not fully known, that is, whether they are pure frontier towns, but they are in an area that is an obvious source of wood, and we know spruce was imported to Cahokia, as well as furs, and this region was one of the centers of the historic fur trade. Additionally, the Red Wing area was the approximate location of the Sioux Rendezvous before it shifted west to the area of Sioux City, Iowa, on the Missouri River, in the nineteenth century (Blakeslee 1975, figure 1) and was a major trading locus in the protohistoric period.

It can not be accidental that Mississippian temple-mound communities are so militarily and commercially placed. No dried fish or fur pelts or copper ore could move from the Lake Superior region without passing a town on its way south. Nothing or no one could move down the Mississippi River, via the Rock or Illinois Rivers, without being monitored or controlled by fortified towns. Having said that, what evidence is there of potential tribute extraction?

First, we know the major towns were all fortified, and fortifications are only necessary in an environment of war, conflict, and exploitation. Second, in a recent intriguing study of petroglyphs at the Gottschall site in southwestern Wisconsin, on the south side of the Wisconsin River, Salzer (1987, 418–72) has recorded painted Middle Mississippian figures decorated with Mississippian symbols including sun symbols upon their foreheads. He argues these scenes are pictoral renderings of the Ioway and Winnebago myths of the struggles of Red Horn. To the Winnebago, for example, Red Horn led his people against the giants who, among other things, were cannibals. Mississippians at Aztalan practiced cannibalism and Salzer believes the myth reflects an extended historic struggle between northern Oneota peoples like the Win-nebago and southern Cahokia-affiliated Middle Mississippians. Thus, these intrusive Mississippians are in a power situation in the regions north of Cahokia.

Two hundred miles directly west of Cahokia up the Missouri River, in the Kansas City area, are the Steed-Kisker sites. Wedel noted (1943, 211–14) their strong relationship to Cahokia and possession of both "Old Village" and "Trappist" traits in the 1940s. Between Steed-Kisker and Cahokia a variety of Cahokian ceramic materials (pottery and spindle whorls), as well as finely knapped projectile points, have been found in the Ozarks, es-pecially on the Gasconade drainage. This area was used by many people in the surrounding region, including Cahokians, for hunt-ing expeditions and other resource sorties. Interestingly, there is no evidence of warfare in this region, and indeed, the Steed-Kisker population may only be farmers within Cahokia's hinter-land. They are located to control the movement of goods into the Central Plains at the juncture of the Missouri and Kansas rivers.

Sites of the Over Focus, situated in southeastern South Dakota, have an amazing array of ceramics related to Cahokia's Ramey Incised, and those sites very likely were the source of widely traded pelts and feathers from predatory birds, and may be the initial source for bison products coming to Cahokia. Over Focus and Mill Creek sites are related and all their major communities are fortified villages. Tiffany (in press) has argued Mill Creek is ancestoral Mandan Indian and Cahokia derivative. Fortifications again point to war.

Due to the north-south trending nature of rivers in Illinois there are no direct riverine links due east of Cahokia, but an old trail heads due east from Cahokia to the Great Salt Spring in south-eastern Illinois and to the Cumberland regions. At the same time Cahokia's role to the south is unclear. Many small fortified tem-ple-mound towns are found south on the Mississippi River near the earlier mentioned Union County chert quarries, but their exact associations with Cahokia (aside from chert importation) are unknown. Collections available from those sites at the Smith-sonian consist of extruded rim, shell-tempered plain jars, "Ca-hokia crud" or Stumpware, and lobed and/or noded shell-tem-pered vessels. The former are associated with the early "Fairmont" phases at Cahokia while the latter would be later in time and more Lower Mississippian in character. Also present are two copper plates—one with an eagle man and the other with two dancing (?) warriors. These data suggest an early Cahokia relationship with a later independence from the site.

Phillips (1970, 557), while noting the similarity of an unclassified incised ware to Ramey Incised in the Shell Bluff "Complex" of the Lake George site near Yazoo City in Mississippi, points out how little is known of the "Old Village" phase of Cahokia in the lower Mississippi River drainage. More recently, Brain (1969, 1978, 344–47) is convinced that Winterville and other Mississippian sites in the Yazoo Basin of the Mississippi received direct contact from Cahokia and that a proselytizing religious elite was involved.

Incomplete as the information is, recent work by Morse (1975) in northeastern Arkansas at the Zebree site presents further tantalizing clues. This site is a small palisaded intrusive Mississippian village lacking a temple mound. Because of similarities in house construction, burial, raw material used, the microlith industry, ceramic temper, shapes and decoration, and so forth, Morse (1975, 214) feels the site is closely related to Cahokia's Fairmont phase (dating A.D. 900–1050) and is an example of "cultural colonization" (Morse 1975, 227). Again a fortified community points to warfare. Cahokian influences up the Ohio River are recorded at the Kincaid site in southeastern Illinois and at the Angel site east of Kincaid in Indiana (Honerkamp 1975, 311), but their nature is obscure at this time.

From this brief and incomplete summary, we can see that Cahokia's influences were extensive over a wide area of the northern and western half of the American Middle West but also occurred to the south down the Mississippi. When these influences occur they are represented by either trade items or more commonly the borrowing of ceramic traits, especially those associated with the ceremonial ceramic type Ramey Incised, or there is evidence of direct colonization and in some cases the establishment of fortified temple-mound towns. This being so, how do these data relate to the question of tribute?

At the start of this discussion it was suggested that differentiating trade from tribute would be difficult, but we do know that materials were coming from situations in which armed communities were invaded. This means conflict, and situations of conflict are inescapably exploitative.

In addition, one powerful piece of data exists from Cahokia itself. With the burial of an elite man in Mound 72 at Cahokia (Fowler 1974, 21–22) were discovered over 200 sacrificed humans, mostly young women, and a great many elaborate exotic grave offerings. The exotics included a massive pile of sheet mica from western North Carolina, about a dozen polished chucky stones, a staff sheathed with copper, copper and shell beads, and hundreds of beautifully made arrowheads.

Available commercial slides of the burials reveal that the arrowheads, which were clustered, probably represent the remains of bundles of arrows. The points are made of exotic cherts coming from as far away as Wisconsin and the Caddo area of eastern Texas or Oklahoma and western Arkansas. This same distribution occurs with the styles of the points also. A reasonable interpretation of the arrowheads is that they represent bundles of arrows sent by various Indian polities at this elite personage's death. They are probably symbolic of the warriors whose allegiance was pledged to him. If this interpretation is correct, they can be seen as tribute in men.

The sacrificed young women can be local Cahokian women, but they could also represent "tribute in young women" sent to Cahokia's ruler, that is, the equivalent of "dancing girls or concubines" sent along with the warriors. Thus, the offerings in Mound 72 can be interpreted as tribute to the ruler of Cahokia and his relatives in humans as well as tribute in goods or materials, as reflected by the other exotics, and Fowler (1974, 22) himself puts forward this interpretation.

Summary

This examination of Cahokia's economic order reveals several things about a society at the early end of the process of "state transformation." First, as expected, such a society is built upon an efficient agricultural economy—this one being focused on maize and squash production with sunflower, maygrass, and marsh elder grown too. Its hinterland is occupied by farmers who are linked to Cahokia either directly or via communities of ascending orders of complexity—hamlets, villages, and temple-mound towns of various sizes. Indeed, some of those communities are themselves involved in agricultural production. Because the only domestic animal was the dog, dietary protein was acquired through local hunting, fishing, and fowling, but the importation of dried fish and meat from the Great Lakes and the Plains is suggested.

The labor force had some specialists, particularly in the manufacturing of exotic items using exotic materials for elite consumption: shell bead artisans, copper jewelry artisans, lapidaries, flint knappers, potters, and also maybe textile and feather workers. Some of this production involved cottage industries who laborers may have worked seasonally. This is not surprising, for the ultimate development of elaborate systems of labor specialization in agricultural societies must begin with farmers and their families working on other tasks during the off season. Present too were unskilled laborers who constructed the temple mounds, worked in quarries and mines, and transported goods and materials over hundreds of kilometers. The imported materials utilized in this system were often exotics, but there was also the importation of mundane resources like cherts and sandstones, as well as salt.

The trading network linked Cahokian derived communities, some over 900 km from Cahokia, and goods and materials were transported following overland trails and the major waterways within the heart of the American continent. Indeed, important fortified Middle Mississippian communities were strategically placed along these routes to protect the transport of goods.

Some of the goods transported from these areas probably represent tribute to the ruling elite at Cahokia. This is based partly upon their exotic nature but also upon the fact that a tributary relationship, as reflected in the arrow bundles, existed between the Cahokian leadership and peoples of these different regions. Sometime around A.D. 1300 these power relationships shifted, for Cahokia began to decline. That this decline is associated with shifts in Cahokia's military situation is reflected in the historic Red Horn myths of the northern Oneota populations and in increased emphasis on war in the ideological symbolism of the Southern Ceremonial Complex (Brown 1976). The Southern

Ceremonial Complex embodies a majority of elements found in the religion of the Middle Mississippians.

Since no single post-1300 Middle Mississippian society dominated the eastern United States in the same manner as Cahokia, and since many scholars refer to these late societies as "chiefdoms," including with them groups like the historic Cherokee and Natchez, it would seem that the "process of state formation" operating in North America between A.D. 900–1300 was not repeated before the DeSoto's *entrada* into the heart of the Southeast in A.D. 1540.

The author would like to thank a number of individuals who, over a period of years, have read a number of different drafts of manuscripts arguing for Cahokia's statehood. They are Janet Benson, Dena Dincauze, Barry Michie, Harriet and Martin Ottenheimer, Donna C. Roper, and John H. Rowe. They have all made important comments on the logic and organization of this argument.

I also wish to express my appreciation to all the participants of the Symposium on the Economics of the Early State, held in Zagreb, Yugoslavia in July, 1988 under the leadership of Professor Henri Claessen, for their comments and encouragement on a longer draft dealing with some of this issues. I, however, am solely responsible for all the faults of this manuscript.

References

Bareis, Charles J. and James Warren Porter, eds.
1984   *American Bottom Archaeology*. Urbana: University of Illinois Press.
Bell, Robert E.
1953   Lithic Analysis in Archaeological Method. *American Anthropologist* 55:299–301.
Bennett, John W.
1945   *Archaeological Explorations in Jo Daviess County Illinois*. Chicago: University of Chicago Press.
1952   The Prehistory of the Northern Mississippi Valley. In *Archaeology of the Eastern United States*, ed. James B. Griffin, 108–23. Chicago: University of Chicago Press.
Binford, Lewis R., S. R. Binford, R. Whallon, and M. A. Hardin
1970   *Archaeology at Hatchery West*. Society for American Archaeology, Memoir 24.
Blakeslee, Donald J.
1975   The Plains Interband Trade System: An Ethnohistoric and

Archeological Investigation. Unpublished Ph.D. dissertation. Milwaukee: University of Wisconsin.

Brain, Jeffrey P.
1969   Winterville: A Case Study of Prehistoric Culture Contact in the Lower Mississippi Valley. Ph.D. dissertation, Yale University. Ann Arbor: University Microfilms International.
1978   Late Prehistoric Settlement Patterning in the Yazoo Basin and Natchez Bluffs Regions of the Lower Mississippi Valley. In *Mississippian Settlement Patterns*. Ed. Bruce D. Smith, 422–50. New York: Academic Press.

Brown, James A.
1976   The Southern Cult Reconsidered. *Midcontinental Journal of Archaeology* 1:115–35.

Childe, V. Gordon
1950   The Urban Revolution. *The Town Planning Review* 21 (1):3–17.

Chmurny, William W.
1973   The Ecology of the Middle Mississippian Occupation of the American Bottom. Unpublished Ph.D. dissertation. Urbana: University of Illinois.

Claessen, Henri J. M. and Pieter van de Velde
1987   *Early State Dynamics* Leiden: E. J. Brill.

Conner, Michael D., editor
1985   *The Hill Creek Homestead and the Late Mississippian Settlement in the Lower Illinois Valley.* Center for American Archeology, Kampsville Archeological Center, Research Series, Vol. 1.

Crawford, H. E. W.
1973   Mesopotamia's Invisible Exports in the Third Millennium B. C. *World Archeology* 5 (2):232–41.

Cremin, William M.
1980   Sand Point (20Bg14): A Lakes Phase Site on the Keweenaw Peninsula, Baraga County, Michigan. *The Michigan Archaeologist* 26 (3–4):7–16.

Cushing, Frank H.
1894   Primitive Copper Working: An Experimental Study. *American Anthropologist* o.s. 7:93–117.

De Peso, Charles C.
1980   The Northern Sector of the Mesoamerican World System. Paper read at the Society for Historical Archaeology and Conference on Underwater Archaeology, Albuquerque, New Mexico, January 8–11, 1980.

Dorothy, Lawrence, G.
1980   The Ceramics of the Sand Point Site (20Bg14) Baraga

County, Michigan: A Preliminary Description. *The Michigan Archaeologist* 26 (3–4):39–90.

Ferguson, Leland G.
1978   Prehistoric Mica Mines in the Southern Appalachians. *South Carolina Antiquities: The First Ten Years*, Vols. 1–10, pp. 211–17.

Ford, Richard I.
1974   Northeastern Archaeology: Past and Future Directions. *Annual Review of Anthropology* 3:385–413.

Foster, J. W. and J. D. Whitney
1850   Report on the Geology and Topography of a Portion of the Lake Superior Land District, in the State of Michigan. Part 1: Copper Lands. 31st Congress, 1st Session, Ex. Doc. No. 69. Washington, D.C.

Fowler, Melvin L.
1969   Middle Mississippian Agricultural Fields. *American Antiquity* 34 (4):365–75.
1974   *Cahokia: Ancient Capital of the Midwest*. Addison-Wesley Module in Anthropology, No. 48.

Gibbon, Guy E.
1974   A Model of Mississippian Development and Its Implications for the Red Wing Area. In *Aspects of Upper Great Lakes Anthropology: Papers in Honor of Lloyd A. Wilford*, ed. Elden Johnson, 129–37. St. Paul: Minnesota Historical Society.

Gillman, Henry
1874   The Mound-builders and Platycnemism in Michigan. In *The Annual Report of 1873 of the Smithsonian Institution*. Washington, D.C.: Smithsonian Institution

Gregg, Michael L.
1975a   Settlement Morphology and Production Specialization: The Horseshoe Lake Site, A Case Study. Ph.D. dissertation, University of Wisconsin-Milwaukee. Ann Arbor: University Microfilms International.
1975b   A Population Estimate for Cahokia. In *Perspectives in Cahokia Archaeology*, ed. Melvin L. Fowler. 126–36. Urbana: Illinois Archaeological Survey, Bulletin 10.

Griffith, Roberta J.
1981   *Ramey Incised Pottery*. Urbana: Illinois Archaeological Survey, Circular No. 5.

Haas, Jonathan.
1982   *The Evolution of the Prehistoric State*. New York: Columbia University Press.

Hall, Robert L.
1972   The Cahokia Presence Outside of the American Bottoms. Paper read at the Annual Meeting of the Central States

Anthropological Society, St. Louis, Missouri, April 12–14, 1972.

Harn, Alan D.
1971   *Archaeological Surveys of the American Bottoms and Adjacent Bluffs, Illinois: Part 2.* Springfield: Illinois State Museum, Reports of Investigations No. 21.
1975   Cahokia and the Mississippian Emergence in the Spoon River Area of Illinois. *Transactions of the Illinois Academy of Science* 68:414–34.

Hines, Philip
1977   On Social Organization in the Middle Mississippian: States or Chiefdom? *Current Anthropology* 18 (2):337–38.
1978   On Middle Mississippian Social Organization. *Current Anthropology* 19 (2):407–408.

Holmes, William H.
1896   Prehistoric Textile Art of Eastern United States. *13th Annual Report of the Bureau of American Ethnology*, 13–46. Washington, D.C.: Smithsonian Institution.

Honerkamp, Marjory W.
1975   The Angel Phase: Analysis of a Middle Mississippian Occupation in Southern Indiana. Ph.D. dissertation, University of Indiana. Ann Arbor: University Microfilms International.

Howard, James H.
1968   *The Southeastern ceremonial complex and its interpretation.* Columbia: Missouri Archaeological Society Memoir 6.

Hoxie, R. David.
1980   An Analysis of the Late Woodland Copper Assemblage from the Sand Point Site, Baraga Co., Michigan. *Michigan Archaeologist* 26:25–38.

Hudson, Charles.
1976   *The Southeastern Indians.* Knoxville: University of Tennessee Press.

Ives, David J.
1975   The Crescent Hills Prehistoric Quarrying Area. University of Missouri, Museum of Anthropology, *Museum Brief* No. 22.

Johannessen, Sissel
1984   Paleobotany. In *American Bottom Archaeology*, ed. C. J. Bareis and J. W. Porter, 197–214. Urbana: University of Illinois Press.

Kelly, Lucretia S.
1979   Animal Resource Exploitation by Early Cahokia Populations on the Merrell Tract. Urbana: Illinois Archaeological Survey, Circular 4.

Keslin, Richard O.
1964   Archaeological Implications on the Role of Salt as an Ele-
             ment of Cultural Diffusion. *Missouri Archaeologist* 26:1–
             188.
Lewis, R. Barry.
1974   Mississippian Exploitative Strategies: A Southeast Mis-
             souri Example. Columbia: Missouri Archaeological So-
             ciety, Research Series 11.
1982   *Two Mississippian Hamlets; Cairo Lowland, Missouri.* Ur-
             bana: Illinois Archaeological Survey, Special Publication
             No. 2.
Lewis, T. H.
1889   Copper Mines Worked by the Mound Builders. *The Amer-
             ican Antiquarian* 11:293–96.
Mair, Lucy
1977   *African Kingdoms.* Oxford: Clarendon Press.
McAdams, William
1880   Ancient Mounds of Illinois. *Proceedings of the American
             Association for the Advancement of Science*, 29:710–20.
Mehrer, Mark W.
1982   A Mississippian Community at the Range Site (11-S-47),
             St. Clair County, Illinois. Unpublished M.A. thesis. Ur-
             bana: University of Illinois.
1988   The Settlement Patterns and Social Power of Cahokia's
             Hinterland Households. Unpublished Ph.D. dissertation.
             Urbana: University of Illinois
Mochon, Marion J.
1972   Toward Urbanism: The Cultural Dynamics of the Prehis-
             toric and Historic Societies of the American Southeast.
             Ph.D. dissertation, University of Wisconsin-Milwaukee.
             Ann Arbor: University Microfilms International.
Morse, Dan F.
1975   Report of Excavations at the Zebree Site 1969. Fayette-
             ville: Arkansas Archeological Survey, *Research Report No.
             4,*
Muller, Jon.
1984   Mississippian Specialization and Salt. *American Antiquity*
             49:489–507.
Myer, William E.
1928   *Indian Trails of the Southeast.* 42nd Annual Report of the
             Bureau of American Ethnology 1924–1925, 727–857.
             Washington, D.C.: Smithsonian Institution.
O'Brien, Patricia J.
1972a   Urbanism, Cahokia and Middle Mississippian. *Archaeol-
             ogy* 25 (3): 188–97.
1972b   A Formal Analysis of Cahokia Ceramics Powell Tract.

Urbana: Illinois Archaeological Survey, Monograph No. 3.

1978   Steed-Kisker: A Western Mississippian Settlement System. In *Mississippian Settlement Patterns*, ed. B. D. Smith, 1–19. New York: Academic Press, Inc.

n.d.   Cahokia: The Political Capital of the 'Ramey' State? Paper submitted to the *North American Archaeologist*.

O'Brien, P. J. and W. P. McHugh.

1987   Mississippian Solstice Shrines and a Cahokian Calendar: An Hypothesis Based on Archaeology and Ethnohistory. *North American Archaeologist* 8 (3):227–47.

Peebles, Christopher and Susan M. Kus

1977   Some Archaeological Correlates of Ranked Societies. *American Antiquity* 42 (3):421–48.

Perazio, Philip A.

1981   Analysis of Burned Hour Floor Assemblages—Settlement C of the Orendorf Site, Vol. 1. In *The Orendorf Site: Preliminary Working Papers 1981, Vols. 1–3*, compiled by D. Esarey and L. A. Conrad, 82–116. Macomb: Western Illinois University, Archaeological Research Laboratory.

Phillips, Philip

1970   Archaeological Survey in the Lower Yazoo Basin, Mississippi, 1949–1955: Part I. *Papers of the Peabody Museum of American Archaeology and Ethnology* 60. Cambridge:

Phillips, W. A.

1900   Aboriginal Quarries and shops at Mill Creek, Illinois. *American Anthropologist* 2, n.s.:37–52.

Polanyi, Karl

1968   Ports of Trade in Early Societies. In *Primitive, Archaic and Modern Economies*, ed. George Dalton, 238–60. New York: Anchor Books, Doubleday and Co.

Porter, James Warren

1969   The Mitchell Site and Prehistoric Exchange Systems at Cahokia: A.D.1000–1300. In *Explorations into Cahokia Archaeology*, ed. Melvin L. Fowler, 137–64. Urbana: Illinois Archaeological Survey, Bulletin 7.

1974   Cahokia Archaeology as Viewed From the Mitchell Site: A Satellite Community at A.D. 1150–1200. Unpublished Ph.D. dissertation. Madison: University of Wisconsin.

1976   Thin Section Analysis of Cahokia Area Ceramics. Paper presented at the 41st Annual Meeting of the Society for American Archaeology, May 6–8, 1976, in St. Louis, Missouri.

1983   *Thin Section Analysis of Ceramics from the Robinson's Lake Site*. Urbana: University of Illinois, FAI-270 Archaeological Mitigation Project, Petrographic Report No. 1.

Prentice, Guy.
1983   Cottage Industries: Concepts and Implications. *Midcontinental Journal of Archaeology* 8:17–48.
Price, James E. and James B. Griffin
1979   The Snodgrass Site of the Powers Phase of Southeast Missouri. *Museum of Anthropology, Anthropological Papers* No. 66. Ann Arbor: University of Michigan.
Riley, Thomas J. and Glen Freimuth
1979   Field Systems and Frost Drainage in the Prehistoric Agriculture of the Upper Great Lakes. *American Antiquity* 44 (2):271–85.
Salzer, Robert J.
1987   Preliminary Report on the Gottschall Site (47Ia80). *Wisconsin Archaeologist* 66 (4): 418–72.
Schoolcraft, Henry R.
1821   *Narrative Journal of Travels from Detroit Northwest through the Great Chain of American Lakes to the Sources of the Mississippi River in the Year 1820.* Ann Arbor: 1966 reprint by University Microfilms, Inc.
Sears, William
1968   The State and Settlement Patterns in the New World. In *Settlement Archaeology*, ed. K. C. Chang, 134–53. Palo Alto: National Press Books.
Smith, Bruce D.
1975   Middle Mississippi Exploitation of Animal Populations. *Museum of Anthropology, Anthropological Papers* No. 57. Ann Arbor: University of Michigan.
1978a   *Prehistoric Patterns of Human Behavior.* New York: Academic Press, Inc.
1978b   *Mississippian Settlement Patterns.* New York: Academic Press, Inc.
Southard, Michael E.
1973   Sources of Chert Present at Towosahgy State Archaeological Site. *Newsletter* No. 273. Columbia: Missouri Archaeological Society
Stimmell, Carole and Robert Helmann
1981   Cultural Implications of Ceramic Technology in the Mississippi Valley. Paper read at the 46th Annual Meeting of the Society for American Archaeology, San Diego, California, April 30–May 2, 1981.
Stimmell, Carole, Robert Helmann, and R. G. V. Hancock.
1982   Indian Pottery from the Mississippi Valley: Coping with Bad Raw Materials. In *Archaeological Ceramics*, ed. J. S. Olin and A. D. Franklin, 219–28. Washington: Smithsonian Institution Press.

Swanton, John R.
1946   Indians of the Southeastern United States. *Bureau of American Ethnology*, Bulletin 137. Washington, D.C.: Smithsonian Institution.
Tiffany, Joseph A.
In press   Modeling Mill Creek-Mississippian Interaction. In *New Perspectives on Cahokia: Views from the Peripheries*, ed. James B. Stoltman. Ann Arbor: University of Michigan Press.
Titterington, P. F.
1938   *The Cahokia Mound Group and Its Village Site Materials.* St. Louis: Private Printing.
Trouwborst, Albert A.
1987   From Tribute to Taxation: On the Dynamics of the Early State. In *Early State Dynamics*, ed. by H. J. M. Claessen and P. van de Velde, 129–37. Leiden: E. J. Brill.
Wagner, Mark J.
1986   *The Bonnie Creek Site: A Late Mississippian Homestead in the Upper Galum Creek Valley, Perry County, Illinois.* Carbondale: American Resources Group, Ltd., Preservation Series 3.
Walthall, John A.
1981   *Galena and Aboriginal Trade in Eastern North America.* Springfield: Illinois State Museum, Scientific Papers 17.
Watson, Virginia.
1950   *The Wulfing Plates, Products of Prehistoric Americans.* St. Louis: Washington University Studies, n.s., Social and Philosophical Studies 8.
Wedel, Waldo R.
1943   *Archaeological Investigations in Platte and Clay Counties Missouri.* United States National Museum, Bulletin 183. Washington D.C.: Smithsonian Institution.
Wittry, Warren L. and Joseph O. Vogel
1962   Illinois State Museum Projects. In *American Bottoms Archaeology July 1, 1961—June 30, 1962*, ed. Melvin Fowler, 14–30. Urbana: Illinois Archaeological Survey.
Woods, W. I. and N. H. Lopinot
1989   Dynamic Patterns of Food Production at Cahokia. Paper read at the 54th Annual Meeting of the Society for American Archaeology, Denver, April 8, 1989.
Yerkes, Richard W.
1983   Microwear, Microdrills, and Mississippian Craft Specialization. *American Antiquity* 48:499–518.

7

Tribute and Commerce in Imperial Cities: The Case of Xaltocan, Mexico

Elizabeth M. Brumfiel

The character of imperial cities is not well understood. Some scholars, most notably Sjoberg (1960), regard the imperial city as a political entity: a clustering of ruling elites and their servants drawn together to facilitate elite rule and governance. Others, such as Jacobs (1969), regard all cities, even imperial capitals, as economic centers where the concentration of human labor and production facilities promotes the efficient manufacture and distribution of goods. The two images of what imperial cities are suggest different means by which they might interact with their hinterlands. The political model leads to an emphasis upon tribute extraction; the economic model implies primary dependence upon exchange. As Hassig (1985, 85) points out, tribute and trade may be regarded as functional alternatives, relying upon different institutions (the military and the market) to exercise different forms of compliance (coercion versus remuneration) to procure nonlocal goods.

Tenochtitlan, the Aztec capital, has sometimes been characterized as an economic center and sometimes as a political center. For example, Sanders, Parsons, and Santley (1979, 180) and Hassig (1985, 130–33) suggest that Tenochtitlan contained numerous craft specialists who supported themselves by supplying goods to a rural population of agriculturalists. In contrast, Lombardo (1973, 212), Brumfiel (1980, 466) and Rojas (1986, 282–83) argue that the bulk of the city's population was made up of elite administrators, warriors, priests, merchants, craft specialists dealing in elite goods, and urban service workers.

To an extent, the difference between these positions is one of emphasis as all agree that the city contained some political elites and some specialist producers of utilitarian goods. And yet, even the compromise position that imperial capitals are somewhat dependent on political function and somewhat on economic function is unsatisfactory for two reasons. First, it does not draw attention to the changes in the function of imperial cities that might occur in the course of their development. For example, Rojas (1986, 35) suggests that Tenochtitlan changed from an earlier reliance on trade to a later dependence on tribute. Second, stating that both economics and politics are important perpetuates the analytical separation of the two, despite theoretical arguments against such a separation (by Polanyi 1957 and Wolf 1982, among others) and despite a growing body of literature on the Aztec economy that affirms the interaction of trade and tribute (Molins Fábrega 1954–55; Litvak King 1971; Kurtz 1974; Berdan 1975; Calnek 1978; Brumfiel 1980; Hassig 1985; Rojas 1986; Hicks 1987).

The purpose of this paper is to suggest the need for an interactive model of trade and tribute in imperial cities. Such a model would recognize that trade and tribute are mutually supportive and that, instead of being functional alternatives, trade and tribute often interact to provide rapidly expanding supplies of nonlocal products to an urban population. This thesis is tested by examining the history of political and economic change at Xaltocan, an early, small imperial capital in the Late Postclassic Valley of Mexico.

Until the end of the fourteenth century, Xaltocan was an important, tribute-receiving imperial capital; afterwards it became a tribute-paying provincial town, administered by a military governor sent by the ruler of Tenochtitlan. This paper attempts to define the economic consequences of this transition. If tribute and trade were functional alternatives, then Xaltocan's loss of tribute receipts at the end of the fourteenth century should have been compensated for by an increased level of marketing activity. However, because trade and tribute are interactive and interdependent, Xaltocan's loss of tribute was not accompanied by an increase in market activity. Market activity declined sharply. A degree of market participation was sustained, but only because a strong commercial impulse emanating from Tenochtitlan, the rapidly expanding Aztec capital, drew Xaltocan into a valleywide market network.

Xaltocan's Political History

Xaltocan is a low island in an ancient lakebed in the northern Valley of Mexico (figure 7.1). In prehistoric times, Lake Xaltocan was shallow, marshy, and brackish, although a spring fed flow of fresh water from the east shore of the lake permitted a small concentration of agricultural *chinampas* (ridged fields) at Xaltocan (Alvarado Tezozómoc 1949, 38; Armillas 1971, 661; Sanders, Parsons, and Santley 1979, 280–81). Archaeological materials recovered in 1987 suggest a continuous occupation of Xaltocan since the Middle Formative, but the town reached its maximum size (68 hectare) during the Middle Postclassic, A.D. 1150–1350. This agrees well with the evidence of ethnohistory, which indicates a role of regional importance for Xaltocan during the thirteenth and fourteenth centuries.

According to native historical narratives, Xaltocan's rise to power was preceded by two events: the decline of Tula and the arrival of Otomí-speaking peoples from the Mazahua area to the west (Carrasco 1950, 241–55). By the first half of the thirteenth century, Xaltocan had established itself as the capital of Otomí-speaking peoples in the southern Hidalgo-northern Valley of Mexico region, and Xaltocan's ruler was recognized as "King and ruler of the Otomí nation" (Alva Ixtlilxochitl 1975–77, 1:321). The Códice Vaticano-Ríos states that, along with Culhuacan and Tenayuca, Xaltocan dominated the pre-Aztec Valley of Mexico (quoted in Carrasco 1950, 260–61). Chimalpahin and Sahagún also affirm Xaltocan's regional importance during the pre-Aztec era (Davies 1980, 144–45).

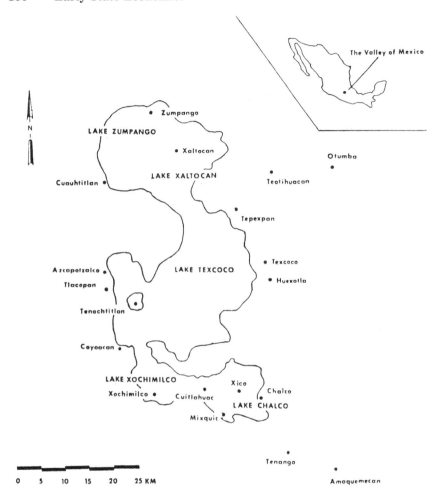

FIGURE 7.1
The Valley of Mexico during the Late Postclassic, showing the locations
of Xaltocan, Tenochtitlan and some other major settlements (after
Gibson 1964 [end-paper]).

Carrasco (1984) has demonstrated that the marriage patterns of political elites in Central Mexico are a good barometer of their power. Thus, information on Xaltocan's royal marriages provides a means of corroborating the more general statements concerning Xaltocan's regional importance. The marriages do suggest that

Xaltocan occupied a high position in regional politics. Its rulers are said to have taken wives from the prestigeous centers of Tollan and Tenayuca and to have given their daughters in marriage to the founders of ruling lineages at Huexotla and Chalco (Nazareo 1940, 124; Alva Ixtlilxochitl 1975–77, 2:17, 18, 51; Berlin and Barlow 1948, 28). Xaltocan's rulers were also wife givers to an early ruler of Azcapotzalco, a town whose growing importance eventually put an end to indigenous rule at Xaltocan (Berlin and Barlow 1948, 28).

These textual allusions to Xaltocan's importance establish a credible basis for the sixteenth century claim by Pablo Nazareo (1940) that Xaltocan at one time controlled an extensive territory in southern Hidalgo and the northern Valley of Mexico. Nazareo claimed Xaltocan's dominion over forty-nine towns (figure 7.2) and its control of tribute fields in twenty-four communities (figure 7.3). A more restricted list of Xaltocan's holdings appearing in Velazquez (1945, 24) includes almost the entire cachement of the northern lakebed (figure 7.4). Nazareo's longer list may represent the extent of Xaltocan's influence while the shorter lists define the area under Xaltocan's direct control. These areas represent considerable potential for tribute extraction. This can be appreciated by examining the tribute which Triple Alliance rulers were able to draw from the area 125 years after Xaltocan's decline (table 7.1). Tribute goods included large quantities of cotton and maguey-fiber textiles, elaborate feather embroidered warriors' costumes, bins of maize, beans, amaranth, and chia, large jars of thick maguey syrup, and from Oxitipan, far to the north, dried chile and live eagles (Barlow 1949). The tribute paid the Triple Alliance rulers was the result of conquest and subjugation; it was probably far more than the tribute paid to Xaltocan rendered as "gifts" in recognition of Xaltocan's overlordship (see chapter 8 for a discussion of gifts and tribute in Aztec Mexico).

One tribute good yielded by the region but not appearing in the Aztec tribute lists is obsidian. Obsidian blades were given to Triple Alliance rulers by the towns of Cempoala and Epazoyuca (Obregon 1949–57), almost certainly from the nearby Cerro de las Navajas source. Otumba, a second important source of obsidian for the Valley of Mexico (Charlton and Spence 1982), is also said to have fallen within Xaltocan's sphere of dominance.

FIGURE 7.2
The extent of Xaltocan's dominion during the thirteenth and fourteenth centuries, according to Nazareo, 1940 (after Carrasco 1950, 259).

Xaltocan's political decline began in the mid-thirteenth century when Xaltocan entered a lengthy war against neighboring Cuauht-itlan. In 1395 Cuauhtitlan, then a part of the Tepanec empire and considerably strengthened by Tepanec reinforcements, defeated Xaltocan (Velazquez 1945, 22–34, Alva Ixtlilxochitl 1975–77, 1:322–23). The initial result was the depopulation of the town. According to Velazquez (1945, 50), the town actually lay deserted for 30 years before it was repopulated:

In this year 8-reed those who today are called xaltocamecas, the

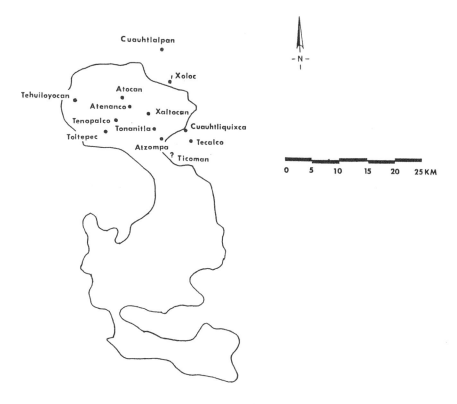

FIGURE 7.3
Xaltocan's tribute fields, according to Nazareo (1940).

acolmantlaca, the colhuas, the tenochcas and otomis, who are entirely outsiders, took up residence. But no ruling house was established until the Spanish came to have a hand in it. When the rulership was destroyed forever, it was because when the xalatocamecas were defeated by the cuauhtitlaneses they were routed and poured into Metztitlan and Tlaxcala. For thirty-one years after the xaltocamecas were thus routed Xaltocan was depopulated and nobody lived there.

Xaltocan's lands were divided between the rulers of Azcapotzalco and Texcoco (Alva Ixtlilxochitl 1975–77, 1:323). The Mexica, as allies of Azcapotzalco, were alloted some holdings in Xaltocan (Alva Ixtlilxochitl 1975, 2:36); this is probably the time when the tribute fields claimed by Nazareo which were among

FIGURE 7.4
Xaltocan's boundaries in 1395, according to the *Anales de Cuauhtitlan*
(Velazquez 1945, 24).

the holdings of Tenochtitlan and Tlatelolco at the time of conquest (Gibson 1964, 371–75) changed hands.

Xaltocan's situation improved little when Azcapotzalco was defeated by the Aztec Triple Alliance in 1428. The Aztecs installed a military ruler (*cuauhtlatoani*) to govern Xaltocan (Nazareo 1940, 125), and Xaltocan paid tribute to both the ruler of Texcoco and the ruler of Tenochtitlan (Alva Ixtlilxochitl 1975–77, 1:380; Nazareo 1940, 120). Stripped of most of its depend-

TABLE 7.1
**Tribute Paid to the Aztec Triple Alliance by Provinces Formerly within Xaltocan's Dominion
(after Barlow 1949).**
Provinces: Xocotitlan, Axocopan, Hueypochtla, Atotonolco el Grande, Acolhuacan (northern half of the province), and Oxitipan.

Type	Quantity	Description
Textiles:	800	loads of little, embroidered, maguey-fibre mantles
	800	loads of maguey-fibre mantles with a black and white border
	4800	loads of white, maguey-fibre mantles
	800	loads of little decorated mantles
	1600	loads of rich, little mantles
	800	loads of little mantles with a black and white border
	1600	loads of white mantles
	1200	loads of rich, thin mantles, in three styles
	2000	loads of large white "twisted" mantles
	1612	loads of large mantles, striped red, blue and yellow
	4020	loads of large mantles, each two varas long
	400	loads of loincloth
	1200	loads of skirts and blouses
Food:	4½	bins of maize
	4½	bins of beans
	4½	bins of chiau
	4½	bins of huauhtli
	1600	large jars of thick, maguey honey
	400	loads of chile
Other:	168	feather embroidered warrior's costumes with shields
	1	or more live eagles, as they were caught.

encies, Xaltocan's economy must have concentrated upon local resource extraction. Fishing, hunting ducks and other water fowl, processing mineral lime, weaving reed mats, and cultivating maize on nearby *chinampas* are all mentioned by sixteenth-century colonial documents. The documents also cite such purely colonial industries as extracting *tequisquitl* (soda ash) for soap and cloth dying and extracting salitre (saltpeter) for gunpowder (Hicks personal communication 1987; Contreras 1979, 31; García 1897, 96; Lopez de Ribera 1979, 176; Gibson 1964, 338–43). Xaltocan's reduced circumstances are reflected demographically. Archaeological remains suggest that the Aztec period population was about 17% smaller than the pre-Aztec population.

Economic Change at Xaltocan

Data received in a recent archaeological investigation of Xaltocan enables us to reconstruct the economic impact of the town's political decline. Artifacts were gathered during an intensive systematic surface collection of the site. The entire site was mapped on to a grid of 7m × 7m squares, and one square from each block of nine squares was slated for collection. A total of 1003 collections were taken from 44.7 hectares, constituting an 11% sample of artifacts on the site surface. A 23.3 hectare area in the center of town could not be sampled because of modern settlement.

The collections include materials that reflect both Xaltocan's capacity to procure nonlocal goods and the volume of its production for market sale. Its capacity to procure nonlocal goods is indicated by the quantities of obsidian present in the collections. Obsidian, used for a variety of cutting and scraping tasks, occurs at a limited number of sources in Central Mexico: Cerro del los Navajas in Hidalgo, Otumba in Mexico, Zinapecuaro in Michoacan, and Pico de Orizaba in Puebla (Zeitlin 1982). Obsidian has been an item of regional exchange in Central Mexico since the Early Formative (Charlton 1984), and, at least in Aztec times, it was one of the goods carried by professional long distance traders and sold in markets (Sahagún 1950–69 bk.9 ch.5, bk.10 ch.24). Its status as an item of tribute has already been mentioned. Obsidian provides an excellent indicator of Xaltocan's capacity to procure nonlocal goods from both within and outside its area of political dominion.

Xaltocan's production for market sale is indicated by the abundance of fabric-marked pottery. This poorly finished, friable ceramic ware is associated with salt production and transport (Charlton 1969). In the Valley of Mexico, fabric-marked pottery occurs in very heavy concentrations at places of salt production (Espejo

1946; Tolstoy 1958; Mayer-Oakes 1959), and it occurs in very light concentrations at places of salt consumption (Brumfiel 1980). At Xaltocan, fabric-marked pottery occurs in moderate concentrations; it is 1.7% of the total ceramic assemblage. This indicates high levels of salt consumption. Current practices at Xaltocan suggest that salt was used extensively in commercial fish processing. Today, fresh fish are heavily salted, wrapped in corn husks or maguey leaf parchment, roasted, and sold in markets at Zumpango, Otumba, and Pachuca. The ratio of salt to fish is high; one kg of salt is needed for every 10–15 kg of fish according to one informant. The salt prolongs the market life of the fish. The preparation of fish for market sale has a long history in the Valley of Mexico. Cortés (1970, 63) found salted fish for sale in the Tlatelolco market, and Sahagún (1950–69 bk. 10 ch. 22) reports that the vendor of fish sold "toasted fish wrapped in maize husks." Although levels of dietary salt consumption can vary widely over time (Marcus 1984), it seems highly plausible that changing quantities of fabric-marked pottery at Xaltocan are related to rises and falls in levels of commercial fish processing.

Obsidian and fabric-marked pottery occur in association with both Early Aztec (A.D. 1150–1350) and Late Aztec (A.D. 1350–1520) ceramics at Xaltocan. Patterns of economic change emerge when the frequencies of obsidian and fabric-marked pottery in collections with predominantly Early Aztec ceramics are compared with the frequencies of obsidian and fabric-marked pottery in collections with predominantly Late Aztec ceramics. Increased frequencies imply a greater procurement of nonlocal goods and market participation; decreased frequencies imply a reduced procurement of nonlocal goods and market participation.

Obsidian

Analysis of the obsidian from Xaltocan is still under way. However, a coherent picture of obsidian procurement has emerged from the work which has been completed thus far.

Preliminary figures from Xaltocan suggest that the community enjoyed preferential access to obsidian during its period of political dominance. The Early Aztec collections contain an average of 189 g of obsidian per 100 rim sherds, far more than the amount

TABLE 7.2

**Obsidian at Valley of Mexico sites, Early Aztec and Late Aztec Periods
(in total grams—figures in parentheses are grams per 100 rim sherds)**

Site	Navajas Obsidian	Other Obsidian	Total Obsidian
EARLY AZTEC			
Xaltocan—all Early			
Aztec Units	10,986 (175)	883 (14)	11,869 (189)[1]
Xaltocan—workshops			
excluded	7456 (119)	770 (12)	8226 (131)[2]
Huexotla	2419 (67)	516 (14)	2935 (83)[3]
Xico	243 (5)	636 (12)	879 (17)[4]
LATE AZTEC			
Xaltocan—all Late			
Aztec units	4575 (79)	629 (11)	5204 (90)[5]
Huexotla	21,385 (77)	3,882 (14)	25,267 (91)[6]
Xico	268 (12)	251 (11)	519 (23)[7]

[1]Number of rim sherds = 6282
[2]Number of rim sherds = 5878
[3]Number of rim sherds = 3582
[4]Number of rim sherds = 5062
[5]Number of rim sherds = 5784
[6]Number of rim sherds = 27,720
[7]Number of rim sherds = 2247.

of obsidian in some other Early Aztec contexts in the Valley of Mexico (table 7.2). Almost entirely, the greater abundance of obsidian at Xaltocan is due to large quantities of obsidian from the Cerro de las Navajas source. There is an average of 175 g of Navajas obsidian per 100 rim sherds in the Early Aztec collections. This is twice the quantity of Navajas obsidian at Early Aztec Huexotla and more than 10 times the quantity of Navajas obsidian at Early Aztec Xico. Intersite differences in the quantities of obsidian from other sources are much smaller.

The great majority of Navajas obsidian at Xaltocan is concentrated in two workshop areas. Debris from these workshops account for 32% of the Navajas obsidian occurring in Early Aztec contexts at the site. The density of debris at these workshops is moderate: up to 46 pieces per m². Similar densities occur in workshops at Late Postclassic Teotihuacan, and Spence (1985) suggests that such moderate densities are indicative of part-time specialization. At Xaltocan (and at Spence's workshops at Teotihuacan), most of the debris is related to prismatic blade production. The low numbers of large percussion flakes suggest that blade cores were manufactured elsewhere and brought to Xaltocan in an already prepared form (Tamara Salcedo, personal communication, 1988). Such cores may have been rendered as gifts to the ruler of Xaltocan by "subject" rulers in the Navajas region. Or they may have been procured through market exchange. The existence of comparable obsidian workshops at Late Postclassic Teotihuacan, a community that made no political claims upon Navajas region towns, suggests that both Teotihuacan and Xaltocan procured obsidian cores through trade and market networks.

Outside the workshop areas, the Early Aztec pattern of obsidian consumption is much the same at Xaltocan as it is elsewhere in the Valley of Mexico. Navajas obsidian constitutes 91% of the obsidian found in household contexts, and total obsidian consumption is 131 g per 100 rim sherds. Although the rate of household consumption was high, it may not have absorbed the full output of the Xaltocan workshops. Like the workshops at Late Postclassic Teotihuacan, the Xaltocan workshops probably supplied the needs of the local region: generally, the communities bordering Lakes Zumpango-Xaltocan. It is also possible that blades were produced for export through long distance trade; trade is suggested by small quantities of Huastec sherds at Xaltocan and by the presence of small spindle whorls, presumably used to spin cotton imported from the lowlands (Parsons 1972).

The collections of Late Aztec materials from Xaltocan suggest major changes in patterns of obsidian procurement and consumption. On the average, there is less obsidian at Xaltocan, only 90 g per 100 rim sherds (table 7.2). Most of the decrease can be attributed to the 55% drop in quantities of Navajas obsidian. This, in turn, is associated with the absence of obsidian workshops in Late Aztec Xaltocan. In nonworkshop (domestic) contexts, obsidian was also less plentiful than before; the Late Aztec average of 90 g obsidian per 100 rim sherds is 31% lower than the Early Aztec nonworkshop average of 131 g per 100 rim sherds. Virtually all this obsidian must have been obtained via the market system.

TABLE 7.3
**Fabric-Marked Sherds at Central Mexican Sites, Early Aztec and Late
Aztec Periods**
(figures in parentheses are frequencies per 100 rim sherds.)

Site	Early Aztec	Late Aztec
Xaltocan	1210 (19)[1]	821 (14)[2]
Xico	372 (7)[3]	407 (18)[4]
Huexotla	30 (1)[5]	792 (3)[6]
Coatlan Viejo		404 (7)[7]

[1]Number of rim sherds = 6282
[2]Number of rim sherds = 5784
[3]Number of rim sherds = 5062
[4]Number of rim sherds = 2247
[5]Number of rim sherds = 3582
[6]Number of rim sherds = 27,720
[7]Number of rim sherds = 5408.

Fabric-Marked Pottery

The frequencies of fabric-marked pottery at Xaltocan are high in comparison to other Late Postclassic sites in the Valley of Mexico (table 7.3). The Early Aztec collections at Xaltocan yield an average of 19 pieces of fabric-marked pottery per 100 rim sherds as opposed to only 7 pieces per 100 rim sherds in Early Aztec collections at Xico and 1 piece per 100 rim sherds in Early Aztec collections at Huexotla. This can reasonably be attributed to an active, market-oriented commercial fish processing industry at Xaltocan and its absence at Xico and Huexotla. The absence of commercial fish processing at Huexotla can be understood in environmental terms (Huexotla is landlocked), but its minimal development at Xico must stem from Xico's marginal participation in market exchange (also evident in the limited quantities of obsidian present in Early Aztec collections from the site).

The Late Aztec collections at Xaltocan yield an average of 14 pieces of fabric-marked pottery per 100 rim sherds. This constitutes a 23% decrease in the frequency of fabric-marked pottery from Early Aztec times, but the frequency is still high. This suggests a somewhat diminished but still active commercial fish processing industry. Elevated frequencies of fabric-marked pottery in Late Aztec collections from Xico indicate that Xico, too, developed an active fish processing industry in Late Aztec times. The low frequencies of fabric-marked pottery at Late Aztec Huexotla and Coatlan Viejo in Morelos (Mason 1980) suggest that, as before, salt use in these communities was confined to dietary consumption.

Discussion

The data from Xaltocan provide an instructive picture of the relationship between trade and tribute in imperial economies. The decline in the abundance of both obsidian and fabric-marked pottery point to a decline in market involvement with the loss of imperial status. Even so, a degree of market activity was sustained; both obsidian and fabric-marked pottery are significantly more abundant at Late Aztec Xaltocan than at Early Aztec Xico, whose low frequencies of obsidian and fabric-marked pottery seem to represent a minimum level of participation in market exchange. Continuing market involvent at Late Aztec Xaltocan might be understood as relating to regionwide changes in market activity that accompanied imperial expansion and urban growth at the Aztec capital, Tenochtitlan (Smith 1974; Brumfiel 1976, 213–14; Hicks 1982; Hassig 1985, 73).

Hicks (1981) and Hassig (1985) have both discussed the character of markets in the Early Aztec Valley of Mexico. Hicks (1981, 3–4) argues that these markets operated under heavy political control:

> Market places (*tianquiztli*) belonged to kings. They were usually located adjacent to the royal palaces, and the king received as tribute a portion of the goods brought by sellers. Trade outside the market place was forbidden. Kings, I believe, viewed their *tianquiztli* as places where goods from the city's immediate hinterland were brought and exchanged, where the city's long-distance merchants brought their exotic goods after giving the king his due, and where these same merchants obtained the goods they took to trade.

Because of the exercise of political power, market activity was monopolized by a single higher level market near the ruler's palace, and the market region was bounded by political borders.

The volume of commercial activity in these markets was probably low. Exchanges between craftsmen and food producers within the market region would have been minimal because most craft specialists were part-time specialists who also raised food, and the few full-time craft specialists were attached to the ruler's household (Brumfiel 1987). Exchanges between commoners and the ruler were accomplished by tribute payment and gift giving (chapter 8). Exchanges of utilitarian goods between part-time specialists probably occurred, but the redundancy of natural resources within the region would not have encouraged it. The real attraction of a region's central market would have been the availability of nonlocal goods: precious goods for elite households on the one hand, but also a variety of nonlocal products for commoners such as reed mats, salt, obsidian, chile, and grinding stones. Professional merchants, the vendors of nonlocal goods, were primarily attracted to a market by the prospects for low volume, high value elite goods. Thus, the presence of a ruler and his tribute wealth attracted professional merchants to the local market, the availability of nonlocal goods attracted many shoppers, and the presence of a crowd of buyers attracted many part-time local specialists to sell their goods.

This interactive model of trade and tribute accounts for variation in the level of commercial participation in the Valley of Mexico during Early Aztec times. At Xaltocan, the presence of a ruler of regional importance and his tribute wealth and his gifts attracted professional merchants to buy and sell precious goods. The merchants also brought obsidian cores which they exchanged for roasted, salted fish (destined to be consumed by people living away from the lakeshore). Local part-time specialists worked the cores into blades for sale to peasant consumers. At Early Aztec Teotihuacan, the ruler's wealth underwrote a similar level of commercial activity with comparable levels of obsidian procurement and blade production. At Early Aztec Xico, there was no ruler to attract professional merchants, and the levels of obsidian procurement and commercial fish processing were low.

By Late Aztec times, local rule had been abolished at Xaltocan. The local market was probably bypassed by professional merchants, and the obsidian blade workshops ceased to function. I suspect that, had all other things been equal, commercial activity would have diminished to the level observed at Early Aztec Xico, as predicted by the interactive model. All other things were not equal, however, because the tribute from Xaltocan and other regional polities did not just disappear. It was redirected into the coffers of the Triple Alliance capitals where it created urban growth and a demand for marketed food (Calnek 1975; Parsons 1976). Tribute wealth also attracted craftsmen and long-distance traders (Hassig 1985, 131–13), centralizing the supply of nonlocal products. A very strong commercial impulse radiated from Tenochtitlan that was transmitted to much of the Valley of Mexico. The result was the expansion of the Tenochtitlan market hinterland, with foodstuffs flowing from rural producers to urban consumers in Tenochtitlan and craft goods and nonlocal goods flowing from Tenochtitlan to rural consumers in communities such as Xaltocan (Brumfiel 1980; Hassig 1985; Rojas 1986; Nichols and Charlton 1988).

For Late Aztec Xaltocan, urban markets at Tenochtitlan provided a new outlet for roasted, salted fish and a new source of obsidian blades. At Late Aztec Teotihuacan, however, a local ruler remained after incorporation into the Aztec empire, and the vitality of the local market was maintained or even enhanced. Teotihuacan retained its obsidian workshops in Late Aztec times. At Late Aztec Xico, there was still no local ruler, but market-oriented commercial fish processing developed anyway in response to the demand for food at Aztec Tenochtitlan.

Table 7.4 summarizes the pattern of tribute payment and commercial activity at Late Postclassic Xaltocan, Teotihuacan, and Xico.

Conclusions

The data from Xaltocan appear to sustain the hypothesis that trade and tribute are interactive. The transformation of Xaltocan from a tribute-receiving to a tribute-paying community is accompanied by a moderate decline in commercial activity. In addition, the hypothesis is also sustained in the wider regional view. The collection of moderate amounts of tribute by Xaltocan's ruler (much of it coming as "gifts") was accompanied by moderate levels of commercial activity in this small imperial capital. Much

TABLE 7.4
Tribute and market participation at Valley of Mexico sites, Early and Late Aztec Periods

Site	Xaltocan	Teotihuacan	Xico
EARLY AZTEC			
Tribute extraction	moderate	moderate	none
Market participation	moderate	moderate	low
LATE AZTEC			
Tribute extraction	none	moderate	none
Market participation	moderate[1]	moderate[2]	moderate[1]

[1]Principally extractive industries
[2]Retains craft production.

greater amounts of tribute gathered through Triple Alliance conquests was paralleled by much higher levels of commercial activity in the Aztec capital. The commercial impulse radiating from the capital was strong enough to maintain a degree of commercial activity in Xaltocan, though not at Early Aztec levels. This suggests a significant increase in commercial activity for the Valley of Mexico as a whole.

Of course the interaction of trade and tribute has qualitative as well as quantitative consequences. These emerge quite clearly from our data. At Xaltocan, the loss of tribute receipts reduced the possibilities for long-distance trade and craft production. At Tenochtitlan, the reverse was true (Hassig 1985, 131–13). We can conclude that the distinctive character of imperial cities is determined not only by the level of commercial activity but also its particular composition. In Postclassic Central Mexico, it was the collection of tribute that helped cities acquire this distinctive commercial mix.

References

Alva Ixtlilxochitl, Fernando de
1975–77   *Obras históricas*. Ed. E. O'Gorman. 2 vols. México, D.F.: Universidad Nacional Autónoma de México.

Alvarado Tezozómoc, Fernando
1949   *Crónica Medicáyotl*. Trans. A. Léon. México, D.F.: Universidad Nacional Autónoma de México.
Armillas, Pedro
1971   Gardens in swamps. *Science* 174:653–61.
Barlow, Robert H.
1949   *The extent of the empire of the Culhua-Mexica*. Ibero-Americana, Vol. 28. Berkeley: University of California Press.
Berdan, Frances F.
1975   *Trade, tribute and market in the Aztec empire*. Ann Arbor: University Microfilms.
Berlin, H. and R. Barlow, trans.
1948   *Anales de Tlatelolco*. México, D.F.: Universidad Nacional Autónoma de México.
Brumfiel, Elizabeth M.
1976   *Specialization and exchange at the Late Postclassic (Aztec) community of Huexotla, Mexico*. Ann Arbor: University Microfilms.
1980   Specialization, market exchange, and the Aztec state: A view from Huexotla. *Current Anthropology* 21:459–78.
1987   Elite and utilitarian crafts in the Aztec state. In *Specialization, exchange and complex societies*, ed. E. M. Brumfiel and T. K. Earle, 102–18. Cambridge: Cambridge University Press.
Calnek, Edward E.
1975   Organización de los sistemas de abastecimiento urbano de alimentos: El caso de Tecochtitlán. In *Las ciudades de América Latina y sus areas de influencia a través de la historia*, ed. J. E. Hardy and R. P. Schaedel, 41–60. Buenos Aires: Ediciones SIAP.
1978   El sistema de mercado en Tenochtitlán. In *Economía política e ideología en el México Prehispánico*, ed. P. Carrasco and J. Broda, 97–114. México, D.F.: Nueva Imagen.
Carrasco, Pedro
1950   *Los Otomíes: Cultura e historia prehispánicas de los pueblos mesoaméricanos de habla Otomiana*. México. D.F.: Universidad Nacional Autónoma de México.
1984   Royal marriages in ancient Mexico. In *Explorations in ethnohistory*, ed. H. R. Harvey and H. J. Prem, 41–81. Albuquerque: University of New Mexico Press.
Charlton, Thomas H.
1969   Texcoco fabric-marked pottery, tlatels and salt making. *American Antiquity* 34:73–76.
1984   Production and exchange: Variables in the evolution of a civilization. In *Trade and exchange in early Mesoamerica*,

ed. K. C. Hirth, 17–42. Albuquerque: University of New Mexico Press.

Charlton, Thomas H. and Michael W. Spence,
1982   Obsidian exploitation and civilization in the Basin of Mexico. *Anthropology* 6:7–86.

Contreras Figueroa, Alonso de
1979   Relación de Ueipuchtla y su partido. In *Relaciones geográficas de México*, ed. F. del Paso y Troncoso, 12–38. México, D.F.: Cosmos.

Cortés, Hernan
1970   *Cartas de relación*. México, D.F.: Porrúa.

Davies, Nigel
1980   *The Toltec heritage*. Norman: University of Oklahoma Press.

Espejo, Antonieta
1946   Exploraciones arqueológicas en Santiago, Tlateloloco. *Tlatelolco a Través de los Tiempos* 7:8–28.

García Pimentel, Luis de, ed.
1897   *Descripción del Arzobispado de México Hecha en 1570 y otros documentos*. Mécico, D.F.: J. J. Terrazas y Hijos.

Gibson, Charles
1964   *The Aztec state under Spanish rule*. Stanford: Stanford University Press.

Hassig, Ross
1985   *Trade, tribute and transportation: The sixteenth century political economy of the Valley of Mexico*. Norman: University of Oklahoma Press.

Hicks, Frederic
1981   Merchant barrios and the balance of trade in prehispanic Mesoamerica. Paper presented at the 80th Annual Meeting of the American Anthropological Association, Los Angeles, U.S.A., 2–6 December 1981.
1982   Acolman and Tepechpan: Tribute and market in the Aztec heartland. Paper presented at the 44th International Congress of Americanists, Manchester, United Kingdom, 12–14 April 1982.
1987   First steps toward a market-integrated economy in Aztec Mexico. In *Early state dynamics*, ed. H. J. M. Claessen and P. van de Velde, 91–107. Leiden: Brill.

Jacobs, Jane
1969   *The economy of cities*. New York: Random House.

Kurtz, Donald V.
1974   Peripheral and transitional markets: The Aztec case. *American Ethnologist* 1:685–705.

Litvak, King, Jaime
1971   *Cihuatlan y Tepecoacuilco: Provincias tributarias de Méx-*

ico en el siglo XVI. México, D.F.: Universidad Nacional Autónoma de México.

Lombardo de Ruiz, Sonia
1973   *Desarollo urbano de México-Tenochtitlan.* México, D.F.: Instituto Nacional de Anthropología e Historia.

Lopez de Ribera, Pedro
1979   Relación de Chiconauhtla y su partido. In *Relaciones geográficas de México*, ed. F. del Paso y Troncoso, 167–77. México, D.F.: Cosmos.

Marcus, Joyce
1984   Reply to Hammond and Andrews. *American Antiquity* 49:829–33.

Mason, Roger D.
1980   *Economic and social organization of an Aztec provincial center: Archaeological research at Coatlan Viejo, Morelos, Mexico.* Ph.D. dissertation, University of Texas.

Mayer-Oakes, William J.
1959   A stratigraphic excavation at El Risco, Mexico. *Proceedings of the American Philosophical Society* 103 (3):334–73.

Molins-Fábrega, N.
1954–55   El Códice Mendocino y la economía de Tenochtitlan. *Revista Mexicana de Estudios Antropológicos* 16:303–36.

Nazareo de Xaltocan, Don Pablo
1940   Carta al Rey Don Felip II. In *Epistolario de Nueva España*, ed. F. del Paso y Troncoso. 10:109–29. México, D.F.: Antigua Librería Robredo.

Nichols, Deborah L. and Thomas H. Charlton,
1988   Processes of state formation: Core versus periphery in the Late Postclassic Basin of Mexico. Paper presented at the 53rd Annual Meeting of the Society for American Archaeology, Memphis, 12 April.

Obregon, Luis
1949–57   Relacíon de Zempoala y su partido, 1580. Ed. R. H. Barlow. *Tlalocan* 3:29–41.

Offner, Jerome A.
1983   *Law and politics in Aztec Texcoco.* Cambridge: Cambridge University Press.

Parsons, Jeffrey R.
1976   The role of chinampa agriculture in the food supply of Aztec Tenochtitlan. In *Culture and continuity*, ed. C. Cleland, 233–62. New York: Academic Press.

Parsons, Mary H.
1972   Spindle whorls from the Teotihuacan Valley, Mexico. In *Miscellaneous studies in Mexican prehistory*, ed. M. W. Spence, J. R. Parsons, and M. H. Parsons, 81–164. Ann

Arbor, University of Michigan Museum of Anthropology, Anthropological Papers, 45.

Polanyi, Karl
1957   *The great transformation*. Boston: Beacon Press.

Rojas, José Luis de
1986   *México-Tenochtitlan: Economía y sociedad en el siglo XVI*. México, D.F.: Fondo de Cultura Economica.

Sahagún, Fray Bernardino de
1950–69   *Florentine Codex: General history of the things of New Spain*. Trans. A. J. O. Anderson and C. E. Dibble. 12 vols. Santa Fe: School of American Research and the University of Utah.

Sanders, William T., Jeffrey R. Parsons and Robert S. Santley
1979   *The Basin of Mexico: Ecological processes in the evolution of a civilization*. New York: Academic Press.

Sjoberg, Gideon
1960   *The preindustrial city*. New York: Free Press.

Smith, Carol
1974   Economics of marketing systems: Models from economic geography. *Annual Review of Anthropology* 3:167–201.

Spence, Michael W.
1985   Specialized production in rural Aztec society: Obsidian workshops of the Teotihuacan Valley. In *Contributions to the archaeology and ethnohistory of Greater Mesoamerica*. ed. W. J. Folan, 76–125. Carbondale: Southern Illinois University Press.

Tolstoy, Paul
1958   Surface survey of the northern Valley of Mexico: The Classic and Postclassic periods. *Transactions of the American Philosophical Society*, N.S. 48, pt. 5:1–101.

Velazquez, P. F., trans.
1945   Anales de Cuauhtitlan. In: *Códice Chimalpopoca*, 1–118. México D.F.: Universidad Nacional Autónoma de México.

Wolf, Eric
1982   *Europe and the people without history*. Berkeley: University of California Press.

Zeitlin, Robert N.
1982   Toward a more comprehensive model of interregional commodity production. *American Antiquity* 42:260–75.

8

Gift and Tribute: Relations of Dependency in Aztec Mexico

Frederic Hicks

The role of gift exchange in ordering social relations and creating ties of dependency has received a lot of attention in recent years. Most often, gifts are discussed in the context of economic structure and are, therefore, contrasted with commodities (Brumfiel 1987, 112ff.; Gregory 1982; Racine 1979). When discussed in the context of political structure, the comparable contrast is usually between reciprocity (or simply "exchange") and some of forcible extraction: tax or tribute (Trouwborst 1987; Godelier 1978). In discussing the contrast for Aztec Mexico, I will express it as a distinction between gift and tribute, because that is the way it is most often expressed in the early sources. I think that this contrast will be useful for understanding the political economy of ancient Mexico, as it has been for other regions, because these were two ways that dependent inferiors related to superiors.

The basic difference is this: when a superior accepts a gift or favor from an inferior, a gift that is given "voluntarily," he is under obligation to reciprocate in some way (see Orenstein 1980,

69–70 for references to support this generalization). When he forcibly extracts goods or labor from an inferior, which is given "involuntarily," he is under no such obligation. In ancient Mexico, superiors received both kinds of prestations from inferiors. Forcible extraction was the way the greatest amount of supplies was transferred from the inferior to the superior. Gifts accounted for a smaller net transfer, but were necessary to keep the system of stratification in operation. In Aztec Mexico, a major objective of empire building was to increase the proportion of the population whose prestations were forcibly extracted.

In actual practice, it may often have been difficult to tell whether a given prestation was a voluntary gift or involuntary tribute. Sometimes an inferior was expected to give a "gift" of a specified quantity of certain goods on specific occasions, and if they were not received, things could go badly for him. Yet so long as they were defined as "gifts," the receiver had some obligations to the giver, and there was a limit to what he could properly demand of him. Also, even though an inferior was forced to give a specified quantity of goods or labor to his superiors as tribute, the receiver had to provide him with at least the means to survive, produce the goods demanded, and reproduce his productive capacity. Yet so long as they were defined as "forcibly extracted," the receiver had no actual obligation to give anything in return, and there were few limits on what he could properly demand of him.

What I mean by "properly" requires some explanation. In stratified societies, elites develop an ideology that justifies their position of dominance and provides a socially accepted framework within which the surplus goods and labor of the nonelite may be appropriated. In most societies, this ideology stresses the benevolence of the elites and the benefits to the masses of their leadership and deemphasizes class antagonisms.[1] Godelier (1978, 767) has pointed out that most often, relations of dominance and exploitation are presented as if they were exchanges of services. Scott (1985) has observed that such an ideology will be accepted, at least outwardly, by the nonelite to the extent they can use it to negotiate for better conditions in terms acceptable to the elite, or to rally support against elites who fail to live up to it. The elites must therefore back up the ideology by appropriate behavior often enough not to jeopardize its usefulness, which means they must restrain their demands on their subordinates (Scott [1985] discusses these matters at length). The ideology of gift exchange means that the masses should fulfill their obligations willingly and voluntarily, the elite should reciprocate and not abuse this willingness, and there is no need for class antagonism.

The elite cannot dominate by physical force alone, so they must make use of the element of voluntarism embodied in the ideology of gift exchange. This limits how much surplus production and labor they can appropriate without straining the ideology beyond acceptability. The ideology of forcible extraction provides an entirely different justification for appropriating the surplus, but it requires a greater ability to dominate by physical force. It does not actually imply a total rejection of reciprocity. Scott (1985) has pointed out, as have others, that any working person, no matter what his status or how poorly he is compensated, sees himself as doing socially useful work and therefore deserving a degree of respect from others of his community. I presume this was true also of ancient Mexico, though I know of no specific statements to that effect. The lords may not have been obligated to give their coerced subordinates more than the minimum necessary for them to work and reproduce their status, but they did owe them at least that. There is, moreover, no good evidence that peasants whose surplus was "forcibly extracted" were seen as socially inferior to those whose surplus was given "voluntarily." Nevertheless, to the extent that the elite were able to dispense with the restraint and delicacy required by the gift exchange ideology, they could justify extracting much more from the labor resources at their disposal.

The distinction between gift and coercion will prove useful, I hope, for analyzing "precapitalist" states. Most such states, Aztec Mexico among them, were characterized by what Eric Wolf (1982, 79–82) calls (borrowing a term from Samir Amin) the "tributary mode of production." By this he means that the surplus is transfered from the producers to the elites primarily by political means, as some form of tax or tribute, rather than by economic means. Wolf notes there are two polar extremes. In one, the central power is strong because it controls some strategic element in the process of production, such as waterworks, and also some strategic element of coercion, such as a standing army of superior military capability, and so can collect the tribute directly without having to depend on local elites. (This has been called the "Asiatic mode of production.") In the other, the central power is relatively weak, because strategic elements of production (for example, land) and means of coercion are in the hands of local elites, who take much of the tribute for themselves. (This has been called the "Feudal mode of production.") Aztec Mexico, I believe, was a bit closer to the "feudal" end of the continuum than to the "Asiatic." The principal strategic resource was land, which was controlled largely by local elites, and local rulers also had their own military forces. Therefore, although a patronage system channeled power toward the apex, it was still necessary to rely in many ways on the norm of reciprocity, as will be explained in the pages to follow. (For the economy and political system of Aztec Mexico, see especially Carrasco 1978; Calnek 1982; Brumfiel 1983; Hicks 1986.)

Now let us turn to the case of Mexico. From the paramount rulers of the Aztec Empire down to the lowliest peasant in a small peripheral state, class relations were marked by prestations, in goods and services. Most scholars have focussed their attention on the flow from bottom to top; only recently have some scholars (most notably Brumfiel 1987) begun to examine more closely, the flow from the top down. Also, when treating the flow from the bottom up, most modern scholars, like most Spanish colonial administrators before them, have been content to treat the flow of goods and services as a single phenomenon: tribute. But a close reading of the primary sources indicates that to the Aztec, there were two kinds of prestations, though Spanish sources are inconsistent in the way they express the distinction. In early colonial court cases, when Indian peasants (through their Spanish lawyers) claim to have made only "voluntary" prestations to their pre-Spanish lords, they sometimes express it by saying they gave "regalos" (gifts) and not "tributo" (tribute) (Hicks 1984b, 237, 249), and sometimes that they gave "tributo" but not "terrazgo" (feudal rent) (Hicks 1978, 145). In Aztec Mexico, peasants did not "own" land; they received use rights to it. The peasants who gave "voluntary" prestations received use rights to community land (*calpollalli*), while those whose prestations were "coerced" had the right to (generally smaller) plots on land that belonged to the lord or institution they served (Dyckerhoff and Prem 1978, 191, 195). They are generally called "terrazgueros" (renters) in the Spanish sources.[2] As for the rulers of states conquered by the Aztec (or the descendants or spokesmen of these rulers), they regularly deny having given "tribute" to the imperial rulers; the latter were their friends, they say, to whom they gave only "presents" (Anunciación 1940; Motolinía and Olarte 1975, 229; Paso y Troncoso 1905, 4:47–48, 127; 5:14, 59).

If peasants gave their lords gifts, the lords of course had to reciprocate. There are many references to gifts given to peasants by kings or high ranking noblemen, usually as a reward for an extraordinary service, or for a required service that was especially well done (Brumfiel 1987). Most often, however, what the peasant was given was simply use rights to land, on which he could raise food for subsistence and a small surplus to sell in the market. This is what peasants whose prestations were "forcibly extracted" were also given, but the evidence is that, by and large, peasants whose prestations were "voluntary" received more land. One would expect that their obligations were lighter, giving them more time to work it, but the evidence for this is ambiguous (Carrasco 1964, 187; Hicks 1976, 72–73; Harvey 1988, 348–51).

There were, then, two kinds of dependency relations: those marked by the transfer of "gifts" and those marked by the involuntary transfer of what I will call "tribute." I have elsewhere used the term *political subjection* for the form of subordination that was marked by giving "gifts", and *tributary subjection* for that marked by giving "tribute" (Hicks 1984b). It is not entirely clear whether it was an individual household or the small "barrio" that was in one or the other form of subjection. The available data on the household level suggest it was the household, but other data suggest it was the barrio. It may even turn out that in some cases, the same household was in political dependency to one lord and tributary dependency to another, but I know of no actual cases of that.

In any case, we can get one view of the way the system worked by looking at the small "barrio," or what Carrasco (1964) has called a "minor ward" (see also Hicks 1982; 1984a). This was a small community, one of several kinds that could be called *calpolli*, which contained anywhere from 3 to 50 households, but on the average about 10 (Hinz, Hartau, and Heimann-Koenen 1983; Dyckerhoff and Prem 1976, 163). It was not politically autonomous; in physical form it was usually a rural village, but it could also be a small ward in a larger city. Quite often, all the people of such a barrio were in the same kind of subjection to the same lord, but there were exceptions. Many barrios were headed by low-ranking noblemen who lived in the barrio, and in such cases, some of the households might be in tributary subjection to him, while the rest were in political subjection. The former worked on the noblemen's fields and, for their own subsistence, were given a bit of his land to cultivate. The latter did not work directly for the noblemen and worked community land for their own subsistence (Hinz, Hartau, and Heimann-Koenen 1983). Some barrios appear to have had no nobles at all and may even have been headed by elder kinsmen of the other residents. Others were made up entirely of households in tributary subjection to one of the imperial rulers, and they were headed by stewards (*calpixqueh*), who supervised their labor and collected their tribute (Hicks 1978, 1982).

The difference between the two kinds of subjection is illustrated by the case of Temascalapa, in the northern Valley of Mexico. Temascalapa was a town subject to the king of Tepexpan. In the Aztec Empire, the king of Tepexpan was a dependent of the king of Texcoco, one of the empire's three paramount rulers. However, Temascalapa also had obligations to Tenochtitlan, whose kings were the most powerful of the empire, and these obligations were of a different kind. We do not have data on the barrio level from Temascalapa, only on the state level, but what we do have is very instructive. The obligations of Temascalapa to Tepexpan and Texcoco were based on the gift principle, while its obligations to Tenochtitlan were based on the principle of forcible extraction.

The data on Temascalapa come from the proceedings of a series of sixteenth century legal disputes which I have described elsewhere (Hicks 1984b). What Temascalapa owed to Tepexpan, and through it to Texcoco, was military service, corvée labor for special projects, and goods such as mats, blankets, fish, and rabbits, but witnesses in the legal dispute insisted that these were not tribute, only gifts. The hierarchy through which these goods and services were given apparently went from the local community to

the titled nobleman who governed Temascalapa on behalf of Tepexpan, from him to the king of Tepexpan, and through the king
of Tepexpan to the king of Texcoco.

What it owed to Tenochtitlan was cloth, cacao, and personal
service of a routine nature (as distinct from corvée labor for
special projects). The hierarchy through which these goods and
services were delivered went from the local community to an
imperial steward (*calpixqui*), stationed in the town of Cempoala,
and from him to the official in Tenochtitlan (also a *calpixqui*)
who received and stored the tribute from Cempoala. Temascalapa
was one of eleven towns that delivered their tribute to Cempoala.
We have the names of only five of them, and of those, Temascalapa is the only one that was subject to Tepexpan, though some
of the others were subject to other dependencies of Texcoco. It
is significant that this tribute to Tenochtitlan did not pass through
the kings of Tepexpan or Texcoco, nor through the governor of
Temascalapa. As head of state, the king of Tepexpan doubtless
was responsible for seeing to it that his subjects fulfilled their
obligations, including their obligations to the tribute collectors of
Tenochtitlan, but the king and his nobles did not themselves give
or even handle tribute. They gave only "gifts."

The evidence from ancient Mexico generally seems to be that
when tribute was demanded, certain lands were set aside to provide it, or certain small "barrios" were designated to give it. It
is interesting to note that, over the years, Tenochtitlan increased
its demands for tribute from Cempoala and the towns subject to
it, including Temascalapa, and as it did so, it also took additional
lands in the region. I would infer that by this process, communities
of commoners were reduced to tributary dependency; the land
they farmed was no longer community land, but land of the king
of Tenochtitlan (or of the noble to whom he may have redistributed it). Their prestations (now to Tenochtitlan) were "forcibly
extracted," and ideologically, nothing was owed them in return.

There is no evidence that peasants in tributary subjection were
any more bound to the land than were peasants in political subjection. Rulers did have authority to resettle peasants from one
area to another, as several historical instances show (Pomar 1941,
7; Alvarado Tezozómoc 1975, 533–34; Durán 1967, 238–39), but
they evidently exercised this power over peasants of either status.

As we have seen, they could also reduce peasants from political to tributary subjection. Peasants had the option of leaving, however, if they could find someplace to go, and, as in any economy where a lord's power depended on the manpower at his disposal, there must have been a perpetual labor shortage (as explained by Kula 1976, 108ff.), so they could probably find another lord on whose lands they could settle. This was possibly the major restraint on what lords could "forcibly extract" from their peasants.

There was another status, below that of peasants in tributary subjection. These were lone individuals, who did not belong to any community, and who had no group of kin. Some may have been survivors of the devastation of wars, some may have been fugitives from punishment, some may have been evicted for some sort of malfeasance, or condemned to slavery for wrongdoing. Often they came into the hands of merchants, who sold them. Unlike the peasants in political or tributary dependency, they did not form communities. In the sources, they appear as individuals or couples attached to someone else's household (Carrasco 1964, 205–6; Hinz, Hartau, and Heimann-Koenen 1983, 1:xvii–xviii). They were not numerous, but the existence of this status may have served to remind those in tributary subjection that a still worse fate could befall them.

We have so far been talking about the relations of peasants to nobles; let us now turn to the relation of nobles to each other. Nobles in ancient Mexico were such by virtue of their birth into a noble lineage, and there was a hierarchy of nobles within each lineage (Carrasco 1976). Within a state, some lineages were more powerful than others. The highest rank of nobility was that of *tlahtoani*, which is most often translated as "king"; but because this was actually a rank of nobility, there could be more than one king in a state (Hicks 1986, 42–44). In addition, the three paramount kings of the Aztec Empire, those of Tenochtitlan, Texcoco, and Tacuba, each dominated the kings of the states they had conquered or otherwise brought into the empire. Sometimes a dominated king in turn dominated the kings of several lesser states, so there could be several levels of kings, each of a different noble lineage (or branch thereof).

These kings all related to each other through gift exchange and so did nobles of different rank within the same noble lineage. Nobles of the subject states were expected to bring gifts for the emperors when they visited the imperial capitals, which they were expected to do three times a year, sometimes also on other occasions. These gifts were likely to be quite lavish, consisting of jewelry, precious raw materials, fine textiles, and the like—luxury goods suitable to give to a powerful king, goods that reflected the status of the giver as well as the receiver, or the status the giver wished to project. The imperial rulers reciprocated with gifts that were probably even more lavish than those they received; again, the gift had to reflect the status the giver wished to project. The more lavish the gift, the greater the obligation of the receiver. We don't have any figures, needless to say, but it seems likely that on balance, the total of gifts given by the imperial rulers to their noble subordinates were of greater value than those given by the subordinates to their superiors. Gifts could be redistributed, traded, or sold (Brumfiel 1987, 112ff.; Calnek 1982, 57–58; Smith 1986, 73–74).

The Aztec Empire was held together by these two kinds of dependency relations: that based on gift exchange and that based on forcible extraction. Dependency based on gift exchange provided the elite with a population of commoners available for military service, for corvée labor, and to provide enough material goods and routine labor to enable a lord and his family to live comfortably. In return these commoners got a measure of security, use rights to land, and perhaps occasional extraordinary favors. Since small wars occurred frequently in Central Mexico before it was united under imperial rule, and peasants not united under a respected lord would have been at the mercy of raiders from other towns, it seems reasonable to suppose that, for the most part, these peasants served their lords without much complaint. It cost a lord relatively little to retain their service and loyalty, but it did not yield a very large surplus.

Dependency based on forcible extraction provided the elite not only with military service and corvée labor, but also with routine labor on a regular basis at whatever task the lord assigned. People in this form of dependency were not expected to serve their lords with any great willingness; they worked under relatively close supervision, backed up by coercive force. Because of this, it cost a lord more to retain their services, but it yielded a larger surplus (that is, surplus labor: the man-hours available in a peasant household after it has provided for its own essential needs).

The stability of the empire required a judicious balance between these two kinds of subjection. To have reduced all of the peasants to tributary subjection would have required more coercive resources than the empire could have marshalled; to have left them all in political subjection would have yielded too little appropriated surplus to have justified the expense. The creation of ties of dependency based on forcible extraction was, however, a major object of empire building. As the empire grew, more and more small communities were reduced to tributary subjection, and labored under the supervision of an imperial *calpixqui* or a local steward. Some 68% of the commoners of Huexotzinco, in the Valley of Puebla, were identified as "terrazgueros" in the mid-sixteenth century (Carrasco 1974, 8), and it is likely that the percentage was higher in the Valley of Mexico by the time of the Spanish conquest. Smith (1986) has argued, and I basically agree (see Hicks 1988 for minor reservations), that a major function of the Aztec empire was to unite the nobility, and to provide a framework within which they could cooperate in the economic exploitation of their own commoners. The form this exploitation took was tributary subjection, or dependency based on forcible extraction, and the empire provided the force necessary to maintain it. Different lords, each with his own military force, cooperated in this, with their efforts coordinated through the imperial center. Should the peasants of one lord rebel, the peasants of another could be called in as an armed force to restore the status quo.

There was no standing army in Aztec Mexico, but military service was an obligation of commoners, who received training in the youths' houses (*telpochcalli*) of their communities, and who were mobilized for war through these youths' houses (Alvarado Tezozómoc 1975, 291, 551; Sahagún 1952, appendix, ch. 5). It is not really clear whether all commoners, those in tributary subjection as well as those in political subjection, gave military service or attended the youths' houses. Hassig (1988, 30, 59) evidently thinks they were, but his evidence is not clear.[3] Since military service is mentioned as an obligation of political subjection, I suspect that lords organizing military expeditions called upon those of their commoners that were in political subjection first, and used their "terrazgueros" for actual combat only if the need was especially great or for defense.

By the time of the Spanish conquest, many communities had indeed been placed in tributary subjection, but many others were still in political subjection. These communities had various functions in craftsmanship, production for the market, and any activity that is done best when done willingly and freely. Possibly this included serving in coercive forces against recalcitrant peasants of their own city, but the sources do not actually tell us so. Apparently most commoners who were permanent residents of Tenochtitlan-Tlatelolco, most of whom were warriors or specialists of one sort or another were in political subjection (Scholes and Adams 1958, 20, 30–34, 51–52; Rojas 1986). However, commoners who were there only temporarily, as servants of visiting nobles from afar, may have been in tributary subjection to these nobles.

As we have noted, relations of domination and subordination have often been disguised as reciprocity. This was true in Inca Peru, among other places, but Toland (1987) has described the strains placed on the credibility and acceptability of this ideology as the empire grew and the state found itself increasingly unable to keep up its side of the bargain; the resulting "moral bankruptcy" in turn threatened other aspects of its legitimizing ideology. But the Inca system did not include ideologically distinct categories of subjection. Peasants in ancient Peru labored for the state or its officials in a variety of statuses, under a variety of different conditions, some more oppressive than others (Rowe 1982; LeVine 1987), but the same legitimizing ideology seems to have applied to all. The Aztec state, by making use of two different legitimizing ideologies, may have been better able to follow through on its obligations to reciprocate, because it had no such obligations to an increasingly large portion of its subjects.

Notes

1. These are the basic elements of elite (or "conservative") ideology in most modern societies also, and one occasionally encounters them in scholarly writing. For instance, the oppressed are assumed not to

mind being oppressed unless there is specific evidence to the contrary, preferably evidence of violent confrontation. I suggest it is more reasonable to assume that the oppressed do mind being oppressed and to require evidence to support statements to the contrary. In any case, where elites write the history (as they did in Mesoamerica; even the Spanish regarded data from Indian nobles to be of much higher quality than data from Indian peasants), they are not likely to acknowledge class struggle as such, and the best indications that the oppressed resisted their oppression are data on measures taken by elites to secure their advantages.

2. The distinction made by Zorita (1941, 142–45) between "calpoleque" and "mayeque" may refer at least partly to this distinction, though his terminology is misleading.

3. In an earlier paper of my own, I find the statement that "mayeque" fought just as did "calpoleque" (Hicks 1976, 74), but no reference is given, and I do not now know where I got that information.

References

Alvarado Tezozómoc, Fernando
1975   Crónica mexicana. México: Editorial Porrúa.
Anunciación, Fr. Domingo de la
1940   Parecer de Fray Domingo de la Anunciación sobre el modo
            que tenían los indios en tiempo de la gentilidad, Chimal-
            huacán, Chalco, 20 set. 1554. In Epistolario de la Nueva
            España 1505–1818, ed. F. del Paso y Troncoso, 259–66.
            México: Porrúa e Hijos.
Brumfiel, Elizabeth
1983   Aztec state making: Ecology, structure, and the origin of
            the state. American Anthropologist 85:261–84.
1987   Elite and utilitarian crafts in the Aztec state. In Speciali-
            zation, exchange, and complex societies, ed. E. Brumfiel
            and T. K. Earle, 102–18. Cambridge: Cambridge Uni-
            versity Press.
Calnek, Edward E.
1982   Patterns of empire formation in the Valley of Mexico, Late
            Postclassic Period, 1200–1521. In The Inca and Aztec states
            1400–1800, ed. G. A. Collier, R. I. Rosaldo, and J. D.
            Wirth, 43–62. New York: Academic Press.
Carrasco, Pedro
1964   Family structure of sixteenth-century Tepoztlán. In Proc-
            ess and pattern in culture: Essays in honor of Julian H.
            Steward, ed. R. A. Manners, 185–210, Chicago: Aldine.
1974   Introducción: La Matrícula de Huexotzinco como fuente
            sociológica. In Matrícula de Huexotzinco, ed. H. J. Prem,
            1–16. Graz: Akademische Druck- und Verlagsanstalt.

1976   Los linajes nobles del México antiguo. In *Estratificación social en la Mesoamérica prehispánica*, ed. P. Carrasco and J. Broda, 19–36. México: SEP Instituto Nacional de Anthropología e Historia.

1978   La economía del México prehispánico. In *Economía política e ideología en el México prehispánico*, ed. P. Carrasco and J. Broda, 15–76. México: Editorial Nueva Imagen.

Durán, Fr. Diego

1976   *Historia de las Indias de Nueva España e las islas de la tierra firme*. Vol. 2. México: Editorial Porrúa.

Dyckerhoff, Ursula and Hanns J. Prem,

1976   La estratificación social en Huexotzinco. In *Estratificación social en la Mesoamérica prehispánica*, ed. P. Carrasco and J. Broda, 157–80. México: SEP-INAH.

1978   Der vorspanische Landbesitz in Zentralmexiko. *Zeitschrift für Ethnologie* 103:186–238.

Godelier, Maurice

1978   Infrastructures, societies, and history. *Current Anthropology* 19:763–71.

Gregory, C. A.

1982   *Gifts and commodities*. London: Academic Press.

Harvey, H. R.

1988   The Oztoticpac Lands map: A re-evaluation. In *Arqueología de las Américas*, (Memorias del 45° Congreso Internacional de Americanistas), ed. E. Reichel Dolmatoff, 339–53. Bogotá: Banco Popular, Fondo de Promoción de la Cultura.

Hassig, Ross

1988   *Aztec warfare: Imperial expansion and political control*. Norman: University of Oklahoma Press.

Hicks, Frederic

1976   Mayeque y calpuleque en el sistema de clases del México antiguo. In *Estratificación social en la Mesoamérica prehispánica*, ed. P. Carrasco and J. Broda, 67–77. México: SEP-INAH.

1978   Los calpixque de Nezahualcóyotl. *Estudios de Cultura Náhuatl* 13:129–52.

1982   Tetzcoco in the early 16th century: The state, the city, and the calpolli. *American Ethnologist* 9:230–49.

1984a   Rotational labor and urban development in Prehispanic Tetzcoco. In *Explorations in ethnohistory: Indians of Central Mexico in the sixteenth century*, ed. H. R. Harvey and H. J. Prem, 147–74. Albuquerque: University of New Mexico Press.

1984b   La posición de Temascalapan en la Triple Alianza. *Estudios de Cultura Náhuatl* 17:235–60.

1986   Prehispanic background of Colonial political and eco-
              nomic organization in Central Mexico. In *Supplement to
              the Handbook of Middle American Indians*, Vol. 4, *Eth-
              nohistory*, ed. R. Spores, 35–54. Austin: University of
              Texas Press.
1988   Alliance and intervention in Aztec imperial expansion.
              Paper presented at the 46th International Congress of
              Americanists. Amsterdam, 20 July 1988
Hinz, Eike, Caludine Hartau, and Marie-Luise Heimann-Koenen,
1983   *Aztekischer Zenzus: Zur indianischen Wirtschaft und Ge-
              sellschaft im Marquesado um 1540.* 2 vols. Hannover: Ver-
              lag für Ethnologie.
Kula, Witold
1976   *An economic theory of the feudal system.* London: Law-
              rence and Wishart.
LeVine, Terry Yarov
1987   Inca labor service at the regional level: The functional
              reality. *Ethnohistory* 34:14–46.
Motolinía, Fr. Toribio de, and Fr. Diego de Olarte
1975   Carta parecer de Fray Toribio de Motolinía y de Fray
              Diego de Olarte a Don Luis de Velasco el primero, Chol-
              ula, 27 ago. 1554. In *Documentos inéditos del siglo XVI
              para la historia de México*, ed. M. Cuevas, S. J., 228–32.
              México: Editorial Porrúa.
Orenstein, Henry
1980   Asymmetrical reciprocity: A contribution to the theory of
              political legitimacy. *Current Anthropology* 21:69–91.
Paso y Troncoso, Francisco del
1905   *Papeles de Nueva España*, Vols. 4 and 5. Madrid: Suce-
              sores de Rivadeneyra.
Pomar, Juan Bautista
1941   Relación de Tezcoco. In: *Nueva colección de documentos
              para la historia de México*, ed. J. G. Icazbalceta, pp. 3–
              64. México: Salvador Chávez Hayhoe.
Racine, Luc
1979   *Théories de l'échange et circulation des produits sociaux.*
              Montréal: Presses de l'Université de Montréal.
Rojas, José Luis de
1986   Cuantificaciones referentes a la ciudad de Tenochtitlan en
              1519. *Historia Mexicana* 36:213–50.
Rowe, John H.
1982   Inca policies and institutions relating to the cultural uni-
              fication of the empire. In *The Inca and Aztec states 1400–
              1800*, ed. G. A. Collier, R. I. Rosaldo, and J. D. Wirth,
              93–118. New York: Academic Press.

Sahagún, Fr. Bernardino de
1952 *Florentine Codex*, Part 4, Book 3, *The origin of the gods.* Trans. Ch. E. Dibble and A. J. O. Anderson. Santa Fe: School of American Research and University of Utah Press.
Scholes, France V., and Eleanor B. Adams eds.
1958 *Sobre el modo de tributar los indios de Nueva España a Su Majestad, 1561–1564.* Documentos para la historia del México colonial, 5. México: José Porrúa y Hijos.
Scott, James C.
1985 *Weapons of the weak; Everyday forms of peasant resistance.* New Haven: Yale University Press.
Smith, Michael E.
1986 The role of social stratification in the Aztec empire; A view from the provinces. *American Anthropologist* 88:70–91.
Toland, Judith D.
1987 Discrepancies and dissolution: Breakdown of the early Inca state. In *Early state dynamics*, ed. H. J. M. Claessen and P. van de Velde, 138–53. Leiden: Brill.
Torquemada, Fr. Juan de
1975 *Monarquía indiana.* 3 vols. México: Editorial Porrúa.
Trouwborst, Albert A.
1987 From tribute to taxation: On the dynamics of the early state. In *Early state dynamics*, ed. H. J. M. Claessen and P. van de Velde, 129–37. Leiden: Brill.
Wolf, Eric
1982 *Europe and the people without history.* Berkeley: University of California Press.
Zorita, Alonso de
1941 Breve y sumaria relación de los señores y maneras y diferencias que había de ellos en la Nueva España. In *Nueva colección de documentos para la historia de México*, ed. J. G. Icazbalceta, 67–205. México: Salvador Chávez Hayhoe.

9

Divide and Pool: Early State Economics and the Classic Maya

Rien Ploeg

Studies of the early state and of Maya culture have several things in common. Therefore the almost mutual ignorance of each other's results with respect to the development of complex societies is surprising, as in Maya studies concepts such as chiefdom and early state are applied, while in early state studies but little attention is given to this Mesoamerican region with its multitude of cultures spread both temporally and spatially, and characterized by recurrent patterns of development into complex societies (Fash 1988; Hirth 1984; Benson 1986). It might therefore be useful to bring together these separate fields of research. Here a start is made to create such a connection by an analysis of early state economics in the Maya Lowland area during the Preclassic and Classic periods.

Interestingly, progress made in Maya studies parallels developments within studies on the early state, especially when it is recognized that the development of sociopolitical organization and leadership is a complex matter that is not adequately understood by studying it from the economic domain of society only (see Claessen and Van de Velde 1985, 246ff.; Culbert 1988a; Lowe 1985). Yet, in this article it will be argued that by concentrating on the economy, and more specifically on the role of subsistence and trade in complex societies, important contributions can be expected in understanding the development of sociopolitical organization in the Maya culture area.

The development of Maya culture has to be viewed both from a geographic and a historical point of view. Geographically seen, Maya civilization developed in an area encompassing the Yucatan Peninsula (covering the modern Mexican states of Yucatan, Campeche, and Quintana Roo); portions of the Mexican states of Chiapas and Tabasco; Belize; Guatemala (mainly in the Petén region and the lower Motagua River valley); the Copan River region in Honduras and parts of western El Salvador. The southern and southeastern parts (Chiapas, Belize, the Petén, the Motagua Valley, and the Copan region) are generally referred to as the Lowland Maya area. Historically it has now become possible to date early state formation in the Maya Lowlands. Through epigraphy and iconography it is known that by A.D. 534 the Lowland Maya state was experiencing expansion both in its geographical and ideological impact (Marcus 1976).

Although we now know with some certainty when Maya state formation took place, it is still hard to account for the how and why. In order to get a better understanding of the development of sociopolitical organization in the Maya culture area, the developments will be viewed here from the perspective of subsistence production and trade.

In explaining the development of the state, Mayanists were guided by the cultural ecological approach, for a long time the dominant paradigm in American archaeology. In this approach economy is more or less equated with technology and man's adaptation to the physical environment (Hirth 1984, 283). This resulted in testing ideas on adaptation of complex societies in the humid tropics—the environment in which Maya civilization prospered. The results of the investigations opened new perspectives on ecology and state formation in the Maya area (Culbert 1983; Harrison and Turner 1978). At that time it was generally assumed that humid tropics formed a hostile and resource poor environment, preventing the development of complex societies *in situ* (Willey 1987, 189ff.). Semiarid regions were thought to be more suitable. These same ideas prevailed in the case of the Maya, and cultural development was attributed to areas outside the Lowlands. However, these ideas proved to be wrong. Research on soil fertility, agricultural techniques, subsistence strategies, and the like indicated that humid tropical environments were suited for the development of complex societies (Miller 1983, 13–47). For the study of Maya culture this led to a reconsideration of the role of subsistence and trade in the development of sociopolitical organization. In this article the hypothesis will be explored whether it is possible to analyze the role of subsistence and trade in terms of "divide and pool"—"divide" defined here as acknowledging the division of the region in political autonomous entities, and "pool" as recognizing the mutual benefits in sharing those resources which are needed and valued in other localities and regions.

As studies of the early state indicate, trade is important for the development of complex society. It can, however, not be considered as a "prime mover," or a "sole mover," and in order to understand the development of complex society other factors have to be brought into the analysis as well (Claessen and Van de Velde (1985, 249). In Maya studies major efforts were recently initiated to explore subsistence potentials in relation to trade in order to gain a more realistic perspective on the development of sociopolitical organization (Harrison and Turner 1978; Flannery 1982).

With respect to subsistence activities, development in the Maya area can be traced back as far as 8000 B.C. with data on small hunting and gathering camps in the Belizean area (Marcus 1983, 457). Little is known of the hunting and gathering period. Between 3000 and 2000 B.C. agricultural societies developed in the Maya Lowlands. These early dates led to the recognition that Maya culture developed *in situ*. This view differed greatly from earlier hypotheses, stating that development should have originated outside the area and been introduced here through migration and the intrusion of foreigners (Marcus 1983, 461). In this period food supply became more localized while at the same time settlement studies indicated a steady growth of population and increasing complexity of society (Ashmore 1981). From the Late Preclassic (250 B.C.) through the Late Classic (up to A.D. 900) Periods the general trend was toward increasing population, monumental architecture, and elaboration in art, script, and the like, reflecting a growing complexity of society and sociopolitical organization (Culbert 1988a). This raised questions on the relations between, among other things, population growth, subsistence production, and trade. There can be no doubt that trade was of some importance in these developments, but recent research redirected attention to the quality of subsistence strategies in the Lowlands. This view led to the consideration of trade as a secondary factor in the explanation of the development of Maya culture (Weaver 1981, 268–74ff.)

From the previous remarks it follows that the role of subsistence systems as explanatory factor changed considerably when it could be demonstrated that ecological zones within the Lowlands had rich subsistence potentials, and when the existence of a great variety in subsistence technologies and production could be demonstrated (Harrison and Turner 1978). The main changes in the views on the role of Maya subsistence systems can be expressed best in the form of two statements:

Statement I summarizes the traditional view that the Lowland Maya lived in a homogeneous, resource poor ecological area in which they practised extensive slash-and-burn agriculture with maize as the staple crop. In Maya studies this is known as the "swidden-thesis" (Harrison and Turner 1978, 13–23).

Statement II summarizes the more recent view that the Lowland Maya lived in a heterogeneous resource rich ecological area in which they practised intensive agriculture using various subsistence strategies along with slash-and-burn techniques with not only maize, but also root crops and other products, of which cacao and cotton were regarded as export crops (Harrison and Turner 1978, 337–73).

According to statement I this type of subsistence could not sustain a large population density and could not account for the development of complex societies. In this approach trade was considered the main factor in explaining the development of sociopolitical organization as this would have been the instrument of control and (re)distribution of goods and valuables in the Lowland area (Adams 1977). Settlement studies, however, proved that population densities contradicted statement I, presenting a totally different picture of the relation between population and subsistence (Ashmore 1981, 185); further research turned the argument upside-down, demonstrating that intensive forms of production could sustain here a complex society and thus internal development could explain the rise of Maya states.

The views on the role of trade, however, did not change so drastically. As part of the economic system trade is considered important for the provision of goods needed in society (Sabloff 1981, 3–27). Following the views expressed in statement I, long-distance trade would have been crucial, for a homogeneous resource poor environment would not stimulate local exchange and would lack important resources. In such an environment long-distance trade would be stimulated, creating an outward looking society. Under influence of the views expressed in statement II the study of trade in Maya society has recently begun to change focus. As this change in focus takes place only slowly , it is difficult already to assess the impact of these new views on trade on the study of the development of Maya culture. The change in focus directs empirical research to interregional and intraregional trade with special attention to intersite and intrasite levels of exchange. Initial observations indicate that regions of exchange are smaller than those postulated before, and confined to exchange within the Maya area—thus suggesting an inward looking society (Marcus 1983, 477). This asks for a thorough revision of the opinions on Maya development defended thus far.

Early studies in this field were dominated by the so-called Priest-Peasant-Model (PPM) of sociopolitical organization, which was based on the concept of the theocratic state (Becker 1979). This model held that priests were crucial in directing agriculture in such a high-risk environment. The agricultural surplus was invested mainly in the development of sociopolitical organization. It was, however, not the production of a surplus, but the fear of shortages that lay at the bottom of this model of development, in which trade played an important role.

As data from archaeology and related fields of research increased in number, it became apparent that the PPM needed revision, for the findings, summarized in statement II, revealed a far more complex type of development and composition of Maya society than was thought possible till then. As in the case of the slash-and-burn method of production, there was also a lot more to add to the priest and the peasant. The data needed here was obtained mainly from the findings of iconography and epigraphy. Here it was demonstrated that the term "priests" should be replaced by the term "rulers"; rulers characterized by some form of sacred kingship, thus bringing back ideology in the center of the study of the development of Maya sociopolitical organization (Schele and Miller 1986, 63ff.). It is now possible with the help of the new data to establish the existence of dynasties, based on lists of names of important rulers and their ancestors. A certain fame in these studies acquired, among other rulers, a certain Pacal, belonging to a late Classic dynasty in Palenque (Schele and Miller 1986, 268ff.). It should be deomonstrated also that in the royal rituals the offering of human blood was of crucial importance (Schele and Miller 1986). Compared to the PPM, in which subsistence and trade was considered as being more important than ideology, recent research gives more weight to the ideological factor, much to the detriment of the presumed central role of agriculture and trade (Culbert 1988a).

This turning of the arguments and the changing emphasis in topics is indicative of the critical phase Maya studies are experiencing nowadays both in terms of future research and the development of theory (Willey 1987, 2). It also underlines the existing uncertainties about the nature of the political, economic, and social relations in Classic Maya society (see also Sabloff 1985, 40ff.). This is evidenced by the possibility of formulating different scenarios for the development of Maya society using population growth, methods of subsistence production, trade, and ideology as their main variables. As they all result in the existence of the complex Preclassic and Classic Maya societies, there is no need here to describe these scenarios separately. Instead they will be included in the following analysis of state development in the Lowlands, viewed from the perspective of subsistence production and trade (Turner and Harrison 1983, 353–68).

There can be found in the Lowlands, from the very beginning, the existence of two contradictory tendencies. On the one hand Lowland societies were capable of maintaining a form of regional autonomy (Solorzano 1987). On the other, cultural unification becomes evident from at least Preclassic times, culminating in the Late Classic Period (Adams 1977). From the perspective of subsistence production, societies were capable of producing a regular surplus. The heterogeneous environment must have resulted in a diversity of products, inducing the many local and regional units to develop exchange relationships in order to benefit in a complementary way from each other's resources (Harrison and Turner 1978, 157–68; Hirth 1984, 1–11).

In terms of control of production and distribution there was little necessity for regional dominance, as every region could stay more or less independent, relying on its own subsistence potential and/or shifting exchange relations (Tainter 1988, 153ff.). Increasing population, however, could become problematical. This could be forestalled by intensification of agriculture. The question then becomes, up to what level? To answer this question "we are still far from understanding the geographical distribution, interrelationships, and relative importance of the various methods of food procurement that sustained Maya civilization" (Harris 1978, 308). Evidence shows that some regions like the Rio Bec, and northern and western Belize, seem to have developed more (large scale) intensive agriculture than other regions (Adams 1977, 77ff.; Harrison and Turner 1978, 345ff.). This suggests specialized crop growing beyond the subsistence needs of the regions in question. This probably indicates a kind of arrangement between the ruling elites of regions to fully benefit from the ecological differences in terms of specialized food production. Such an arrangement would make it possible to sustain a growing population. Regarding these arrangements it should be emphasized that to try to separate the economic from the sacred, military and "political function of the Maya elite would be futile; to try to assign them an order of priority would be even more so. They all seem to have been merged together" (Farris 1984, 145). Most probably such arrangements were based on kin relations and marriage alliances between the ruling elites of separate polities, thereby creating mutual economic and political interests (Fox and Justeson 1986, 7,19; Farris 1984, 119ff.; Freidel and Schele 1988, 90ff.).

Concentrating on economics, research in Belize testifies to the phenomenon of intensive agriculture and specialized food production. Instructive here are the findings in the Pulltrouser Swamp in northern Belize. An interdisciplinary research group demonstrated the existence here of raised fields during the Late Preclassic and Classic Periods (Turner and Harrison 1983). Raised fields require a relatively large and continuous labor investment. To balance this investment it is suggested that mainly plants giving high returns were cultivated. The comparison of pollen tests with ethnohistorical data indicates that "any crop could have been used, regardless of habitat requirements or market value". It is suspected, however, that crops like ananas, gossypium, nicotiana, theobroma, vanilla, and zea were selected for planting, "because of their transportability and market value" (Turner and Harrison 1983, 117).

When different regions have an elaborate exchange system in specialized food products or other valued products, trade then becomes an important instrument in the process of increasing inequalities in political power (cf. Rands 1969). But again, the heterogeneous environment and the possibilities of shifting trade relations might hamper such a process. Relationships are thus fragile because of the inbuilt flexibility of inter and intraregional food procurement. This flexibility possibly explains the sociopolitical developments in the Lowland region during the Preclassic and Classic Periods. Suggestive in this respect is Wiseman's Maximum Habitat Model (Harrison and Turner 1978, 105–19). This model relates site location in the Maya area and the orientation of centers towards soil boundaries. The varied use of local habitats and microenvironments contributed to the development of a more diversified subsistence base. This use of ecology creates an "environmental advantage," effective if managed locally through allocation of labor and the subsequent (re)distribution of its produce (Lowe 1985, 120, 204). From this situation one might hypothesize an acknowledgement of the idea that divide and pool would benefit more than unite and rule.

The control of production and distribution of subsistence goods and other products may explain also the existence of the many centers developed in the Preclassic and Classic Periods (Lowe 1985, 113ff.). Consequently, competition between centers in order to gain more control over the distributive network as it developed throughout the Maya area would not be improbable.

Moreover, due to ecological strategic advantages some centers would expand more than others. But, although it was recognized that these centers formed a vital link in the exchange network, alternative routes for exchange were possibly available. Thus dominance of centers was limited in this respect, too (Flannery 1982, 90; Sharer and Sedat 1987, 449ff.). In other words: "with relatively uniform productivity over large areas of the Lowlands, there was no economic basis for any center to achieve dominance over another; to this it might be added that there was also no advantage to doing so" (Tainter 1988, 164). In this setting several centers were in a position to try to gain prominence, and, if all of them were to develop their potentials in this direction at the same time, no one would really benefit in the end. Again the idea of divide and pool instead of unite and rule might be operative here in acknowledging each other's contribution in the exchange network. This would also imply that there had developed certain arrangements to regulate the (re)distribution of goods. Another possibility might have been the alternation of trade routes in order to ensure each of the participating centers an equal share in the long run.

The production of subsistence goods and trade, developing in a heterogeneous resource rich environment, thus gave a specific dynamic impulse to the economic and political processes in Maya society. It seems probable that production and distribution were coordinated by political leaders who regulated the control and (re)distribution of economic resources on the premise of alternating power positions between centers. Culbert (1988b) envisions here the development of stronger types of authority based on the control of agricultural intensification, specialization, and trade. Concentrating on the collapse of the Classic Maya societies, Culbert also expected rulers to find alternate sources of goods and wealth (1988b, 78ff.). In his view, the population-subsistence balance, giving more weight to agriculture than trade, became endangered to a point where a too dense population "covered an area too large to allow adjustment through relocation or emigration" (Culbert 1988b, 99). Assuming long-term environmental degradation, he admits, however, that "given the tight interconnections of [these] factors and the paucity of precise data, one could construct almost any scenario of agricultural failure" (1988b,

100). The paucity of data, together with the growing awareness of the continuation of the large and densely populated settlements during the "collapse" of the rainforest polities, may lead to a different interpretation of the interplay between population, trade, subsistence production, and Maya sociopolitical organization (Hammond et al. 1988; Culbert 1988b, 87; Sabloff 1985, 43). One might think, for example, in terms of a situation in which the development from an early state level to a mature state was frustrated because of the fact that the dynamic input of subsistence goods and trade "tolerated too much 'movement' on the regional levels to promote a mature state organization for the regulation of economic activity" (Bargatzky 1987, 30; cf. Lowe 1985, 180ff.).

This point is best illustrated by the fact that during the Preclassic and Classic Periods through increasing population, the production of subsistence goods and trade experienced intensification—thus creating better opportunities for individual centers to gain more prominence and sustain their dominant position over other centers for a long period of time. A Preclassic center such as El Mirador, and Classic centers such as Tikal, Yaxchilan, and Copan testify to this inferred development. Though becoming more prominent, the idea of divide and pool and the dynamics inherent to that view, gave rise to a more extreme competition between centers to gain, as it seems, dominance over each other (Miller 1986; Willey 1987, 7ff.). A closer consideration of the role of pre-Hispanic Maya trade in food is imperative in view of the enthnohistorical evidence of Maya interest in commercial agricultural production. Also the location of the large settlements of Nakum, midway between the larger sites of Tikal, Maranjo, Uaxactun, and Naachtun on the route between Calakmul and Tikal, suggests cooperation in realizing nodes for the exchange of products needed in the large settlements, experiencing a situation of increasing population densities, and probably at the same time diminishing opportunities to be self-supporting (Lowe 1985, 154; Flannery 1982, 153; Miller 1983, 83–99; Shortman and Urban 1983, 60; Harrison and Turner 1978, 353).

Apart from the inferred dynamic input from the production of subsistence goods and trading activities to the development of Maya society, what other evidence is there to reflect the idea of alternating political power and the subsequent struggles of centers to become an independent locus of power? There are several lines of evidence. One such a line is based on ethnohistorical sources in which the rotation of political dominance is a major theme. The sources indicate an alternation of power positions between a group of allied centers (Freidel 1983, 1986a, 1986b). In all likelihood, this theme of power rotation reflects the initial stages of political development in the Maya area (see also de Montmollin 1987). Another line of evidence is archaeological and is based on settlement studies which indicate an alternating development of and between centers, possibly reflecting forms of political arrangements (Lowe 1985, 9ff.). A third line of evidence is embedded in iconographic and epigraphic analyses. Recent research demonstrates that centers were involved in heavy power politics, especially in the Late Classic Period (Fox and Justeson 1986; Freidel and Schele 1988; Marcus 1976; Miller 1986). It seems that they tried to unite and rule in getting rid of the restrictions posed by the notions of divide and pool. This view finds some confirmation in Culbert's study of the relations between centers which were highly competitive (Culbert 1988a).

The idea of alternating power positions finds support in the fact that conflict and competition is found to occur almost exclusively between local centers which were situated on alternative trade routes. They seem to be struggling for political prominence, while at the same time being part of a political hierarchy of centers (Marcus 1976). Examples are the struggles between Yaxchilan and Piedras Negras in the Usumacintha region; Tikal and Uaxactun in the Petén region; and more recent research in highlighting the relations between Copan and Quirigua in the southeastern region (Beaudry 1984; Fash 1988; Adams 1977, 151–54). Study of these intersettlement conflicts gives additional data for the understanding of the dynamics behind the sociopolitical development of the Lowland (Classic) Maya. Especially promising is the above mentioned relationship between Copan and Quirigua. In the Late Classic Period they were among the many flourishing centers in the southern and southeastern parts of the area. This period is characterized by intensive communication and trade within and beyond the regions (Sabloff and Andrews 1986, 454–56). It is interesting to see how Copan, situated on the southeastern margin of the Maya culture area, becomes a part of the

Maya political hierarchy, developing a politically inward-looking attitude. At the same time, however, Copan directs its trade activities in a geographically opposite direction, towards western El Salvador—thus developing an outward-looking economic attitude. This might imply a diversion of the system of altneration of political and economic power. The consequences of the (supposed) defeat of Copan by Quirigua at least point in this direction, because from this time onwards Copan became economically isolated, while Quirigua gained greater dominance (Beaudry 1984; Robinson 1987; Urban and Shortman 1986; see also Fash 1988).

A pattern of hostile relations between centers is obvious throughout the Maya area (Freidel 1986a); more and comparative studies are needed in order to determine the impact of the production of subsistence goods and networks of trade on the development of sociopolitical organization—and the reverse. Especially interesting is the question of how the severe competition between centers in the ideological and political domain relates to the suggested cooperation between centers in the economic domain, both diachronically and synchronically. To substantiate the assumed relation between agricultural intensification and trade on the one hand and the development of sociopolitical organization on the other more research is needed. It seems possible, on the basis of the data gathered thus far, to suspect that, in the course of the development of the Maya civilization, periods of cooperation—here termed divide and pool—alternated with periods of struggle and competition—termed here unite and rule. This view would make it possible to explain at least some findings which hitherto were difficult to square with the view of perpetual struggle.

References

Adams, Richard E. W. ed.
1977   *The origins of Maya civilization*. Albuquerque: University of New Mexico Press.
Ashmore, W. ed.
1981   *Lowland Maya settlement patterns*. Albuquerque: University of New Mexico Press.
Bargatzky, Thomas
1987   Upward evolution, suprasystem dominance, and the Ma-

ture State. In *Early State dynamics*, ed. H. J. M. Claessen and P. van de Velde, 24–38. Leiden: Brill.

Beaudry, M. P.
1984   *Ceramic production and distribution in the southeastern Maya periphery*. Oxford: BAR International Series 203.

Becker, M. J.
1979   Priests, peasants, and ceremonial centers: the intellectual history of a model. In *Maya archaeology and ethnohistory*, ed. N. Hammond and G. R. Willey, 3–20. Austin: University of Texas Press.

Benson, E. P. ed.
1986   *City states of the Maya: Art and architecture*. Denver: Rocky Mountain Institute for Pre-Columbian Studies.

Claessen, Henri J. M. and Pieter van de Velde
1985   Sociopolitical evolution as complex interaction. In *Development and decline; The evolution of sociopolitical organization*, H. J. M. Claessen, P. van de Velde, and M. E. Smith, 246–63. South Hadley: Bergin and Garvey.

Culbert, P. T.
1988a   Political history and the decipherment of Maya glyphs. *Antiquity* 62:135–52.
1988b   The collapse of Classic Maya civilization. In *The collapse of ancient states and civilizations*, ed. N. Yoffee and G. L. Cowgill, 69–101. Tucson: University of Arizona Press.

Culbert, P. T. ed.
1983   *The Classic Maya collapse*. 3rd ed. Albuquerque: University of New Mexico Press.

Farris, N. M.
1984   *Maya society under colonial rule*. Princeton, N.J.: Princeton University Press.

Fash jr, W. L.
1988   A new look at Maya statecraft from Copan, Honduras. *Antiquity* 62:157–69.

Flannery, K. V. ed.
1982   *Maya subsistence. Studies in memory of Dennis E. Puleston*. New York: Academic Press.

Fox, J. A. and J. S. Justeson
1986   Classic Maya alliance and succession. In *Ethnohistory. Supplement to the Handbook of Middle American Indians*, ed. R. Spores, 7–34. Austin: University of Texas Press.

Freidel, David A.
1983   Political systems in Lowland Yucatan: dynamics and structure in Maya settlement. In *Prehistoric settlement patterns: Essays in honor of Gordon R. Willey*, ed. E. Z. Vogt and

R. M. Leventhal, 375–86. Albuquerque: University of New Mexico Press.

1986a   Maya warfare: An example of peer polity interaction. In *Peer polity interaction and socio-political change*, ed. C. Renfrew and J. D. Cherry, 93–108. Cambridge: Cambridge University Press.

1986b   Terminal Classic lowland Maya: Successes, failures, and aftermaths. In *Late Lowland Maya civilization: Classic to Postclassic*, ed. J. A. Sabloff and E. W. Andrews, 409–30. Albuquerque: University of New Mexico Press.

Freidel, David A. and Linda Schele,
1988   Symbol and power: A history of the Lowland Maya cosmogram. In *Maya iconography*, ed. E. P. Benson and G. G. Griffin, 44–93. Princeton, N. J.: Princeton University Press.

Hammond, Norman, David Stuart, and Ernestene Green
1988   Excavations and survey at Nohmul, Belize, 1986. *Journal of Field Archaeology* 15:1–15.

Harris, D. R.
1978   The agricultural foundations of Lowland Maya civilization: A critique. In *Pre-Hispanic Maya agriculture*, ed. P. D. Harrison and B. L. Turner II, 301–23. Albuquerque: University of New Mexico Press.

Harrison, P. D. and B. L. Turner II, eds.
1978   *Pre-Hispanic Maya agriculture*. Albuquerque: University of New Mexico Press.

Hirth, K. G. ed.
1984   *Trade and exchange in early Mesoamerica*. Albuquerque: University of New Mexico Press.

Lowe, J. W. G.
1985   *The dynamics of apocalypse. A system simulation of the Classic Maya collapse*. Albuquerque: University of New Mexico Press.

Marcus, J.
1976   *Emblem and state in the Classic Maya Lowlands: An epigraphic approach to territorial organization*. Washington: Dumbarton Oaks.

1983   Lowland Maya archaeology at the crossroads. *American Antiquity* 48:454–88.

Miller, A. G.
1986   *Maya rulers of time: A study of architectural sculpture at Tikal, Guatemala*. Philadelphia: University of Philadelphia Press.

Miller, A. G. ed.
1983   *Highland-Lowland interaction in Mesoamerica*. Washington: Dumbarton Oaks.

Montmollin, Olivier de
1987   *Temporal and social scales in Prehispanic Mesoamerica.*
               Cambridge: Centre of Latin American Studies.
Rands, Robert L.
1969   *Maya ecology and trade.* Carbondale, Ill.: University Mu-
               seum, Southern Illinois University.
Robinson, E. J. ed.
1987   *Interaction on the southeast Mesoamerican frontier.* Vols.
               1 and 2. Oxford: British Archaelogical Records, Inter-
               national Series 237.
Sabloff, Jeremy A.
1985   Ancient Maya civilization. In *Maya; Treasures of an an-
               cient civilization*, ed. Ch. Gallenkamp and R. E. Johnson,
               34–46. Albuquerque: Albuquerque Museum.
Sabloff, Jeremy A. ed.
1981   *Supplement to the Handbook of Middle American Indians.*
               . *Archaeology.* Austin: University of Texas Press.
Sabloff, Jeremy A. and E. W. Andrews, eds.
1986   *Late Lowland Maya civilization. Classic to Postclassic.* Al-
               buquerque: University of New Mexico Press.
Schele, Linda and Mary Ellen Miller,
1986   *The blood of kings. Dynasty and ritual in Maya art.* Fort
               Worth: Kimbell Art Museum.
Shortman, E. M. and P. A. Urban, eds.
1983   *Quirigua reports.* Vol. 2. Papers 6–15. Philadelphia: The
               University Museum, University of Pennsylvania.
Sharer, R. J. and D. W. Sedat
1987   *Archaeological investigations in the northern Maya high-
               lands, Guatemala. Interaction and the development of Maya
               civilization.* Philadelphia: The University Museum, Uni-
               versity of Philadelphia.
Solorzano, F.
1987   De la sociedad prehispanica al régimen colonial en Centro
               América (siglos 16–17). *Revista Occidental, Estudios La-
               tinoamericanos* 12:147–79.
Tainter, Joseph B.
1988   *The collapse of complex societies.* Cambridge: Cambridge
               University Press.
Turner II, B. L. and P. D. Harrison, eds.
1983   *Pulltrouser Swamp. Ancient Maya habitat, agriculture, and
               settlement in Northern Belize.* Austin: University of Texas
               Press.
Urban, P. A. and E. M. Shortman, eds.
1986   *The southeast Maya periphery.* Austin: University of Texas
               Press.

Weaver, M. P.
1981   *The Aztecs, Maya, and their predecessors*. 2nd. ed. New
                York and London: Academic Press.
Willey, Gordon R.
1987   *Essays in Maya archaeology*. Albuquerque: University of
                New Mexico Press.

10

State and Community: Changing Relations of Production after the Unification of Nepal

Joanna Pfaff-Czarnecka

During the first half of the eighteenth century over sixty different political units existed in the present Nepalese territory.[1] From 1744 onwards a small and economically weak principality of Gorkha under the Shah rulers[2] succeeded in conquering the surrounding areas, founding a kingdom with rulers claiming a high status within the Hindu caste hierarchy, one half of the subjects belonging to a variety of ethnic groups the other half being Hindu. Gorkha's military expansion lasted until the second decade of the nineteenth century.[3] It was put to an end by a war with the British East India Company. The powerful "unification" of Nepal and the consolidation of the Shah's rule initiated a variety of processes causing changes in power and authority relations, in the extraction of surpluses, and in the division of labour, creating new relations of political economy within the emerging "Nepalese" society. The important questions arising in this context refer to:

1. The nature of the processes causing changes and the measures

231

taken by the rulers in order to maximise the surplus extraction from the subjects immediately after the "unification," and:

2. The effects the rulers' efforts in maximizing the surplus extraction had on the relations of production within local societies in different parts of Nepalese territory

The period in question (1769–1846) is the time immediately after the unification, known also as the Shah era.

In the beginning of this article an attempt is made to describe the Shah's difficulties in coping with the initial lack of centralization and—more generally—the difficulties the rulers had to face in order to strengthen their control over the subjects and over the economic resources. It will be shown how fragmentary the system of economic control was in this time, with its different forms of dependence and surplus extraction.

In the following section attention is paid to measures taken by the central government in order to increase the surplus extraction and to centralize the state apparatus. In this context, to encourage the Hindu population, skilled in plough agriculture, to migrate into tribal areas where barter trade, swidden cultivation and/or pastoralism were practiced, proved crucial for the increase of production, the lion share of which was gradually appropriated by the ruling class. In the same time the promotion of migration was instrumental for the establishment of law and order in remote areas of the country.

Thus, the consequences of the state's intervention in the relations within the putative "autonomous village communities" will be of interest in the concluding part of this article. It will be argued that despite their weakness the Shah rulers succeeded in establishing foundations for a future system of revenue administration, the emergence of new local élites at village level being an important consequence of their efforts. While production was increased, the rulers' *divide et impera* policy proved successful in controlling the new and the old local élites, as well as their subjects.

In the Nepalese ethnohistory the concept of the "local community" has not yet been discussed. Nevertheless, several authors convey the impression that local societies either remained unaffected by changes on the state level or passively suffered the hardships inflicted on them by the ruling class. Even though it is widely approved that the ruling family, the competing élites, and the army divided the lion share (at least theoretically, see below) of the economic surplus produced within the Nepalese boundaries[4] among themselves, the local societies are not examined in this context or are merely seen as abstract victims of the central policies. It is not surprising then, that the tremendous stream of population migrating from west to east after the unification of Nepal is not perceived as a constituent factor in the processes of changing power relations within local societies. Thus, the relation between state and community usually tends to be viewed from above. At first, this article also adopts the view from above, as it starts with a discussion of central policies. The relations within some local societies though will be examined with regard to their effect on central policies.

Lack of Centralization

Nepal under the Shahs (1769–1846) was a redistributive state commanded by gentry and military officials; besides landowners,[5] prebendaries were an important section of the ruling class. The term "redistributive" illuminates the nature of the relationship of the state to producers and traders in the sense that the state holds property and consequently has rights over the product.

According to Hodgson, who was a British resident in Nepal during the later half of the Shah-era: ". . . there is no specific aggrandisement, district, or zilla," therefore no district-level administration (Regmi 1984, 40). Only the subsequent Rana government (1846–1951) "had acquired the power to enforce uniformity of government in all parts of the empire" and the state "was sustained by its ability to appropriate a large portion of the economic surplus generated within its frontiers" (Singh 1988, 299). Gradually, after the Shah era, a centralized system of administration was established and a far-reaching monetization was achieved so that since the second half of the nineteenth century the offices were paid for in cash, replacing gradually payments in kind.

Although the Shah rulers regarded the economic resources within the Nepalese boundaries as the "entire possessions of the king of Gorkha" (Burghart 1984, 103) they did not prove successful in extracting an essential part of the surplus during the period in question. The rulers had the delicate task of integrating different conflicting communities and various indigenous sociopolitical systems. At the same time they acknowledged the existence of various units ("countries") within their territory where the subjects claimed "certain rights to their land and way of life on the basis of ancestral authority" (Burghart, 1984, 103). In these various political subunits, the relationship between the rulers and their subjects was perceived in different ways. Being a subject entailed making specific payments to the king, which indicated the respective grade of inferiority towards him. Considering oneself a "younger brother of the king"[6] and thus paying a rather symbolic tribute was very different from being compelled to a variety of payments and services as was the case in the centrally located parts of the Nepalese territory. Thus, the "sovereignty" of the Gorkha rulers had different meanings all around the country in the time of the unification, depending on how the different groups were subjugated and how difficult it was for the rulers to extend their control over each specific territory. The lack of uniformity and integration, and the difficulty of centralizing the administration, were, among other things, due to the fact that between 1774 and 1816 the "societal format" of the Gorkha state multiplied several times. It expanded from a small principality of approximately 12,000 inhabitants to a state "able to resist the English and Chinese (Gaborieau 1978a, 30).[7]

The multiple growth of the Nepalese territory, the increase of the population, and the population movements required manifold organizational adaptations.[8] Due to the lacking organizational infrastructure the revenue collection system could not be centralized and the surplus at the state's disposal was scarce. The quest for landed property (in addition to the control of trading routes, the main source of income) destabilized the central government. Because of the unstable political situation in the center, the rulers were striving to establish durable links with their entourage and had to reward followers lavishly—while their revenue collection system was still inefficient. The resources at the rulers' disposal were scarce, among other things, because they had not succeeded in building up an effective administrative infrastructure, and also because they failed to control the competing élites. In fact, not the kings but heads of different political factions were subsequent de facto rulers—unable however to establish a durable rule; it was only achieved by the Ranas—one of the competing sections—in 1846 (until 1951). As a consequence, different political factions were fighting for the control of the scarce resources. There was no administrative hierarchy as it had developed in the Mughal state (North India) in the seventeenth century.[9] One of the main problems was the fragmented control of the land.

Control of the Land

"Rather than attempt to collect revenues in grain, transport them to government granaries, and disperse grain in payment for services rendered by various individuals to the state, the government assigned specific fields in specific villages to its various government servants and authorised them to collect the revenues due from these fields" (Stiller 1976, 294). As stated before, from the point of view of the central élites, the land was always scarce. A great bulk of land was controlled by the ruling family and the dignitaries having the key ranks in the administrative-military system (*sera* and *birta*[10]). Further lands were distributed to the religious specialists (*birta*) and institutions (mainly *guthi*[11]), because of the crucial importance of their support (communication with the gods) throughout the military expansion (Hasrat 1970, 82). During the period of the military conquests a large amount of land was distributed to the officers and to the standing army as *jagirs*.[12] After the defeat by the British East India Company, to which the Gorkhas had lost some of the conquered territories, the army was still growing, although there was no prospect of further expansion (Stiller 1976, 293). The army was now needed in order to solve internal problems. Only under the Ranas, however, the military administration proved to play a crucial role in tax collection on the other form of state lands (*raikar*[13]). The most vehement quarrels took place on the fertile Terai lands (southern area of Nepal) which were slowly cleared up after the war against the British. More lands were made arable in the hill area, usually on the basis of forced labor. The area of agricultural land expanded further at the expense of other forms of production (pastoralism and shifting cultivation), the entire nineteenth century being characterised by the gradual change from other forms of livelihood to agriculture.

The land at the central élites' disposal was also scarce due to the fact that "ownership rights" in agricultural lands and forests were transferred to individuals and groups for political reasons. The Gorkhali rulers did not achieve political unification solely through military conquest, and often political compromises with various communal groups, as well as with the rulers of different principalities, were considered more expedient. *Kipat* was a form of communal land ownership, under which each person had the right to the exclusive use of a particular piece of land. However, his rights to dispose of the land were restricted on the theory that the land belonged to the community as a whole.[14] The *rajya* system of the western hill region may be cited as an example of similar compromises with the rulers of principalities who exchanged their independence for vassal status under Gorkha's suzerainty. The term *raja* literally means a king, and *rajya*, a kingdom. In post-1770 Nepali historiography, however, *rajya* means a vassal principality in the Gorkhali empire, which usually enjoyed a substantial measure of local autonomy" (Regmi 1984, 18).

To the central government, the distribution of lands not only meant the loss of its product but also the loss of political control to an important degree: ". . . the lands assigned as *jagir* and *birta* were more or less permanently removed from the area of government controlled lands. The *jagirdar* or *birta* owner became the 'government' in these tracts, and the villager had no direct access to government in the normal business of life. In most instances the landlord's word was law" (Stiller 1976, 295). Thus, direct state administration was confined to the subjects living on *raikar* lands.

The described types of land ownership and land tenure were the main forms of land control throughout the Shah rule. Whereas the *raikars* and *jagirs* were state lands, the extensive *birtas, guthis, rajyas* and *kipats* were removed from state control. In reality the control of the state lands proved to be difficult, too. Nevertheless, the rulers succeeded in reducing the land controlled by the priesthood[15] and by the remote ethnic groups and to extend the state controlled lands (*raikar* and *jagir*) instead. Still, until the end of the Shah era, the organization of land distribution and exploitation was characterized by its fragmentary nature, lack of an effective administrative infrastructure, and a very low degree of monetization. In this relation some important aspects must be pointed out.

Corresponding to the fragmentary character of the land system, the revenue system (taxes and/or rents) was even more complicated. On each land form different methods of revenue collection were practiced which called for a large variety of revenue officials, depending also on the sort of land (dry or wet cultivation) and the form of payments (either a part—usually half—of the product or a quantity of the product which was agreed on in advance—under the Shah a transition from the former to the latter took place). There were different forms of revenue collection in different parts of the country. Most parts of the country probably shared common traits in their land revenue system:[16] the rents did not fall below half of the crops; the payments were done in kind rather than in cash; finally, in most parts of the country, under the Shah, the revenue was collected by *ijaradars* (revenue collectors) appointed to the government for a certain number of years—the payable amount was agreed on and sometimes even paid in advance.

The payment of the land revenue was not the only burden on the peasants. Despite the loss of the land revenue the state still controlled other economic activities conducted by their subjects. The state:

imposed taxes on commodities offered for sale,
recruited the villagers for the army,
forced the villagers to compulsory labor (Regmi 1984, 29ff.), the
    obligations being either occasional or imposed on peasants to
    supply specified commodities or to provide specified labor serv-
    ices, for example, porterage services for the transportation of
    mail or goods (that is, of guns).

In addition to the rents, the peasants had to make further payments and tributes, that is, taxes (homestead, cattle), occasional payments (on coronations, initiation of princes, royal weddings), and they had to supply game, skins, goods (pots, paper), fodder, charcoal, and so forth. However, the state control in this field varied greatly from region to region.

Due to the land scarcity, the land-controlling groups were increasing their pressure on the peasants. Stiller (1976) describes an important period (1816–1839) of the Shah rule as a time of subjects' "silent cry." An immense migration of the Nepalese subjects to British India is one important indicator of the situation of the peasants[17] in this time. Countless complaints to the central government are further testimony of their severe lot.

Contrary to most *birta*-grants, the *jagir*-grants had temporary character. Thus, many *jagirdars* ". . . tended to be less concerned for the proper use and development of the land. Long-range improvements such as irrigation channels that could only be developed by a planned use of the excess labour of the village were postponed or not taken up at all. The *jagirdar* was primarily concerned with maximizing his return from the land" (Stiller 1976, 295).

The land-controlling groups and their clients not only extracted rents from the peasants but imposed on them the same obligations as those by the state, that is, compulsory labor, tributes, and occasional payments. Due to their judicial authority they also collected fines and fees. Under the Shah the peasants (with few exceptions) didn't have tenurial security. The landlords could always evict them. The situation of the peasants worsened when during the Shah rule the form of rent collection changed from a share of the crop to a fixed amount of the product, leaving the risks of crop failures entirely to the peasant. This was the main reason for the impoverishment of the peasants often leading to bondage and slavery.

The élites controlling the *jagirs* and *birtas* were absentee landlords. Many of them lived in the capital or in local centers and had duties which prevented them from controlling the agricultural activities on their lands themselves. Thus local élites tended to become their middlemen. As will be shown later, under the Shah new local élites emerged in many parts of the country.

Trade

The long-distance trade had been of crucial importance in the principalities on the Nepalese territory—especially in the Kathmandu Valley—long before the unification.[18] Its volume, diminished during the conquest, multiplied from 1816 onwards (Hodgson 1831, 92). The British used the Nepalese trade routes to Tibet and China until the end of the nineteenth century. Before the Shah, the importance of long-distance trade consisted almost entirely in the considerable transit duties; after the conquest the conspicuous consumption of the Nepalese élites was increasing. For their benefit fabrics, precious stones, and European goods (furniture, window glass, and so forth) were imported from India; Chinese silk and wool, gold, musk, and medicinal herbs were brought from China and Tibet. Forest products, especially timber, were the main items to be exported from Nepal to India, as well as cotton and cotton textiles, iron, copper, metal utensils, rice, and paper. Only a few goods like rice, copper, and iron, were sold to Tibet. The bulk of the Nepalese exports consisted of raw materials. The custom duties on the entrepôt trade continued to be the main share of the trade revenue controlled by the rulers. Of minor importance were other sources of revenue: taxes on sales and duties on exports. According to Regmi: "It may be noted that the distinction between transit duties and export duties emerged only during the later years of the nineteenth century; the traditional practice was to collect duties at ferry-points, trade centres, and market-towns irrespective of whether the commodities so taxed were destined to another place inside the frontiers or exported" (1984, 148).

On the routes between north and south, the barter of Tibetan salt for Nepalese grain had a long tradition. Various groups, mostly of Tibetan stock, were involved in this exchange. Under the Shah the Newar community of the Kathmandu Valley expanded in other parts of the hill area: "The Newars had a well established reputation for trading as an independent means of livelihood. . . . Newars had established commercial relations between Tibet and Kathmandu by setting up a Newar colony in Lhasa, Tibet. . . . The early trade probably began as Tibetan salt in exchange for Nepali rice. Eventually other products were also traded" (Iltis 1980, 103ff.). Apart from their participation in the long-distance trade, the Newars are said to have promoted the internal trade. However, according to Regmi (1984) the peasants were left with hardly any means to purchase commodities. They produced goods themselves during the slack agricultural season. Commodities were also produced by occupational castes and exchanged on institutional basis of *jajmani*-type. Most of the goods produced on the household level were locally exchanged, leaving no surplus for the state to extract. The internal trade was conducted mainly between different regions and Kathmandu. The exchanges comprised mainly cotton, ore, and metal utensils (Regmi 1984, 111).

The state was strongly involved in trading institutions and activities. It encouraged foreign traders to work in Nepal (Regmi 1984, 118) as well as to settle in different parts of the country, and it promoted the development of market towns (especially at the southern borders). As stated previously, the control of the custom duties was one of the main governmental activities under the Shah, but, due to the poor centralization, this control couldn't be exerted all over the country. Some examples of rulers issuing instructions and restrictions concerning the trade are known, but in some parts of Nepal they were not able to enforce their rule: in far-western Nepal ". . . restrictions were imposed on the movement of trade from the interior areas in the midhills and Himalayan regions" in order to channel it through market towns known as *mandis* (centers for collection of custom duties). Due to insufficient arrangements "there is no evidence, however, that these restrictions were strictly enforced" (Regmi 1984, 120); it proved still more difficult to extend state control over trading in the northern areas. This region comprised a number of passes connecting the southern slopes in the hill area with the Tibetan plateau. Due to the specific topography, monopolies in trade and duty collection had to be abandoned to local groups, such as the Sherpa of Khumbu or the inhabitants of Tarap (Regmi 1984, 123). Even though the government could determine the trading routes or close them down (mainly in order to prevent Tibetan invasions), a considerable share of the revenue remained with the local communities and did not reach the center. In eastern Nepal, the *golas* (corresponding to the western *mandis* [see above]), situated on the *kipat* territories, were partly controlled by ethnic chiefs in the beginning. During the Shah rule, the *golas* were gradually detached from ethnic control (Regmi 1984, 119). As in other parts of the hill area, however, the rulers were here, too, unable to collect the revenue because of the deficient administrative control over the newly acquired territories. Institutions for revenue collection with appointed, salaried civil servants were not built up yet, the problems being the same as in the agricultural sector. Unlike agriculture, trade, except the barter of salt and grain, seems to have been fully monetized.

As in the agricultural sector, revenue collection in the markets and at custom posts was done by *ijaradars*. The *ijaradars* were often appointed by bidding; the excess revenue belonged to the *ijaradars*, who often had to hand in a specified amount of the revenue to the center in advance. The activities of the *ijaradars* consisted not only in revenue collection. Since many goods like elephants, timber, or cardamom were under revenue monopolies or confined to state trading, they had either to be sold to state appointed individuals or to be bought on fixed prices. In this way the state also tried to increase its income, but the *ijaradars* were the true beneficiaries. According to Regmi (1984, 205f.): ". . . although the *ijara* system may have been a more or less effective means of extracting the economic surplus generated from production and trade through revenue monopolies and state-trading operations, as well as of maximizing revenue from the exploitation of forest resources in the state sector, the lion's share of the benefits accrued to the ijaradar rather than to the state. . . . We may conclude that difficulties of administration hampered the government's objective of maximizing revenue from state intervention in production and trade."

Talking about the fragmentary character of the administrative system within the Nepalese boundaries, it is important to stress that small local units like wards have often been divided into different forms of tenure, the inhabitants being subject to different lords and their middlemen. As Höfer rightly put it: "Legally, neither caste membership nor domicile but a person's tenureship determines to whose jurisdiction he is subject. Thus, over peasants cultivating state land . . . local judicial authority is with agents of the State, such as the village headman, tax-collectors and/or functionaries responsible for organizing public labour service. . . . Tenants under the *birtaa*, *jaagir* and *guthi* tenures are, by contrast, subject to the 'seignory' of their landlord to whom the State granted land or assigned the income from the land" (1979, 201). The great variety of local officials and middlemen appointed in order to meet the revenue requirements had far reaching consequences for the political structure within local societies. Due to different allegiances and thus different patrons from outside the villages, the local societies became factionalized, the local officeholders competing for followers and resources. Among other things, dominant positions within the legal system secured the élites incomes from fees, fines, and bribes. Furthermore, the officials with these charges were able to mobilize large followerships. A similar position of dominance was held by moneylenders who disposed of their debtor's working force as well as of their political support.

Efforts of Time and Space Reduction

As already stated, the changed societal format, especially the manifold growth of the state's territory, is crucial in order to understand the changes within the relations of production in various areas of Nepal. The term "societal format" refers to the population and to the space. Population movements, the increase of the population, and the extension of the controlled area require organizational adaptations to be met by the rulers (Claessen and Van de Velde 1985, 257). Placing a political system in space and time does not only require an examination of its natural environment and its historical background.[19] The consideration of its boundaries and the distances which affect the system of communication (the legitimation system being a part of it), transport, and the administrative and military control is of equal importance. What Marx stated in *Grundrisse* (1857–58, 445) in connection with the expansion of capital as reducing time and space while conquering the whole world was—in a figurative sense—also of crucial importance for the control of resources within the Shah state:

> ". . . while capital must strive on the one hand to tear down every local barrier to traffic, i.e. to exchange and to conquer the whole world as its market, it strives on the other hand to ennihilate space by means of time, i.e. to reduce to a minimum the time required for the movement [of products] from one place to another" (Marx and Engels 1986, 463).

The idea is that, whereas in modern societies the distances between the center and the administrative subunits are equal concerning the time which is required in order to reach them (this holds for the communication system as well as military control), the various parts of Nepal under the Shahs were remote from the center in different extents, sometimes despite the actual distances measured in kilometers. The amount of time that was required to reach the various areas is not a sufficient indicator to understand the difficulties to rule the conquered territory. It is however interesting to note that the furthest parts of Nepal could be reached by relays (*hulak*) within 40 days (but often it took longer).

Analyzing the changed societal format in the Nepalese State, the question arises of how the rulers succeeded in diminishing the distances in space and time in order to increase their control of the economic resources. The lines of division affecting the centralization of Nepal under the Shah were among others:

- topographic barriers, the main divisions being:

  lowland (Terai) very well suited for agriculture but in the Shah era partly densely wooded, timer being a valuable product;[20]
  hill regions (500–2,800 m) with sparse mineral resources, forests, pastures, and soils of varying quality and irrigation possibilities;
  high mountain area (above 2,800 m) with poor soils, pastoralism and trading being the main means for livelihood.

  Whereas the communcation between north and south was possible, allowing for long distance trade (between Indian states, later British India, and Tibet and China) as well as for local trade transactions (barter trade between regions of Nepal and Tibet), furrows of Ganges inflows and deep valleys prevented trade and hindered the communication between west and east. The topographic barriers proved to be especially bothersome in areas of strategic importance;

- different forms of economic activities and production depending on the habitat, especially trading, agriculture, pastoralism, shifting cultivation, hunting, and gathering, each requiring specific forms of control and revenue collection;
- different forms of land tenure;
- previous political boundaries, partly maintained after the unification, the population within which was administered in the form of indirect rule (in the Far West, some of the former princes (*rajas*) were granted the status of vassals, some ethnic groups were granted

a far reaching autonomy); for example, transit duties on rivers and highways continued to be collected as before (Regmi 1972, 14);
- cultural boundaries, with two main population streams: groups speaking Tibeto-Burmese languages coming from the north and northeast and Hindu groups speaking Indo-Aryan languages coming from the south and southwest. Except for the Kathmandu Valley and the Terai, the Hindu were spreading out in the Napalese territory from west to east, gradually subjugating the different tribes[21] who had entered the Nepalese territory before them.
- religious boundaries: even though the Shahs dreamed of Nepal as of "a true Hindustan" (Stiller 1968, 44) not more than half of the population was Hindu.

The divisions listed above seem to be unrelated only at first glance. In reality, important division lines fall together: for the present argument it is important to stress that in the hill area, the main part of the territory with the capital in Kathmandu, plow agriculture was expanding at the same time as Hindu groups, mainly speaking one Indo-Aryan language (Nepali), were spreading from west to east. It is argued here that the proliferation of Hindu groups living on agriculture all over the hill area was important in view of distance reduction, allowing the Nepalese rulers to establish links essential for the control of people and resources. Under the Shah, however, this process has only been initiated.

The expansion of agriculture and the encouragement of trading activities on one hand, deforestation, giving up of shifting cultivation, and pastoralism on the other are important developments under the Shah; furthermore, tremendous population movements took place in the Nepalese territory. It is estimated that some hundred thousand people, mainly of Tibeto-Burmese languages, left Napal during the nineteenth century (Sagant 1978, 93, 101) while Hindu groups have continued their migration from west to east. According to Sagant, "there were three causes, during 1769–1816, pushing the Nepalese on the way of exile . . .: defeat by the Gorkha troops; the emergence of a particularly oppressive state administration; the extension of usury and the indebtedness of the peasants"[22] (1978, 103). The expanding labor market (industry, transportation system, plantations) in British India was another factor boosting the migration movements. Concerning the shift of control in local communities, it is important to stress that mainly the Hindu population was pouring into tribal territories, whereas the tribal population was leaving Nepal. The migration movement has caused considerable changes within the population structure, augmenting the portion of the freshly migrating population to the disadvantage of the earlier settled groups.

There is still not enough data available about the role of the huge standing army that remained and even has grown after the conquest. It can be suggested (but it is still to be proved) that the establishment of local army units in remote parts of the Nepalese area became easier after the high-caste Hindu population had settled down there. Thus, the population movement and the establishment of army units all over the country have reinforced each other.

The examples presented below document clearly that, after the unification, important changes occurred in many parts of the country; with the extension of agriculture and trade new groups achieved control of land and of the peasants. As Sagant indicated, the oppressive situation in the central part of Nepal was one of the main reasons for people to migrate into remote areas of the country, whereas under the Shahs land for cultivation could be cleared all over the conquered territory. Without the backing of the central élites, this far-reaching redistribution would not have been possible. The central élites benefited from the infiltration of Hindu groups into most parts of the country, as it brought about an expansion of their economic resources as well as the effect of reducing distances, allowing the center to increase gradually also their political control. It has to be stressed, however, that some population segments living in remote areas have never come entirely under the command of the Shah government. The rulers were compelled to find special means in order to establish durable relationships, whereby they lost control over the local resources to an important degree. They had, for instance, to face the question of controlling the strategically vulnerable Khumbu area (bordering on Tibet) high up in the mountains where an ethnic group (Sherpas) lived, who controlled the salt-grain barter trade, who payed tributes to Tibetan monasteries and would likely side with Tibet in case of war.

Massive immigration of high caste Hindus, as well as of some ethnic groups from other parts of the country (mainly Newars,

Magars, and Gurungs), split local élites not only because their conflicting interests but also because of (putative or factual) cultural cleavages. The competition of culturally distinct local élites was instrumental for the needs of central élites in the sense of the central rulers *divide et impera* policy—not only because the problem of maintaining law and order in remote areas was in this way at least partly solved, but also because the central élites could demand a higher share of the collected surplus from competing factions.

It is important to ask why the immigration of the Hindu groups into areas hitherto controlled by tribal groups did not cause resistance on a large scale. The existing data (see Sagant 1976, 36ff.) indicates that in the beginning the migrating population was under the rule of local élites. Thus, the local (tribal) élites were even interested in promoting the influx of the migrants, as the migrants had to pay tribute and were subject to their jurisdiction. Furthermore, having abandoned their lands to the settlers, the tribal population thought of this transaction as being only temporary, assuming that the lands could be reclaimed whenever they needed them for themselves. But, from the central government's point of view, the transfer of land that occurred in this way was final. It should be stressed that the central élites were interested in the shift of the cultivated areas from tribal population to the new settlers, because the lands that were transferred could be put under new forms of tenure (from *kipat* to *raikar, jagir* or *birta* see above) thus enlarging the areas from which they could extract surplus. Gradually, the settlers attained a stronger economic and political position. On one hand they were more skillful in the plow agriculture technologies than the bulk of the tribal population, changing slowly from swidden agriculture and/or pastoralism, and they settled in lower, more fertile areas. On the other hand the ethnic population became increasingly indebted to the settlers, losing more land to them and becoming increasingly dependants of the migrating population. In this way new local élites emerged who gradually managed not only to free themselves from the tribal élite's control but also to establish relations of dominance over part of the tribal population. These changes weakened the former élites to the economic advantage of the center in the sense of the *"divide et impera"* policy.

Changing Control Over the Labor Forces and Over the Means of Production: Some Local Examples

Concerning the local élites, Rose and Scholz have stated: ". . . the rest of the country outside of Kathmandu was in general only minimally affected by the near chaos prevailing at times at the royal court. The holder of a state office, and hence of the land-holdings in the districts that went with the office, might change frequently, but the system did not. The local élites developed great skill in adjusting to sudden, dramatic changes in Kathmandu; indeed, the weakening of central authority that usually went along with such developments worked to their advantage" (1980, 25f.). This statement needs closer examination. While it is true that the local élites usually adjusted to the changes in Kathmandu, it is important not to mistake the relationships at the "peripheries" as stable and only marginally affected by the central activities. On the contrary, under the Shah crucial changes took place in most parts of the country. As stated above, after the Gorkha conquest, changes occurred in local "communities" due to economic change, and, in close connection with the former, due to the immigration of Hindu groups into most parts of Nepal. Whereas the majority of the Hindu population shared the lot of being tenant cultivators with ethnic groups, a small Hindu minority tended to acquire dominant positions in most places they settled or they became strong enough to challenge the dominance of the formerly established élites. In order to understand the changes in local communities it is important to bear in mind that: land was cleared for agriculture; the space for shifting cultivation, pastoralism, hunting, and gathering was accordingly diminished; correspondingly, mines were opened up in tribal areas (Fournier 1974); and trade was encouraged. Some examples are presented below in order to show:

how the changing economic structure led to the emergence of new local élites;
that, due to geographical position and the forms of production, the élite-formation processes have varied in different parts of the country, and
(to be seen occasionally) how high caste Hindu groups gradually attained dominance in many parts of the Nepalese area.

Khumbu is an area high up in the **north**, situated on one important Nepal-Tibet trading route northeast from Kathmandu. Due to the specific habitat, Hindu groups never settled in this area. Because of its proximity to Tibet, this area was of strategic importance under the Shahs. Due to the lack of Hindu groups, the central government had to establish good relationships with the Sherpas, who had immigrated into this area from East Tibet since the sixteenth century; because of their regular contacts with Tibetan religious institutions the Khumbu Sherpas preserved their religion and culture to a considerable degree. In order to establish good relationships, the Sherpas were granted various privileges so that some authors even speak of a "Sherpa autonomy" (Oppitz 1968). Apart from being exempt from several taxes and compulsory labor the Khumbu Sherpas held the trade monopoly in this area. As distinct to the Khumbu Sherpas, the Solu Sherpas, who lived further south (in greater vicinity to the hill area), did not enjoy the same privileges. Even though the people of Solu managed to have the former's monopoly abolished in 1810 (Regmi 1984, 123) it was reestablished shortly afterwards because it was important for the government to divide neighbouring people and because it was much easier to control Solu than Khumbu. Due to their monopoly ". . . the [Khumbu] Sherpa's favourable position as middlemen in the trade between Tibet and the lower-lying regions of Nepal enabled them to attain a standard of living far above that of most other Nepalese hill people" (Von Fürer-Haimendorf 1975, 60).

In **western Nepal**, the territory of the former Chaubisi states,[23] the contacts between the ethnic and the Hindu groups had a longer tradition than in central (except the Kathmandu Valley) and in eastern Nepal. Here, the local population had been subjugated from the beginning of this millenium onwards; some remaining independent chiefdoms were conquered only shortly before the Gorkha conquest (Hamilton 1986, 264). Among the western ethnic groups especially two (Gurungs and Magars) had had quite intimate contacts with the Hindu conquerors before the unification, having participated in the political process.[24] After the unification their economic conditions and their former political role deteriorated.

The Gurungs, for instance, were the oldest inhabitants in Samjur, where, during the eighteenth century, other groups (high caste Hindu, Newars, Muslems) settled down. Even though the Gurungs managed to keep their political functions, they gradually lost the control of a big part of their land; ". . . from the middle of last century, the local chief (mahamukhiya) has given the main part of land which was under his direct administration to cultivators from high castes in exchange of gifts . . . and later money"[25] (Gaborieau 1978b, 54). Having disposed of a considerable share of their lands when it was abundant, the Gurung lands became scarce in favor of the high-caste Hindu settlers.

With the unification of Nepal a redistribution of the economic control also took place in Bandipur. When Bandipur came first under the sword of Hindu rulers, it was inhabited mainly by the Magars (Iltis 1980, 83) but also by some Hindu population and other ethnic groups. Shortly after the conquest, merchant Newar families came here from Kathmandu Valley: "This new influx marked the beginning of a major change in subsistence patterns, and absorption of new cultural patterns and traditions into the community, which brought a transformation of a rural hill village into a thriving cosmopolitan trade centre" (Iltis 1980, 103). Their profits enabled the Newars to buy land. Even nowadays the bulk of the Bandipur population is still dependent on Newar families by indebtedness. Today, the Newars also control the mines where mainly members of impoverished ethnic and untouchable families are employed (personal communication, S. Mikesell).

In **Central-Nepalese** "Devikot"[26] at the time of the unification the local rulers were Magars[27] and the population consisted of Magars and Tamangs. None of the various high-caste families currently inhabiting Devikot was living in the village in the time prior to the unification. High caste families moved here only during the Gorkha conquest, some of them being granted *birta* lands for their priestly services. Today, the Hindu families form half of the population, and they control about three quarters of the cultivated area. The village lies northwest from Kathmandu, about 20 km as the crow flies. Its proximity to the capital and its rich soil attracted already very early the attention of the central élites. Devikot, as an example, demonstrates: how diverse external influences have structured a local "village community"; how a new élite emerged; and how the local ethnic population was relegated to inferior positions by the high-caste Hindu, their élites nevertheless being used as a counterbalance to the emerging Hindu élites.

Shortly after Devikot was conquered by the Gorkhas about half of the village was granted as *birta* to the royal brothers. Some other members of the royal family, of central élites and some merchant families from the Kathmandu Valley, were granted lands as well, and some local families were given *birtas*. The remaining land was divided in *jagirs* (to army units and to high army officials) and *guthis* (mainly at the disposal of the local Devi temple). There were also some *raikar* lands, granted to peasants who were working as porters to relays (*hulak*), and some *kipat* land was controlled by the Tamangs (an ethnic group spread all over Central Nepal). Corresponding to this variety of land-tenure forms, different officials and middlemen were needed in order to collect the revenue. Local high-caste *birta* owners as well as Tamang élites were usually middlemen of the absentee landlords, depending upon the location of the fields. Whereas the Hindu middlemen were in control of lands in the lower, more fertile part of the village, the Tamang élites were in charge of the fields in the elevated area. Correspondingly, the tenants consisted either of Tamangs or Hindus, depending upon habitat. The *jagir* rents were collected by middlemen called *dokres*, the revenue on *raikar* by *ijaradars* on nonirrigated fields and by other officials (*jimmawal*) on the irrigated fields. Furthermore, the porterage services were supervised by special porterage headmen, the forest products were collected by other *ijaradars* and on special occasions other functionaries occasionally appeared in the village to collect further rents, tributes and so forth.

The owners of large *birtas* were of course absentee landlords who had to rely on local middlemen to collect the revenue. Amongst the various middlemen, the one in charge of the main part of the royal brothers' *birta* (*dware*) held the key position: he was awarded the function of the village headman; apart from the revenue collection on the royal lands, he had the jurisdiction over the village and was entitled to arrange and lead ritual ceremonies on communal basis (especially the *dasai* festival[28]). Although he was the focus of the local administration, he was by no means the supervisor of the other functionaries, each one having his specific duties and privileges and being accountable only to the various absentee landlords. It is especially interesting to note that the Tamang headmen who collected revenue on the remaining part of the royal lands have not been put entirely under the control of the Hindu village headman (*dware*). Even though they were under his jurisdiction concerning the five most severe crimes (*panc khat*), they were compelled to transport the collected revenue to the royal palace themselves, instead of delivering it to the *dware*. Obviously, the royal family was interested in maintaining direct relationships with all the élites that were in charge of their land. Apart from the fact that in this way the royal family secured itself the possibility to compel their dependants to further obligations and to take them to task in cases of disobedience and arbitrariness, the maintenance of contacts with élites of different cultural background is an other case of the *divide et impera* policy pursued by the center. It is significant to note that even in centrally located Devikot, an area which at least seemed to be easy to control, the rulers divided the local power positions among several officials, thus weakening them and subjecting them to each other's control. It is also intriguing how great the impact of the unification process was on the redistribution of the economic control between the Hindu and ethnic groups in Devikot. Whereas only some Tamangs headmen were left as a counterbalance to the Hindu élites, the Magars gradually lost their lands and charges.

Still, as in other parts of the country, ". . . in view of the absence of a formal machinery of district administration in most parts of the region, one can easily imagine the degree of authority that these functionaries exercised over producers and traders in areas under their jurisdiction" (Regmi 1984, 41). In addition to the product from their own land, the various functionaries had compulsory labor, judicial fines and fees, bribes and tributes at their disposal. The various sources of income enabled them to make further investments: to clear land and to build irrigation channels. They were also sources of credit; a big part of their income stemmed from usury. The fact that today in Devikot four high-caste élite families control 25% of the irrigated land demonstrates how extended the possibilities to widen their economic control have been. Noting the fact that the élite group was large and involved in constant internal competition, it is easily imagined how great the burden on the peasant cultivators must have been.

Prior to the unification only few Hindus inhabited **Eastern Nepal**. In spite of being vassals of Hindu *rajas* already before the unification, the ethnic groups of Kirati stock nevertheless enjoyed independence to a great extent. After the conquest Hindu settlers were encouraged to settle in the East by the government as well as by the local groups who were eager to recruit labor forces and political dependents from among the immigrating population (see above), while changing from shifting cultivation to agriculture. Further do not forget that the central government was urging the local headmen to surrender lands to the migrating population (Sagant 1976). In the beginning, the settlers coming to live in *kipat* areas of the Limbu were under the jurisdiction of the Limbu chiefs. Amongst the Kirati groups, the Limbus were in a privileged position due to the strategic importance of their habitat (their lands bordered on British India). Like the Sherpas of Khumbu, they enjoyed various privileges. Under the Shah their position was stronger than that of the Hindu immigrants. However, the first fights for land took place already as early as 1811 (Regmi 1972, 52), and gradually the state managed to impose ceilings on their lands. It is of interest to stress that later on, under the Rana rule, when Hindu groups possessed an important share of the land, the Limbu lost many of their previous privileges, for instance the jurisdiction rights over the entire area (Jones 1976). Thus, the Limbus enjoyed their privileges as long as the rulers didn't have means to control the resources in their area.

Thus, these examples indicate that in various parts of the Nepalese territory, especially in the middle hills, the population structure was thoroughly or partly changed after the unification of Nepal. With the influx of new population, new relations of production and new power relations were established. Whereas the migrating population initially hoped to escape the central government's grip, the gradually increasing competition between different political factions and population sections strengthened the central control on them once again. To be sure, the growing local élites retained the bulk of the collected surplus themselves, but due to their competition for central élites' favours, they had to be careful to deliver an appropriate share of it to the center.

Except for their political strategies and their ability to control their subjects, to extend their resources and to defend their interests staunchly against their rivals, the local élites had—last but not least—to control the ideology as strategical means.

The Legitimation of Surplus Extraction

The extension of the central élites' control over their subjects and over the resources within the conquered territory and the far-reaching expropriation of the means of production from the subjected population in favor of the central élites and their clients are the main features of the emerging state of Nepal, building a framework within which its consolidation has been achieved. The concomitant change of legimating systems is to be examined against this background. The main aspect of this change during the Shah's (and the subsequent Rana's) rule was the spread of the Hindu religion among the subjected, previously non-Hindu population.

The change of the "societal format" has not only affected the mobilization of control and coercion but has also left the rulers with the difficult task "to legitimate the sectional interests of hegemonic groups" (Giddens 1979, 188) against the rival political factions. The Shahs had to establish a ritual frame within which they would emerge as superior against their political opponents. Furthermore, they aimed at establishing a notion of ritual division of labor, linking privileges with a high position within the caste system and relegating duties and burdens to the population that was not Hindu, placing it within middle and lower ranks of the Hindu hierarchy.[29] The requirements of the legitimation systems were thus twofold: the Shahs had to prove their ritual superiority against their rivals,[30] and it was imperative to establish horizontal cleavages in order to prevent the subjects from claims to participate in the rule. As Gellner (1983, 11) has put it:

> The establishment of horizontal cultural cleavages is not only attractive, in that it furthers the interests of the privileged and the power-holders; it is also feasible, and indeed easy. . . . by externalizing, making absolute and underwriting inequalities, it fortifies them and makes them palatable, by endowing them with the aura of inevitability, permanence and naturalness. That which is inscribed into the nature of things and is perennial, is consequently not personally, individually offensive, nor psychologically intolerable.

According to Burghart: "After 1817 Gorkha saw itself as the only independent Hindu realm in the Sacred Land of the Hindus. The implication of this was that this hitherto peripheral region of the subcontinent had now become the terrestrial centre of the universe" (1984, 106). However, Hinduism by no means embraced the whole society and even the Hindus followed the rules of ritual purity in a rather loose way. To say that the rulers perceived Nepal as a Hindu kingdom does not mean that they were aiming to incorporate the conquered population within a common religious framework. Except for the protection of the cow, the Shahs did not pursue proselytising the non-Hindu population (Höfer 1986). They were trying though to free the country from the stigma of a "country of wilderness," and that is why, especially in the initial period of their rule, they issued decrees in order to render the Hindu population "more orthodox." The Shah pursued the politics of ritual differentiation of the inhabitants according to the Hindu criteria of hierarchy, separation, and the division of labor.[31] They urged ethnic groups (the Gurungs and Tamangs) to employ Brahmin priests (Höfer 1979, 174) and Magars not to accept boiled rice from lower ranking groups (RRS 2:278ff.). Furthermore, especially the high-caste Hindu, the Brahmins, were asked not to accept boiled rice from lower groups and not to plow themselves (RRS 18:77; RRS 11:55); Jaisi-Brahmins were forbidden to perform vedic rituals (RRS 2:278ff.). Also, high-caste Hindus were forbidden to marry their cross-cousins (Höfer 1979, 166) and to have sexual intercourse with their elder brother's wife (RRS 3:2).[32] Another important aspect was the gradual exemption of high-caste Hindus from the compulsory labor obligations for the state (the landlords could compel their tenants to such obligations in spite of their hierarchical status). The Shah determined which groups were allowed to work inside the mines, compelled potter groups to deliver pots, or compelled the cobbler castes to deliver skins, and the smith castes to deliver charcoal (Regmi 1984, 168f.). A division of labor was especially felt in the political center where almost all functions—priests, dignitaries, army officers—belonged to the high-caste Hindu groups (Edwards 1975). There is not enough space to elaborate on the very interesting notion of "the ritual division of labour." It served the interests of the high-caste Hindu élites two-fold: on one hand, the Hindu élites—in the center as well as within local communities—were able to extend their dominance (control over resources and control over people) claiming a higher ritual purity (accompanied, of course, by other means of political control); on the other hand, however, one should not forget that the bulk of the Hindu population belonged, along with the ethnic population, to the dependent peasantry. The Hindu tenants were thus in the peculiar position of being ritually superior towards other tenants but having the same burdens to endure. Thus, the holistic-oriented notion of the ritual division of labor did not correspond to the factual relations of production and because of that has had an important ideological function. Still, such decrees cannot be understood as attempts of extensive Hinduisation of the population. Rather, they had the legitimizing function of making the rulers appear eager to promote the state's ritual purity.

Even when talking of Nepal as a "true Hindustan," the Shahs did neither intend to make themselves understandable to the entire population nor did they try to establish the Hindu religion as a legitimizing system uniting all the subjects. It was far too difficult to legitimize themselves by way of cultural concepts alien to the conquered population, while maintaining and establishing cultural cleavages served their purpose. Furthermore, as set out above, they gradually exploited other means in order to maintain law and order all over the country, such as establishing military camps and promoting Hindu immigration into remote areas. So, it is important to stress in this context that it was not ideology that caused the subjects' compliance, but, in the first place, force:

> Given the general problem of communication in a society based on isolated rural communes, there was no coherent peasant class consciousness which could have mobilised the peasantry against the landlords as a class of oppressors. Material conditions ruled out the development of anything but a localised sense of identity and solidarity. However, even with a definite class consciousness, the peasanty was controlled by the landlord's hold over tenancy of land and by the landlord's monopoly of other means of production, such as mills and dikes. These features of economic control were themselves largely dependent on the superior military strength of the landlords as a class. Hunger, drudgery and disease did the rest. Our argument, then, is that the "extra-economic" factors which Marxists claim were necessary in feudalism for the subordination of peasants had very little

to do with the "political/ideological instance" and a great deal to do with force, the threat of force and the dull compulsion of the economics of everyday life (Abercrombie and Turner 1980, 72).

The growing local élites played a crucial role in subjugating the local population to diverse duties, taxes, and tributes. In spite of their common interests, the local élites were by no means united. They were competing among each other, serving their diverse political patrons who were interested in promoting the *divide et impera* rule. One of the important dividing forces were the cultural cleavages, especially those between the immigrating groups and the earlier inhabitants. Since the rulers were (or at least claimed to be) high-caste Hindu, they established Hindu rules and norms as the language of power. Being in frequent contact with the central élites, the local élites, who were their inferiors, were gradually made to realize that the Hindu symbol system was of crucial strategic importance. They began to realize that showing Hindu symbols and Hindu behavior were instrumental in attaining a higher position within the societal structure. The ethnic élites were compelled to display Hindu symbols because their rivals were mainly high-caste Hindus, who were jealously guarding and extending their privileges. Wherever the presence of Hindu groups became stronger, changes in relations of production in the local communities were accompanied by the spread of the Hindu rules.[32]

Thus, the spread of Hinduism in wide parts of Nepalese territory (especially in the hill area) was not the result of the central government's endeavors, but, within the emerging legitimatory framework, the Hindu rules and norms had become a strategic resource. Because of their keen competition, the local élites had to learn the rulers' language and at least to display Hindu symbols in order to prove loyal and be treated on an equal footing with the emerging Hindu élites. After Hinduism had been established in the center as a binding ideological framework, it was increasingly imported to the local level, serving local élites' purpose as well. Just like the central élites, the local élite aspired to attain a position above their political rivals while dissociating themselves from the majority of the local population by using cultural criteria in order to prevent competition from within their own community. One of the most fascinating examples of such borrowings from the center to the local level was the introduction of the Hindu *dasai* festival. Even where there was no Hindu population, local élites started performing this ritual (with very curious deviations), claiming for themselves such a central position within the local community as if they were kings of Nepal. Thus, as a consequence of the crucial changes in the center, the local élites reproduced the symbolic framework to their own advantage as well.

Until the end of the Shah era the control of economic resources was characterized by the lack of centralized, uniform institutions in order to collect the revenue. The land was divided among competing factions, and the revenue from trading activities remained, up to an important degree, in the hands of local collectors. Whereas the center was not able to secure the flow of revenue, local élites emerged who were strong enough to extract surplus from local producers, leaving them with no more than a bare livelihood. Not being able to centralize the country, the Shah however managed to reduce the distances in time and space mentioned in the beginning: plow agriculture spread out in wide parts of the country (at the expense of shifting cultivation, pastoralism, hunting, and gathering); the extension of trading and mining further contributed to the spread of the Hindu groups, thus blurring the boundaries between Hindu and tribal areas and laying foundations for the adoption of Hindu norms and values. Many processes which were initiated by the Shah, especially the emergence of new local élites, constituted a basis on which the Ranas were able to extend their control, to achieve a far reaching centralization and to reduce the variety of the different forms of dependence and exploitation—but not their extent.

Notes

1. Without the research and publications of Mahesh Chandra Regmi this article would not be possible. The author wishes to express her gratitude to Mr. Regmi, Kristin T. Schnider, and Stephen Mikesell for the many hours of discussion. Possible mistakes and misconceptions, however, are the author's own responsibility.
2. In order to make the text more legible a standardized transliteration according to Turner (1931) has been abandoned.
3. The name "Nepal" referred only to the area of Kathmandu Valley. In the beginning the unified state was called the "State of Gorkha." Since the 1930s, the name "Nepal" has designated the last Hindu

kingdom separating Central from South Asia. In this article the names "Nepal" and "State of Gorkha" are used interchangeably, i.e., the term "Nepal" is used in the modern sense and the term "State of Gorkha" pertains to the political unit after the expansion. Similarly, in this article the terms "Shahs" and "Gorkhas" relate to the same rulers. "Shah" being their family name and Gorkha connoting the locality of their former principality.

4. The notion of "boundaries" in the context of the state under the Shahs has been interestingly discussed by Burghart (1984).

5. In opposition to "owners", the prebendaries here are designated as "possessors."

6. The bulk of the ethnic population was already subjugated by the Hindu long before the unification. There are important reasons to believe that the social distance between the Hindu princes and the ethnic groups was then smaller than after the unification. In some parts of Nepal, however, the process of differentiation between the Hindu rulers and their tribal vassals lasted until long after the Shah era.

7. Translation by the author.

8. Having brought their throne from Gorkha to Kathmandu (Burghart 1984, 111) the Gorhkas were forced to change their political and administrative organization. While in Gorkha, six leading families (*chha thar*) assisted the rulers; after the shift to Kathmandu, the number of offices quickly increased. Correspondingly, more noble families came to Kathmandu from different parts of the hill area. By the time the Gorkha expansion was stopped by the British (1816), the already fierce struggles over the allocation of scarce resources culminated in the center:" . . . stability was most notably absent during much of the period before 1850" (Rose and Scholz 1980, 23). After the death of Prthwi Narayan Shah (1775), the Gorkha king who had started the military conquest, the entire period of the Shah rule was characterized by quarrels over dominance in the center (the Shah kings ascending the throne had been minors since 1777). In the struggles, apart from the feuds within the Shah family, some other families, either Brahmin priests or those claiming the high-caste status of the Kshatriyas, competed for the economic resources and for marriage alliances with the Shah (Lévi 1905, 2:291), as well as for honors and ranks.

9. Singh 1988, 304.

10. "*Birtas* were given to individuals in appreciation of their services to the state, as ritual gifts, or as a mark of patronage. . . . *Birtas* were usually given on an inheritable basis" (Regmi 1984, 19). This was the main form of land ownership. "Sera-Lands [were] assigned for the supply of agricultural commodities to meet the requirements of the royal household" (Regmi 1972, 229).

11. "Guthi-Lands" [were] endowed to temples, monasteries and other

religious and philantropic institutions or for similar purposes" (Regmi 1972, 226).

12. "*Jagirs*. . .were assigned to civil and military employees and government functionaries of different categories as their emoluments. . . . *Jagirs*. . .were valid only during the period when the concerned *jagirdar* remained in governmental service" (Regmi 1972, 226). In this context it is appropriate to talk about "possession" of land.

13. "*Raikar*—State-owned-land" (Regmi 1972, 229), the revenue of which went (at least theoretically) to the state treasury.

14. There is not yet enough evidence to deduce that *kipat* holdings were conferred to groups practicing shifting cultivation, which usually requires other forms of ownership and control than plow agriculture. The collective ownership of land due to this specific form of production might be an alternative or additional reason for the emergence of *kipat* tenure to that given above. However, not more than 5% of the Nepalese population lived on *kipat* lands.

15. While some *birtas* were bestowed upon priests during the conquests, in this time *birta* lands were partly expropriated, mainly from the owners hostile to the Gurkhas. With the end of the military expansion there was no further necessity to bestow lands upon religious specialists.

16. In this context, little is known about the Far West of Nepal.

17. Under the Shah the labor force was in demand. The emigration of Nepalese subjects put land-controlling groups in a difficult position. Regmi (RRS) presented many documents in which escaped peasants are asked to return to Nepal and are promised better tenurial conditions.

18. "La prospérité des royaumes Malla est fondée en grande partie sur le commerce transhimalayen. Située sur l'axe principal qui mène du Tibet au bassin indo-gangétique, la vallée de Kathmandou joue un rôle déterminant dans ces échanges, et ses habitants en retirent des bénéfices substantiels" (The prosperity of the Malla kingdoms is based mainly on the Trans-Himalaya trade. Because of its location on the road which connects Tibet with the Indus-Ganges region, Kathmandu Valley plays a decisive role in this trade, to the great profit of its inhabitants) (Toffin 1984, 40).

19. Questions of space have been convincingly elaborated by Giddens (1979; 1984, 110–61).

20. Until then, the dense malaric forests were thought to be natural barriers, necessary as defense against alien attacks. The clearance of the Terai land went along with the deforestation, timber being sold mainly to the British.

21. There is no space to discuss the processes of ethnogenesis.

22. Translation by the author.

23. The political units in the western part of Nepal before unification

were divided in a Baisi (Far West) and a Chaubisi (West) confederation, the names referring to numbers: 22 and 24 respectively, political units. In most of these principalities the rulers were Hindu. Gorkha was the last principality to be founded (in the mid-sixteenth century) west from Kathmandu Valley.

24. For example in Gorkha, the Magars belonged to the council of the six highest families (*chha thar*). As Rose and Sholz (1980, 21) stated: "Composed exclusively of high-caste Hindu (Kshatriya and Brahman) families, the new courtier class in Kathmandu (after the 'unification') was much less representative of the population of Nepal than the *thar gar* (an other term for *chha thar*) had been of Gorkha (before the 'unification')."

25. Translation by the author.

26. A pseudonym. The data concerning "Devikot" was collected by the author, see Pfaff-Czarnecka 1989.

27. Those Magar *rajas* were vassals of the king of Kathmandu.

28. In places like Devikot, on the tenth *dasai* day the linking of power with the Hindu ritual was as striking as in Nepal's political center.

29. Concerning the inclusion of ethnic groups within the Hindu caste hierarchy, there are significant differences between the Indian and the Nepalese caste system.

30. Already before the unification the Hindu rulers of the various Nepalese principalities conceived themselves as descendants of the Sun and Lunar dynasties, and as being closely related to Indian Rajputs. Similar to the Malla rulers of the Kathmandu Valley before the unification (Toffin 1984, 39) the Shah kings also conceived themselves as the incarnations of the God Vishnu. Having come to Kathmandu they received blessings of the Goddess Taleju (the former tutelary Goddess of the Malla kings; Burghart 1984, 111) and from the Living Goddess Kumari (Lévi 1905, 2:277). The exercise of power was connected with the ritual. It was, for instance, no coincidence that the above mentioned *pajani* (yearly distribution and withdrawal of ranks and emoluments) was held on the tenth day of the great Hindu *dasai* festival.

31. Subsequently the Ranas were able to declare the whole Nepalese society as caste-divided and hierarchised (see Höfer 1979).

32. Today the last four facts are considered by the Nepalese Hindus as extremely ritually polluting.

33. These processes are described in detail in Pfaff-Czarnecka 1989.

References

Abercrombie, N. and B. S. Turner
1980   *The dominant ideology thesis.* Allen and Unwin.

Burghart, R.
1984   The formation of the concept of nation-state in Nepal.
            Journal of Asian Studies 44:101–25.
Claessen, H. J. M. and P. van de Velde
1985   Sociopolitical evolution as complex interaction. In *Devel-
            opment and decline; The evolution of sociopolitical orga-
            nization*, ed. H. J. M. Claessen, P. van de Velde, and M.
            E. Smith. 246–63. South Hadley: Bergin and Garvey.
Edwards, D. W.
1975   Nepal on the eve of the Rana ascendancy. *Contributions
            to Nepalese Studies* 2: 99–118.
Fournier, A.
1974   The role of the priest in Sunuwar society. *Kailash* 2 (3):153–
            166.
Fürer-Haimendorf, C. von
1975   *Himalayan traders*. London: Murray.
Gaborieau, M.
1978a   *Le Népal*. Paris: Editions Complexe.
1978b   Le partage du pouvoir entre les lignages dans une localité
            du Népal central. *l'Homme* 18:37–67.
Gellner, E.
1983   *Nations and nationalism*. Oxford: Blackwell.
Giddens, A.
1979   *Central problems in social theory*. London: Macmillan.
1984   *The constitution of society*. Berkeley: University of Cali-
            fornia Press.
Hamilton, F. B.
1986   *An account of the kingdom of Nepal*. New Delhi: Asian
            Educational Service (orig. ed. 1819).
Hasrat, B.
1970   *History of Nepal as told by its own and contemporary
            chroniclers*. Hoshiarpur: V. V. Research Institute Press.
Hodgson, B. H.
1831   On the commerce of Nepal. In *Essays on the languages,
            literature, and religion of Nepal and Tibet*. New Delhi:
            Mansjuri Publishing House.
Höfer, A.
1979   *The caste hierarchy and the state in Nepal*. Innsbruck: Uni-
            versitätsverlag Wagner.
1986   Wie Hinduisieren sich die Tamang? In *Formen kulturellen
            Wandels und andere Beiträge zur Erforschung des Hima-
            laya*, ed. B. Kölver, 35–55. Sankt Augustin: VGH Wis-
            senschaftsverlag.
Iltis, L.
1980   An ethnohistorical study of Bandipur. *Contributions to
            Nepalese Studies* 8:81–146.

Jones, R. L.
1976   Sanskritization in Eastern Nepal. *Ethnology* 15:63–75.
Lévi, S.
1905   *Le Népal.* 2 vols. Paris: Presses Universitaires de France.
Marx, K.
1857–58   *Grundrisse.* Marx-Engels Werke 42. Berlin: Dietz.
Marx, K. and F. Engels
1986   *Collected works.* Vol. 28. Moscow: Progress Publishers.
Oppitz, M.
1968   *Geschichte und Sozialordnung der Sherpa.* Khumbu Himal,
              Vol. 8. Innsbruck and München: Universitätsverlag Wag-
              ner
Pfaff-Czarnecka, Joanna
1986   Der Himalaya als Kultur-und Sprachregion. Integration
              und Differenzierung in einem aussereuropäischen Ge-
              birgsraum. *Jahresbericht der Akademie für Geisteswissen-
              schaften 1986,* 25–33. Bern: Akademie der Geisteswis-
              senschaften.
1989   *Macht und rituelle Reinheit. Hinduistisches Kastenwesen
              und etnische Beziehungen im Entwicklungsprozess Nepals.*
              Grüsch: Rüegger Verlag.
Regmi, M. C.
1972   *A study in Nepali economic history.* New Delhi: Manjusri
              Publishing House.
1984   *The state and economic surplus.* Varanasi: Nath Publishing
              House.
RRS
1970ff.   *Regmi Research Series.* Historical documents published by
              M. C. Regmi in the English language. Kathmandu: Ratna
              Pustak Bhandar.
Rose, L. E. and J. T. Scholz,
1980   *Nepal; Profile of a Himalayan kingdom* Boulder: West-
              view Press.
Sagant, Ph.
1976   *Le paysan Limbu, sa maison et ses champs.* Paris, La Haye:
              Mouton.
1978   Ampleur et profondeur historique des migrations népa-
              laises. *l'Ethnographie* 120:93–119.
Singh, C.
1988   Centre and periphery in the Mughal state; The case of
              seventeenth century Panjab. *Modern Asian Studies* 22:299–
              318.
Stiller, L. F.
1968   *Prithwinarayan Shah in the light of Dibya Upadesh.* Ran-
              chi: The Catholic Press.

1975   *The rise of the house of Gorkha*. Kathmandu: Ratna Pustak Bhandar.

1976   *The silent cry*. Kathmandu: Sahayogi Prakashan.

Toffin, G.

1984   *Société et religion chez les Néwar du Népal*. Meudon-Bellevue: Editions du Centre National des Recherches Scientifiques.

Turner, R. L.

1931   *Dictionary of the Nepali language*. New Delhi: Allied Publishers Private Limited.

11

The Political Economy of an Early State: Hawaii and Samoa Compared

Martin A. van Bakel

In this chapter I investigate structural features of early state economics. To this end I first provide an ethnographic description of one specific early state: aboriginal Hawaii. This is contrasted with an ethnographic description of a society which certainly is not an early state: aboriginal Samoa. After this comparison I conclude with an assessment of the essential features of the political economy in an Early State.

Before I present the data on the case studies it should be noted that not all scholars agree that aboriginal Hawaii can indeed be classified as an early state. Many (cf. Goldman 1970; Kirch 1986; Sahlins 1958; Service 1975) hold the opinion that in aboriginal times Hawaii was a chiefdom. Hence only after the European discovery of the archipelago, and more or less under Western influence, an early state emerged. Of course it is largely a matter of definition. As I have dwelled on this issue elsewhere (Van Bakel 1988) I shall not repeat the arguments, but only state that I do think that in Hawaii there existed one or more early states before European times (see Seaton 1978 for the same opinion). For this I accept the definition of Claessen and Skalnik (1978, 640):

> The early state is a centralized socio-political organization for the regulation of social relations in a complex, stratified society divided into at least two basic strata—viz. the rulers and the ruled—whose relations are characterized by political dominance of the former and tributary obligations of the latter, legitimized by a common ideology of which reciprocity is the basic principle.

In the following section it will be demonstrated that the political system(s) in aboriginal Hawaii do indeed conform to this definition. There does not seem to be any problem about Samoa; almost all scholars agree that aboriginal Samoa was a chiefdom (but see Bargatzky 1988).

Hawaii

Geography and population

The Hawaiian archipelago, since August 8, 1959 the fiftieth state of the United States, is situated in the northern part of the Pacific Ocean between 18°50′ and 28°15′ North latitude and between 154°40′ and 178°15′ West longitude. It consists of eight large inhabited islands and some 124, mostly uninhabited, lesser islands (most of these no more than little rocks or reefs). The land surface of the archipelago is about 16,638 km²: Hawaii with 10,456 km², Maui 1886 km², Oahu 1535 km², Kauai 1421 km², Molokai 676 km², Lanai 361 km², Niihau 180 km², and Kahoolawe 116 km². The tallest mountains are on the island of Hawaii: Mauna Kea (4206 m) and Mauna Loa (4170 m). All the islands are of volcanic origin; there even are some still active vulcanoes on Hawaii. As most of the larger, inhabited islands are situated south of the Tropic of Cancer, the climate in the lowlands is subtropical, although moderated by the influence of the ocean. Yet in the archipelago almost all climates of the world, from the semi-arctic climate to a semi-desert climate, can be found within a short distance from each other, as climate is not only influenced by geographical location, but also by such factors as altitude and rainfall. In this respect it is important that the length axis of the archipelago as a whole, as well as of each individual island, marked by a very pronounced chain of high mountains, is approximately southeast-northwest. In a region where the northeast trade winds are habitually blowing, this causes a marked contrast between the wet, windward and the dry, leeward side of the islands. From the high central mountain chain, high side chains often branch off most abruptly, ending in the sea. Between these side chains deep and narrow valleys are located. Sometimes we find large coastal plains. On account of the many streams coming from the mountains, none of the high islands is completely surrounded by a lagoon, though sometimes there are little barrier reefs creating a partial lagoon. The valleys and coastal plains are very fertile, unless covered by volcanic ash or lava streams from recent eruptions.

On the basis of the foregoing it is estimated that only 20% of the land is inhabitable and cultivatable (Carter 1981, 205). Kirch (1984, 98) even says that only 10% is cultivatable. This part, even in aboriginal—prewestern—times, was very densely populated. Though the estimates of the population in aboriginal times vary widely—from 700,000 (Cools 1979, 9) to 200,000 (Kirch 1984, 98)—an estimate of about 300,000 people in 1778 seems acceptable. This means a population density of about 18 persons per km². This is not in accordance with our view of Hawaii as a densely populated country. Yet all indicators of an (even too) dense population were found in Hawaii: practices regulating birth such as abortion and infanticide, warfare, agricultural intensification (especially terracing and irrigation), and in certain parts of the archipelago a decline in population (Kirch 1984, 104ff., 246). But if we only take into account the land surface which is cultivatable—which is just 20% or even only 10% of the total—a different picture emerges. Then population density rises to 90 or even 180 persons per km². In favorable spots, that is, where lagoon fishing was also possible, density would have been even higher. In those cases one might rightly speak of population pressure.

Economy

The economy was a subsistence economy based to a large extent on the production of taro, sweet potato, yam, coconut, breadfruit, and bananas, and on fishing. Taro, grown on irrigated terraces, was the primary staple food, and fishing consisted almost entirely of fishing in the lagoon and gathering shell fish and so forth along the coast. Animal husbandry was rare and only involved the rearing of some pigs and chickens. However, these were intended for ceremonial occasions and were only eaten by the elite. The same was true for most of the deep sea fishing and the keeping of fish in the fish ponds. The ecology in the cultivatable parts was relatively uniform and stable, meaning that the same products could be raised almost everywhere, and natural disasters were rare. The most important were droughts, inundations, tidal waves, and volcanic eruptions. These disasters were not only rare, but were also mostly circumscribed and thus generally had but a limited effect. The large scale destruction of the means of production by the conquerors during, and especially after, the frequent wars was of much more significance (Schmitt 1970, 111).

In contrast to almost everywhere else in Polynesia, breadfruit does not seem to have been the basic staple food in Hawaii (Cook 1967, 271, 601). On account of the dense population and the very limited agricultural area, the intensification of agriculture had reached a high level. This led to the dependence on taro as the main staple food and to large scale irrigation and terracing wherever possible (Claessen 1975, 54ff.; Kirch 1984, 116ff.). Fish was the main source of protein in the achipelago but it does not seem to have been available in abundance (Ellis 1826, 10). Perhaps this prompted the construction of fish ponds along the coast (Ellis 1826, 175, 179, 374; Kuykendall 1947, 4; Malo 1971, 45ff.; Wise 1965b, 98). Yet the species of fish found in these ponds indicate that they were not kept for eating by the general population but by the elite (Malo 1971, 45ff.). The same seems to hold for the fish from the deep sea, as well as for the pigs and chickens (Ellis 1826, 321). As in many other societies in Polynesia there existed an extensive corpus of rules leading to an uneven distribution of food in society. These rules worked on two levels: at the levels of production and of consumption. On the first level a distinction existed between elite (*alii*) and commoners. The commoners tilled the fields: both the *kula* lands and the irrigated fields. *Kula* land could be cultivated, but not irrigated. On the *kula* lands dry taro, yam, sweet potato, and sugar cane were the most important crops, with slash and burn cultivation carried out on lands which were considered undifferentiated properly of the ruling *alii*. Each of an *alii*'s subordinates could claim an usufructuary right in *kula* land just by cultivating it. On the irrigated fields (wet) taro was practically the sole crop under cultivation. The elite (the *alii*) received their share of the production in three ways:

part of the land cultivated by a commoner was expropriated from him (though he was obliged to keep on cultivating it) by the *alii* or by his overseer the *konohiki*. The produce of all such parts went directly to the *alii* or the *konohiki*.

apart from this there was a regular as well as an irregular taxation of the commoners. Once a year, during the *makahiki* festival, each commoner had to pay a more or less fixed tax in kind (food and goods) to the highest ruler of the territory. In addition, when an *alii* and his court travelled through his realm, they had to be fed by the commoners along the route. Moreover, first fruits and so on had to be presented to the *alii* and/ or to the gods. Last but not least, at feasts—both religious and secular—food and other offerings had to be delivered by the people.

every commoner regularly had to perform services for the *alii*. At least one day a week was set apart for this purpose. Furthermore, an *alii* could call on the services of his people whenever he wanted.

The second level was governed by taboos, especially taboos on various kinds of food. Certain kinds of food were reserved for the elite (Ellis 1826, 321). They were tabooed for the common people. The same differentiation held true for men and women (Cook 1967, 1181; Kuykendall 1947, 11; Malo 1971, 29; Wise 1965b, 102). Though men habitually prepared the food, they did so in separate ovens for men and women (Cools 1979, 29; Malo 1971, 27). Even every group—the guests, the titled men, the men, and the women with the children—ate separately (Cools 1979, 85, 89; Ellis 1826, 319; Malo 1971, 29; Wise 1965b, 102).

The basic unit of production was the household group consisting normally of a (grand)father and a (grand)mother, their unmarried children, their married sons with their wives (and children), and sometimes some relatives or friends (often those defeated and expelled from their homes), all living together in a house amidst

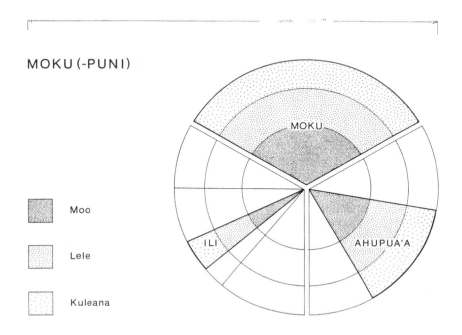

MOKU (-PUNI)

Moo

Lele

Kuleana

FIGURE 11.1
Idealtype of the Political Divisions and Subdivisions in Hawaii

A *moku(puni)* is one island; a *moku* is a district; an *ahupua'a* is a subdistrict, whereas an *ili* is the smallest division in society. The other names are for pieces of land in different ecological zones. (Adapted from Handy 1965)

their fields. Every household group seemed to have at their disposal an *ili lele* (see figure 11.1) consisting of several tracts of land each in another ecological zone—from the sea, the lagoon, the coastal plain or valley floor, the lower and the higher mountain slopes, up to the mountainous interior which was mostly covered by tropical rain forest—and so had the disposal of the production possibilities of the total ecological range of the region (Davenport 1969, 5; Handy 1965, 37; Malo 1971, 16–17).

Though the common people, organized in household groups, were the cultivators of the fields, they were not the owners of the land. In Hawaii we find the most elaborate system of distinctions between "king," elite, and the population of Polynesia as a whole.

This was most pronounced in the division between ownership of the land and the use of it. All the land was the undisputed and inalienable property of the highest governing leader: the *alii ai moku* (the *alii nui*). No matter if he inherited this right by birth or acquired it by conquest:

> all the land belonged to the *Alii Nui* of the island. All land was distributed on conquest or on the coming of a new chief into power. (Wise 1965a, 81)

Upon gaining power the *alii ai moku* divided the land among his loyal followers.

> The division of the land fell to the *Kalaimoku*. . . . It was really like slicing a pie because the islands were more or less round and the lines dividing districts were cut from sea coast to mountain top. These large districts were called *ahupua'a*'s, and were given to high chiefs. The *ahupua'a*'s were parcelled out by these chiefs among their followers in small strips or sections called *ili*. A simple *ili* was a strip running from sea to mountains. (Handy 1965, 37)

The lands his followers received did not become their inalienable property or that of their families, but belonged to the function to which they were appointed by their leader (Wise 1965a, 83). When a follower lost his function, for whatever reason, he also lost all rights to the land. To receive a function one not only had to be a follower but also an *alii*: a status position and a title one received by birthright. The *alii* were the elite, who among themselves were also hierarchically structured. The common people were termed *maka ainana*. They cultivated the land, and among them the division of labor was by sex. Cultivation of the land was practised by the women; fishing by the men (Ellis 1826, 243). According to Cook (1967, 524) and others, the intensification of cultivation was at its maximum and fallowing of land for regeneration was impossible. There were various systems for refertilizing the land with manure. Apart from the fishing along the coast and in the lagoon, there was also some fishing in the open sea, but this appeared to be restricted to two periods each of six weeks during the year (Campbell 1818, 133) and so could not have been of much importance for the daily menu of the common people.

Only one third of the production of the land was intended for the cultivators themselves (Kuykendall 1947, 103). Every three months a part of the production had to be given to the owner of the land (Campbell 1818, 108), culminating in the big annual taxation festival of the *alii nui* (that is the *alii ai moku*). It was called the *makahiki* festival, which lasted about four months (Handy 1965, 38; Malo 1971, 53, 143; Wise 1965a, 91). Apart from these more or less regular taxations, on several other occasions goods and services were required from the population:

> Tenants were called on for contributions in goods or labor on the occasion of any ceremony acquiring offerings, or feast of the *alii*, or war, or other public activity. . . . Tenants were required by the *konohiki* (the steward of the *alii ai ahupua'a*) to labor when work was to be done in building and cleaning of irrigation ditches, making roads, etc. (Handy 1965, 38)

It is estimated (Handy 1965, 38; Malo 1971, 64; Wise 1965a, 91) that the population spent one day a week on services for the *alii*. These corvée services were regulated by taboos on other work (Cools 1979, 95). Apart from the goods and services required by the *alii*, religious services and offerings also laid a considerable claim in production (Davenport 1969, 9, 12, 17; Handy 1965, 38).

Apart from the broad spectrum subsistence economy of the population there was also some specialization in production, especially in the inland regions (Campbell 1818, 135; Ellis 1826, 134, 241). There also are some indications of a market system (Campbell 1818, 135; Cook 1967, 483, 486; Ellis 1826, 241, 296, 376, 390; Malo 1971, 80). It is, however, not clear if this had developed after the coming of the Europeans, but the remarks of Cook (1967, 483 486), among others, indicate that elements of the system already existed before the coming of the Europeans.

Summarizing, we can say that the economy in Hawaii was a subsistence economy with a redistributive system in which the common people were the producers of a surplus and the *alii* and the religious specialists were the consumers; the elite did not produce the food themselves, but only consumed it. In principle it was the *alii ai moku* (the *alii nui*) who collected this surplus and who distributed it among his followers, even in times of scarcity among the common people (Cordy 1981, 21). For this purpose he even had storehouses (Malo 1971, 195). There was some specialization of agricultural production and possibly even some form of monoculture (taro in the irrigated fields). Probably as a consequence of this there was a limited system of trade and a formalized system of taxation. The elite in the society—the *alii*—acquired therefore gradually the character of an officialdom with mainly management functions (Wise 1965a, 83).

Political Economy

The highest political official was the *alii ai moku*, sometimes called *alii nui*. He was considered the owner of all the land in his territory, which most of the times consisted of one island. Before its discovery by the Europeans, the archipelago was divided in some four autonomous territories which were more or less congruent with the four big islands: Hawaii, Kauai, Maui, and Oahu (Ellis 1826, 392). On account of the frequent wars these societies regularly changed in size and numbers.

As both the person and the function of the *alii ai moku* were surrounded by many taboos, some of his functions were taken over by specialists. The most important of them was the *kalai-moku*—on his own account also an *alii*—who acted as a sort of prime minister; he was the primary executive authority. In the religious sphere this was the high priest, the *kahuna nui*. Yet the *alii ai moku* was considered the supreme leader and his were the most important ritual tasks:

> Indeed, the strength and prosperity of the chiefdom was supposed to be positively related to the religiousness of the paramount chief. (Davenport 1969, 6).

> . . . educated in the priestly order that he might perform the temple service required of a king by the old Hawaiian cult. (Kuykendall 1947, 71)

In order to rid himself of many of those taboos, his eldest son was installed as his successor as soon as possible (Cook 1967, 585, 590, 1229). And Campbell related that:

> At the *Macaheite*-festival which I attended on the island, the eldest son of Tamaahmaah, a youngster almost at the age of fifteen years, received the royal paraphernalia and got the same homage as his

father. Which became his place in government I don't know; yet in
the royal power I didn't notice any change. (Campbell 1818, 120)

The territory of the *alii ai moku* was divided among his followers
in districts (*moku*) and subdistricts (*ahupua'a*) (see figure 11.1).
Sometimes the whole territory of the *alii ai moku* was called
moku; then there were only subdistricts. At the head of an *ahupua'a* stood the *alii ai ahupua'a*. His executive was the *konohiki*;
his steward. Sometimes an *ahupua'a* was further divided up into
ili with the *alii ai ili* as the headman. Each *ili* contained several
ili lele, which were the lands cultivated by one household.

Ideologically the political system was structured along kinship
lines, just like everywhere else in Polynesia. But in practice there
were two separated kinship lines: one for the elite, one for the
common people. So in Hawaii there were two clearly separated
levels in society. This was even more accentuated by the fact that
there was no genealogical connection between the cultivators of
the land—the *maka ainana*—and the owners of the land—the
alii. Moreover there was no genealogical connection with their
political leaders either. These leaders were appointed by the *alii
ai moku* as a reward for their support before he came to power.
On account of this they received their functions, including the
ownership of the lands. The relationship between *alii* and *maka
ainana* was based upon the system of patron and client in which
the *konohiki* was the pivot.

Due to the large royal court and the poor infrastructure, the
alii ai moku had to change his residency frequently and was obliged
to travel a great deal about his territory. This not only made
possible a good knowledge of what was going on in his territory
and among his people, but also distributed the burden of feeding
the court more evenly among the population.

But traveling about through their dominions was a common practice
of Hawaiian chiefs. . . . In 1822 Kaahumanu, the *kuhina-nui*, and
her husband Kaumualii, with a train of chiefs and servants numbering
about a thousand persons, spent several months in making a tour of
nearly the whole kingdom. (Kuykendall 1947, 74)

One of the important tasks of the political system described
above was the regulation of the economy and the extraction of a

surplus from the producers, the *maka ainana*. At each level there was an official regulating the production and extracting the surplus. At the top level it was the *kalaimoku* who was responsible for the regulation of the production; at the lowest level—that of a (sub)district—it was the *konohiki*.

These goods gathered at the central level were used not only for its own maintenance, but were also redistributed among the elite, the specialists, and others working for the elite. On account of the existence of some specialization, even in the production of food, there was some trade, but only in a limited form. The famous red feathers in particular, but also certain kinds of food and other things, belonged to the category of prestige goods. Just as everywhere else in Polynesia (Claessen 1975, 55–56), in Hawaii no indication is found that the government had anything to do with the maintenance of the irrigation systems.

Samoa

Geography and population

The Samoan archipelago is situated in the southern part of the Pacific Ocean between 13 and 15° South latitude and 168–173° West longitude. It consists of 9 (10) islands and is now divided into American Samoa—with the islands Ta'u, Ofu, and Olosega (together called the Manu'a archipelago) and the islands Tutuila and Aunu'u—and the independent state (since 1960) of West Samoa—with the islands Upolu, Manono, Apolima, and Savai'i. The total land area of the archipelago is approximately 2800 km²: American Samoa just about 224 km² (the Manu'a archipelago measures about 91 km², and Tutuila with Aunu'u together 133 km²); whereas Western Samoa is about 2600 km² (Savai'i with 1707 km², Upolu with 868 km², but Manono and Apolima are only 8 and 5 km², respectively). The biggest mountain is on Savai'i, at 1800 m. All the other mountains of the central chain are much lower; up to 1000 m. Just as Hawaii the islands of Samoa are of volcanic origin; on Savai'i some volcanoes have only recently died out (Krämer 1901; Meijer 1910). The climate of this archipelago, so near to the equator, is subtropical, as it is moderated by the influence of the ocean. As the length axis of the islands, as well as of the archipelago, is approximately from east to west in a region where the southeast trade winds habitually blow, there is almost no difference between the usually wet, windward and the dry, leeward side of the islands. The rainfall, moreover, is fairly evenly divided over the year, though there is some difference between a wet season—from November to April—and a dry season—from April to November (Holmes 1974, 43; Meijer 1910, 316, 469; Turner 1884, 353). There is no real marked constrast in the temperature between summer and winter; there is only a variation of 1.5°C about a mean temperature of 25.76°C (Meijer 1910, 316). Though there are almost no permanent streams, there is no shortage of drinking water (Rowe 1930, 45; Turner 1884, 2). Yet, with the exception of Upolu, none of the islands has a complete barrier reef and so a complete lagoon; but in many places there are parts of a barrier reef and a partial lagoon. As the interior of the islands, the mountains, are covered with rain forest, the contacts between parts of the islands are mostly by sea. There are few side chains coming from the central mountain chain and so there are few valleys. But instead there are extensive and fertile coastal plains ranging up to 6 kilometers inland (Gilson 1970, 3).

Though the foregoing gives the impression of a paradise (Keesing 1934, 19), it is estimated that only 30% of the land is cultivatable (Carter 1981, 46; Pirie 1972). The other 70% is mountaineous and covered with rain forest. Contrary to the situation in Hawaii, there is no shortage of cultivatable land in Samoa. Carter (1981, 46) even estimates that only 6% of the cultivatable land is in use. The same is thought to have been the case during aboriginal times. Up till now there has not been any commonly accepted explanation why the population of aboriginal Samoa had apparently stopped expanding in such an excellent environment. Whatever might have been the reason for this, almost all scholars (but cf. Ember 1962b, 970; 1966, 166) agree that in aboriginal times the growth of the population had halted fairly well below the carrying capacity of the land (see a.o. Davidson 1979, 102; McArthur 1968; Turner 1884, 49). It is commonly accepted that the aboriginal population counted about 50,000 people (McArthur 1968, 101). Population density then was about 17 persons per km². If we want to compare the situation in Samoa with

Hawaii, we might better use population density per cultivatable km², which for Samoa means some 60 persons per km². This is clearly well below the density in Hawaii, and so might be termed a moderate population density. This is in accordance with what can be found in the literature. Practices regulating births are said to have been almost absent in Samoa, though abortion is said to have been practised to some extent (Turner 1884, 79) and there is some debate about the occurrence of infanticide (cf. Pitt 1970 versus Hjarnø 1980 and Turner 1884). There are no reports of agricultural intensification. As natural disasters—such as cyclones, tidal waves, droughts, inundations, volcanic eruptions, and so forth—seldom occur in Samoa, and when they occur are said to have a limited impact, they cannot be the cause either. In view of the population figures available (McArthur 1968; Freeman 1983, 169) warfare could not have been the real cause either.

Economy

The economy was a subsistence economy, to a large extent based upon the production of breadfruit and taro as the two staple crops, and further upon bananas, coconut, and yam (Krämer 1901, 2:136, 168–69; Tiffany 1975, 269). The crops were cultivated in an extensive manner. There were no extended irrigation systems or permanent cultivated plots. A household dwelled amidst their gardens, and when production faltered they moved on to another plot in the neighborhood. Each household decided on its own concerning the organization and type of its productive efforts. Yet there was some form of communal interest in the production. This was vested in the village *fono*. There the elders (*matai*) of each household gathered, debated and decided about the organization and kind of production. As they could not come within the domain of each individual household, they could only decide about questions involving common interest, such as the building of roads, communal houses, offerings at feasts, and so forth. Fish was only seen as an addition to the main, predominantly vegetarian food. The meat of pigs and chicken only was eaten at ceremonial occasions (Freeman 1983, 49). According to Turner (1884, 107) during one half of the year breadfruit was the staple food, and taro during the other half. Just as in Hawaii, the ecology in the cultivatable parts was relatively uniform and stable. Though there were periods of relative scarcity (McArthur 1968), they seldom seem to have been problematic (Turner 1884, 107). Moreover, in those circumstances one could depend upon the *malaga*; the institution of mutual—ceremonial—visits between villages (or parts thereof). Though the *malaga* was instituted for enhancing mutual social relations, it also could be used to lessen the impact of the periods of scarcity, which were mostly strictly localized and temporary. There are almost no indications of some body of rules causing an uneven distribution of food in society. According to Turner (1884, 115) everyone—men, women, and children—ate together, though Keesing (1956, 79), as well as Krämer (1901, 2:132), tell that first the titled men ate together and only afterwards the rest.

The basic unit of production was the household group consisting, just as in Hawaii, of an extended family and sometimes some additional friends or relatives. Though every household group owned land there were no strict boundaries within a village (consisting of several—often more or less related—household groups).

> Graeffe says land was in part common property, and in part family property, and the various heads of families or *tulafale* came to an agreement in their assemblies as to the portion of land to be cultivated by each. (Williamson 1929, 2:445; 1929, 3:258)

Each household group was autonomous, but there was much cooperation inside the village. And:

> The Samoans clung to the system of common interest in each other's property with great tenacity. Not only a house, but a canoe, a boat, a fine, a dowry, and everything else requiring an extra effort was being subject to the idea. The system entitled them to beg and borrow from each other to any extent. (Williamson 1929, 3:235)

also:

> Property in Samoa was vested in the family, not in the individual. It is true the beggar was supposed to make return, but the obligation was only moral; it could not be, or was not, enforced, and was often disregarded. (Williamson 1929, 3:236)

This was not a real problem in aboriginal times, as there was an excess of cultivatable land and production capacity.

This abundancy of production possibilities, in addition to a great uniformity of both the ecological and the economic system in the whole of the archipelago, offers a possible explanation of the relative low degree of organization and rigidity of the economic system. Reciprocity provided to be the overruling ideology here, as well as the actual practice. Redistribution—as a system of collecting (a part of) the production centrally, and later on redistributing this again among (a part of) the people—proved to be rare and little developed; though formally the control over production and the means of production was in the hands of the *matai*. The *matai*—a titled person and usually the head of a household—formally made the decisions regarding production and everything else regarding his household, yet everything was decided in gatherings of the adult members of the household. The youths—that is all the untitled members, male and female—of the household composed the working force. As there was much interaction in a village and there were many communal tasks, cooperation and regulation of all this was needed. The cooperation in a village was regulated by a council—*fono*—of all the *matai* in the village. Decisions of a village *fono* had to be unanimous, as they could not impinge upon the autonomy of an individual household. On a higher level, the same held true for the decisions of a district—or even the island—*fono*. On its own level each part—be it a household, a village, a subdistrict, or a district—was autonomous and could not be overruled by a higher level, unless one was willing to risk war.

As the means of production, as well as the production itself, were the property of the producers, that is, the individual households, only reciprocity provided the mechanism for the division or redistribution of the production. Each *matai* was dependent for his income first and foremost upon the willingness of his followers—the members of his household—who of course also profited by producing for their household and so for their *matai*. But he could force them only to a very limited extent. Each member of the household had the possibility of changing his membership, each member had many possibilities to choose from. Yet, as long as one was a member of a particular houseshold, one had to fulfill the obligations imposed upon him by the *matai*. The same held for the higher levels, for the relationships between the *matai* themselves. Here too reciprocity was predominant, and could be enforced only to a very limited extent. "Goods and services which pass beyond the village are virtually wholly ceremonial, pertaining to elite interaction" (Keesing 1956, 17).

However as Samoan society was based upon kinship and kinship obligations, much of the production could be gathered in the hands of the *matai* along these lines. Especially as there was heavy competition between "families" concerning their relative status. The status of the family *matai* was crucial in this context. The relative status of these family *matai* was enhanced by lavish "*potlatches*". A great deal of the production was needed for this purpose.

Specialization in the agricultural production process seemed to be almost absent. The same seems to hold for all other sorts of specialization. Specialist functions, such as management, healing the sick, religious functions, and so forth, were most of the time performed by each *matai* for his own household. Apart from this, the *matai* had to perform the same duties as the other members of his household.

In summary we can say that the economy in Samoa was characterized by a subsistence economy and a system based upon reciprocity encompassing the whole society from the lowest up to the highest levels. The producers were the consumers; there was no distinctive group of nonproducers. The few persons who, to a certain degree, might be called specialists—especially the *matai*—performed these specialties only part-time (Gilson 1970; 16; Holmes 1974, 45; Mead 1969, 72; Williamson 1929, 3:344). Moreover they performed many different specialists functions. There was no formalized form of taxation. Trade did not have the form of a market exchange, but of reciprocal exchange. Except at the level of ideology, there was almost no integration of the highly autonomous lower levels of society, the households and the villages, into one centralized societal system.

Political System

In this part we must make a distinction between the political system as ideology and the political system in practice. First I will describe it ideologically, then the practice.

Political system: the ideology. At the level of ideology there was a hierarchical system in Samoa, which might be called in Johnson's (1982) terminology a system of "simultaneous hierarchies." This means a stepped, pyramidal governing and control system with a number of successive, hierarchically ordered, levels of integration. At the lowest level we find the household group governed by a *matai*, a titled family elder, with the power to decide in all matters regarding his household group. At the next higher level we find the village council—the village *fono*—with the power to decide in all matters regarding the village affairs. Membership of the village *fono* comprised all the *matai* in the village, and its president was the headman of the village: the *matai* with the highest title(s) of the village. At this level we also find a distinction between the decision making, the ceremonial power, and the executive power in the differences between *matai* with *alii* and *matai* with *tulafale* titles. Formally the *alii* were the officeholders; they made the decisions. In principle every *alii* had a *tulafale*, of approximately the same rank as his own, as his official speaker. At official gatherings, like the gatherings of a *fono*, the *tulafale* spoke in the place of his *alii*. The *tulafale* were the holders of the executive power, while the *alii* were the (ceremonial) authorities. The village *fono*, formally represented by the village headman (the *alii* with the highest title in the village), decided in all affairs regarding the village.

At the following level we find the district, or sometimes a subdistrict below a district, with the same structure as on the level of the village. The (sub)district *fono* was composed of the highest *alii* and *tulafale* from each of the villages in this (sub)district, acting as representatives of their respective villages. The president of this *fono* again was the *alii* with the highest title(s), with the highest *tulafale* as his official speaker.

These districts—with the exception of Manu'a—were in turn part of one of three regions: A'ana, Atua, and Tuamasanga. These three regions were called after areas on the island of Upolu, but the islands Tutu'ila, Savai'i, Aunu'u, Apolima, and Manono were also parts of one or more of these regions. At this level we find the region *fono* with the same structure as the lower levels.

The *fono of all Samoa* (again with the exception of Manu'a) was at the top level. This *fono* was thought to hold the decision making and the executive power regarding all Samoa. An indication of how this whole structure was primarily only a structure in and for the mind is that as far as we know (Goldman 1970, 272; Mead 1969, 11) the *fono of all Samoa* had never gathered. This is not meant to suggest that therefore it was unimportant for the people or for Samoan society; on the contrary, as anthropologists we have to know this and to take it into account when we want to understand Samoan society or its people.

In a formal sense, the "King of all Samoa" (*tafa'ifa*) was the highest authority and the supreme owner of all lands and land rights in Samoa. Yet only seldom had there ever been an actual *tafa'ifa* in Samoa. As for the right upon the (honorific) title *tafa'ifa*, it was essential that he or she was the bearer of the highest titles of the four most important families—*Salafai, Samalietoa, Satupua*, and *Salevalasi*—in Samoa. As these titles were bestowed by a special board of the highest *tulafale* from the four families, only a few people in Samoan history had ever succeeded in achieving this (Keesing 1956, 22 ff.). Yet even when there was a *tafa'ifa*, though his status was very high, his real power in practice did not exceed that of every other *matai*; his power was in his own lineage and not beyond. Only ideologically he was the supreme head.

Political system: the practice. This is more in accordance with the idea which Johnson (1982) has called "sequential hierarchies." In a system with sequential hierarchies, each level within these hierarchies is to a great extent autonomous, especially the lowest levels. Most of the time the higher levels are absent, and then only exist as a possibility in the mind of the people. Higher levels only are brought to life if, when, and as long as there is a need. The higher the level the less they are needed and so the less they exist in reality.

This is exactly what we see in Samoa. The two lowest levels in society—the household and the village—were the only ones that actually existed in reality all the time. There almost all the interaction, work, and governing took place. A higher level, for example, a district, was brought to life only when there were issues regarding the district as a whole; for instance, threat of war between villages in different districts. When there was a need to assemble the members of a *fono* of the district, we see the following:

The *matai* of the village who felt the need for an assembly of the districts *fono* appealed to the president of this *fono*. The president in turn sent messengers to all the members of the *fono*. They were asked to come to the assembly and were informed about the issue concerned. First of all these members called their own (village) *fono* together to inform their colleagues and to come to a decision about their own point of view regarding the issue. With this mandate the members of the districts *fono* gathered to come to a decision at the level of the district. Decisions in this district *fono* were preferably unanimous; otherwise the decisions only had force of law for those who had agreed. There was no force or power to compel the others to follow the decisions.

As regards the *matai*, it can be said that though they had a high status in society and they held much power, yet their position was not at all comparable to that of the *alii* in Hawaii. A Samoan *matai* first and foremost was a family member; his position was one of the family elder. As such he had received from his family, his fellows, a family title. This title could be taken away from him in the same way as it was bestowed upon him. Their position was primarily based upon consent and not upon power. Moreover almost everybody was eligible to such titles. According to Keesing (1934, 245; 1956, 43) almost every man older than forty years of age was holder of one or more of such family titles. One even could be the holder of titles in different familes (Holmes 1974, 19). The position of *matai* in Samoa so was thus firmly embedded in kinship and the *matai* could not be called a class in contrast to the common people, as was the case in Hawaii.

Economic practice was in accordance with this practice of the political system. Both the ownership of the ground and the ownership of the production was vested in the household. The production itself too was regulated primarily within the individual household. Only for communal tasks in society, within the village, the village *fono*—in which each household had a representative— had a responsibility. Yet a *fono* only could decide something by consent of all the representatives.

Structural Features of Early State Economics

Though in this section discussion will be centered around so-called ideal-types—the ideal-type of the state in opposition to the ideal-type of the chiefdom—it will be clear that every existing chiefdom or state is somewhere in between on the continuum amidst these ideal-types.

The structual differences between a chiefdom and an early state, as can be deduced from the foregoing, are found not so much in the economy proper, but in the domain of political economy. In the economy proper there are only slight, gradual, differences.

In Hawaii we see a great deal of agricultural intensification, the development of monocultural production, some specialization, and the beginning of the development of trade and a market system. Apart from this, a system of regular taxation was developed, apart from and above forms of irregular extraction of production and services from the population.

In Samoa there was almost no form of agricultural intensification; on the contrary, much cultivatable land was not brought into cultivation. Though in Samoa we did find breadfruit gardens, taro fields, and so on, every household produced (almost) all of the different products it needed. There was only a rudimentary form of specialization, whereas trade and markets were absent except in the form of irregular, almost wholly ceremonial, exchange of products along kinship lines. Taxation was absent, whereas the services and goods required by the *matai* or the *fono* were thought of as being in the interest of the people concerned. So, if a *matai* or a *fono* ordered some services rendered or certain goods delivered for a feast or some other occasion, it was not only required that the people concerned gave their consent, but that they would only give their consent when they were convinced that it was advantageous. As said before, tasks as well as production were communal, and products were communal property, regardless of who had produced it. The *matai* and the *fono* were the managers only, and nothing else. Their tasks also were seen as communal and being in the interest of the community. In a chiefdom there is little difference between the population, the food producers, and the consumers of the surplus, the elite. In an early state the differences are clearly marked.

With this we come to the essential structural differences between the economy in an early state and a chiefdom. The first and foremost feature concerns the division of society in clearly distinguished parts in an early state: the people, the producers of the food, and the consumers of the surplus, the elite. The people till the fields, but do not own the land which they work. Moreover, the greater part of their production is not their own; it is reserved for the owner of the land. The owner does not himself produce; he has the right, and the power, to extract as much as he wants from his subordinates. Apart from the regular taxation—in Hawaii predominantly during the *makahiki* festival—he can demand goods and services from his people according to his whim. So, for instance, it is told that at a certain moment in Hawaii there was a shortage of food on account of the greed of the chiefs for European goods; especially firearms. To get these desired goods, the chiefs had to deliver large amounts of precious sandalwood which was growing in the rainforests. The people were ordered to fetch this. In order for this to be accomplished so much work was required from the people that they had no time to till their fields and a famine resulted.

In a chiefdom as Samoa the foregoing would have been impossible. If a *matai* or a *fono* would have required so much work from their subordinates, the people would have looked for some other *matai* or some other village where the stress would have been less severe. And every *matai* and every village would gladly welcome those people. This threat of followers leaving their leaders is a guarantee for the people that their leaders will not make the burden too heavy. In Samoa there is no power invested in the *matai* or in the *fono* to prevent the followers from leaving and from settling elsewhere.

This brings us to the second structural difference between an early state and a chiefdom; coercive power, the use of force, and consensual power, authority. In an early state (coercive) power is vested in the top level of the society, which, moreover, has a monopoly on the use of force. It has the right and the possibilities to use power and to force people to do things; even to the detriment of the people concerned. In a chiefdom, however, the top level has no power; it has authority (consensual power). Of course this authority can be used to let people do certain things, but they cannot be forced by other means than by a certain amount of consent of the people concerned.

A third structural difference between an early state and a chiefdom is that the economic, the social, and the political organization in a chiefdom are almost wholly organized along kinship lines, whereas in an early state kinship has lost much of its importance as a basic organizational structure (though ideologically this is not the case). For instance, in a chiefdom genealogical ties to a leader are essential to be elected to a position. In an early state this is not necessarily so. In Hawaii personal loyalty to a leader is the most essential criterion for this, apart from the membership in a certain class.

A fourth structural difference is the ownership of the means of production. In an early state it is not the food producers who own the means of production. The consumers, the elite, are the owners of the land, of the boats, and so forth. In a chiefdom the food producers are the owners of the land. Here the top level only ideologically is the owner of the land. But this level only owns the land on behalf of the people; it cannot dispose of it or anything else without the consent of the people. Moreover the top level is itself a producer of food. Therefore most of the time its members are only part-time specialists. Also, not only are the other specialists also part-time specialists for most of the time, but there are in general very few specialists in a chiefdom.

On account of this, in an early state there is a well developed system of extracting goods and services from the people on a large scale and, if necessary, by force. In a chiefdom the extraction of a surplus from the people is not only on a more limited scale most of the time but is also governed more by consent than by force.

As can be seen from the foregoing, the essential structural differences between early states and chiefdoms are in the political domain, even where the economy is concerned. Here, too, we find in an early state a division in society between the rulers and the ruled, a division which is nonexistent in a chiefdom.

References

Bakel, M. A. van
1988   Structurele veranderingen tijdens de vorming van de Ha-
            waiiaanse staat. In *Tussen vorst en volk*. ed. H. J. M.
            Claessen, 65–78. Leiden: Institute of Cultural and Social
            Studies (ICA publication no. 81).
Bargatzky, Th.
1988   Evolution, sequential hierarchy and areal integration: the

case of traditional Samoan society. In *State and society: the emergence and development of social hierarchy and political centralization.* J. Gledhill, B. Bender, and M. T. Larsen 43–56. London: Allen & Unwin.

Campbell, A.
1818   *Reize om de wereld in de jaren 1806–1812.* Amsterdam: J. C. van Kesteren.

Carter, J., ed.
1981   *Pacific Islands yearbook.* 14th ed. Sydney: Pacific Publications.

Claessen, H. J. M.
1975   Despotism and irrigation. In *Current anthropology in the Netherlands.* ed. H. J. M. Claessen and P. Kloos, 48–62. Rotterdam: Nederlandse Sociologische en Antropologische Vereniging.

Claessen, H. J. M., and P. Skalník, eds.
1978   *The early state.* Den Haag: Mouton.

Cook, J.
1967   *The Journals of captain James Cook. The voyage of the Resolution and Discovery, 1776–1780.* 2 vols. Ed. and Intro. J. C. Beaglehole. Cambridge: The Hakluyt Society.

Cools, A., ed.
1979   *Histoire de la mission des iles Sandwich ou Hawaii 1825–1838.* Vol. 2 Rome: Sources Historiques S.S.C.C.

Cordy, R. H.
1981   *A study of prehistoric social change. The development of complex societies in the Hawaiian islands.* New York: Academic Press.

Davenport, W.
1969   The "Hawaiian Cultural Revolution": Some political and economic Considerations. *American Anthropologist,* 71:1–20.

Davidson, J. M.
1979   Samoa and Tonga. In *The prehistory of Polynesia.* ed. J. D. Jennings. 82–109. Cambridge: Harvard University Press.

Ellis, W.
1826   *Narrative of a tour through Hawaii, or, Owhyhee; with remarks on the history, traditions, manners, customs, and language of the inhabitants of the Sandwich Islands.* London: H. Fisher, Son, and P. Jackson.

Ember, M.
1962a   The nature of Samoan kinship structure. *Man,* 62:124.
1962b   Political authority and the structure of kinship in aboriginal Samoa. *American Anthropologist,* 64:964–71.
1966   Samoan kinship and political structure; an archaeological test to decide between the two alternative reconstructions

(Ember's versus Freeman's). *American Anthropologist*, 68:163–68.

Freeman, D.
1983   *Margaret Mead and Samoa: The making and unmaking of an anthropological myth*. Cambridge: Harvard University Press.

Gilson, R. P.
1970   *Samoa 1830 to 1900. The politics of a multi-cultural community*. London: Oxford University Press.

Goldman, I.
1970   *Ancient Polynesian society*. Chicago: The University of Chicago Press.

Handy, E. S. C.
1965   Government and society. In *Ancient Hawaiian civilization*, (revised edition), ed. E. S. C. Handy, and M. Kawena Pukui, 35–46. Rutland: Charles E. Tuttle Co.

Hjarnø, J.
1980   Social reproduction. Towards an understanding of aboriginal Samoa. *Folk*, 21/22: 73–123.

Holmes, L. D.
1974   *Samoan village*. New York: Holt, Rinehart and Winston Inc.

Johnson, G. A.
1982   Organizational structure and scalar stress. In *Theory and explanation in archaeology*. ed. C. Renfrew, M. J. Rowlands, and B. A. Segraves. 389–421. New York: Academic Press.

Keesing, F. M.
1934   *Modern Samoa: its government and changing life*. London: Allen and Unwin.

Keesing, F. M. and Keesing, M. M.
1956   *Elite communication in Samoa: A study of leadership*. Stanford: Stanford University Press.

Kirch, P. V.
1984   *The evolution of the Polynesian chiefdoms*. Cambridge: Cambridge University Press.

Kirch, P. V., ed.
1986   *Island societies. Archaeological approaches to evolution and transformation*. Cambridge: Cambridge University Press.

Krämer, A.
1901   *Die Samoa-Inseln: Entwurf einer Monographie mit besonderer Berücksichtigung Deutsch-Samoas*. Stuttgart: Schweizerbartsche Verlagsbuchhandlung.

Kuykendall, R. S.
1947   *The Hawaiian kingdom 1778–1854. Foundation and trans-
               formation.* Honolulu: University of Hawaii Press.
Malo, D.
1971   *Hawaiian antiquities. Moolelo Hawaii.* Ed. N. B. Emer-
               son. Honolulu: Bernice P. Bishop Museum Press.
McArthur, N.
1968   *Island populations of the Pacific.* Canberra: Australian
               National University Press.
Mead, M.
1969   *Social organization of Manu'a.* Honolulu: B.P.B. Museum
               Press. (Orig. 1930).
Meijer, H., ed.
1910   *Das Deutsche Kolonialreich. Eine Länderkunde der
               deutschen Schutzgebiete.* Leipzig: Bibliographisches Insti-
               tut.
Pirie, P.
1972   Population growth in the Pacific Islands; the example of
               W. Samoa. In *Man in the Pacific islands*, ed. R. G. Ward,
               189–218. Oxford: Clarendon Press.
Pitt, D. C.
1970   *Tradition and economic progress in Samoa. A case-study
               of the role of traditional social institutions in economic
               progress.* Oxford: Clarendon Press.
Rowe, N. A.
1930   *Samoa under the sailing gods.* London: Putnam.
Sahlins, M. D.
1958   *Social stratification in Polynesia.* Seattle: University of
               Washington Press.
Schmitt, R. C.
1970   Famine mortality in Hawaii. *The Journal of Pacific His-
               tory*, 5:109–15.
Seaton, L.
1978   The early state in Hawaii. In *The Early State*, ed. H. J.
               M. Claessen and P. Skalník, 269–88. Den Haag: Mouton.
Service, E. R.
1975   *Origins of the state and civilization.* New York: Norton.
Tiffany, S. W.
1975   Giving and receiving: participation in chiefly redistribution
               activities in Samoa. *Ethnology*, 14:267–86.
Turner, G.
1884   *Samoa; a hundred years ago and long before.* London:
               MacMillan and Co.
Williamson, R. W.
1929   *The social and political systems of Central Polynesia.* 3 vols.
               Cambridge: Cambridge University Press.

Wise, J. H.

1965a   The history of land ownership in Hawaii. In *Ancient Hawaiian civilization*, revised edition, eds. E. S. C. Handy and M. Kawena Pukui 81–94. Rutland: Charles E. Tuttle Co.

1965b   Food and its preparation. In *Ancient Hawaiian civilization*, rev. ed., E. S. C. Handy et al, 95–104. Rutland: Charles E. Tuttle Co.

12

State and Economy in Polynesia

Henri J. M. Claessen

In this article I describe and compare the economic system of two early states in eighteenth century Polynesia: Tahiti and Tonga. I shall first provide a description of eighteenth century Tahitian society. I then present information on Tongan society relating to the same period. In the final section I then compare these two societies. The comparison is carried out against the background of supplementary data from other Polynesian societies.

Tahiti

In the eighteenth century the relatively large island of Tahiti (1000 km^2) was divided into a number of more or less autonomous political units (see figure 12.1). Several of these qualify as early states; others may be best described as chiefdoms. Early states were: Papara in the south, Tautira in the east, and Te Porionu'u in the northwest of the island. Other regions, such as Atehuru, Hitia'a, and Fa'a'a, were chiefdoms (Claessen 1988, 89; cf. 1978, 449).

In order to understand the position of the various groups of

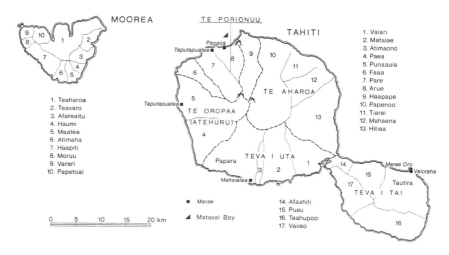

FIGURE 12.1
Tahiti and Moorea

people in the complex social system of the Tahitians, some preliminary remarks must be made on their relative ranking. Con-
ceptually—though in practice many departures from the rule did
occur—Tahitian society was structured along the lines of a ramage system (for details: Sahlins 1958, 140–51; Claessen 1978,
442–47). A *ramage* is a nonexogamous, internally stratified, un-
ilineal—here patrilineal—descent group. Distance from the senior line of descent from the common ancestor is the criterion for
stratification. The "common ancestor" is usually a mythical figure, a descendant of the gods. This descent invests the senior line
of the ramage with sacred powers (*mana*). The mode of succession
in the system is by primogeniture. Furthermore, every brother is
ranked according to the principle of seniority, and sisters may
also be integrated into this hierarchy. This system of ranking is
extended outwards to embrace the whole of society. In theory
each individual occupies a different status position, in accordance
with his or her distance from the senior line of descent in the
group. Tahitian society—as well as Tongan society—can be analyzed as comprising the constituent sections of a single genealogical system at the apex of which stands the sacred ruler, the
direct descendant in the senior line of the reputed founder of the

society as a whole. In practice the all-embracing ramage is split into a number of subramages. One of the subramages may be said to outrank all the others and to supply—in the Tahitian case—the *arii rahi*. This title, however, is also applied to the supreme leaders of some of the subramages. In the course of time the system in which each member of a ramage had his or her own ranking gradually made place for another form of social stratification. The social and economic distance between the senior and junior branches of the same subramage grew so great that marriages between members of these groups were no longer considered attractive, and the following more or less endogamous social strata developed in Tahitian society:

an upper group, or the *arii*,
a middle group, or *raatira*, and
a lower group, or *manahune*.

Generally speaking, there is no problem in allocating people to one of these categories. The borderlines between the groups, however, are rather vague. This may be occasioned by the persistence of ideas pertaining to the ramage structure, in which everybody had his own rank. Higher and lower *arii* are distinguished, based on their relative distance to the oldest descent line. Among the lower *arii* one finds the *iatoai*, that is, the people belonging to the junior branches. *Raatira* as a group are lower than *iatoai*, but a clear dividing line between a low *iatoai* and a high *raatira* is difficult to draw. The same holds for the line of demarcation separating the *raatira* from the *manahune*. The majority of European visitors of the eighteenth century considered the *raatira* as a landed gentry; they were described as the owners of land. As, however, the *arii* were also owners of land, and the *manahune* had claims to land, this criterion is not of much help. Even so, no better criterion exists. Fortunately more can be said on the subject. *Manahune* were often considered to be landless people, as they were found working on the land of *arii* or *raatira*. This was occasioned by the fact, as Queen Marau (1971, 85ff.) stated, that they were mainly entitled to land in the hills and mountains that had only limited access to the sea. Their claims to better land were overruled by the stronger claims of the other groups (the summary of the ramage structure is based on Claessen 1978). In contrast to members of the *arii*, the *raatira* worked their land themselves (Oliver 1974, 769ff.). According to the missionary Ellis (1831, 3:96ff.) there were great differences in status and influence between the members of this category, and their landed property varied from 20 to 100 acres. The highest *raatira* are depicted by him as resembling *iatoai*. The basic unit of Tahitian society was formed by the *mata'eina'a* (household group). A number of such groups constituted a neighborhood, "a cluster of households consisting of one 'principal' household and a number of others—all interconnected by worship at a common marae" (Oliver 1974, 968). The head of a neighborhood was usually a person of *raatira* status (Claessen 1988, 90; cf. Ellis 1831, 3:119). He had the supervision over agricultural activities, fishing, and housebuilding. Through him, a sometimes considerable portion of the local produce was handed over to the ruler as tax. The other household heads were lower *raatira*, or sometimes well-to-do *manahune*.

A number of neighborhoods made up, in the words of Oliver (1974, 976), "a second-order tribe." The precise meaning of this concept is not very clear. According to Oliver, the chief of one of the neighborhoods is also the leader of the others. This formulation gives the impression that such a leader had a position comparable to that of village head or district head in other parts of the world. There are indications that the leader of such a 'district' was an *iatoai*. He had the title of *toofa* (Morrison 1966, 137). As the *raatira* of a neighborhood, the *toofa* had to maintain law and order. Both functionaries had the right to proclaim a *rahui*—a chiefly interdiction or prohibition (with supernatural sanctions) on the use of particular, frequently agricultural, resources (Morrison 1966, 137). The inhabitants of the district had to support their *toofa* with food, goods, and labor. The *toofa* in turn had to support the *arii rahi*. His due, however, was produced by his subjects.

A number of districts formed the "third-order tribes" such as Fa'a'a, or Hitia'a, polities that quality as chiefdoms. The rulers over these chiefdoms were *arii*. In many respects their social status was similar to that of the *arii* ruling the "fourth-order tribes." Politically, however, differences existed. The rulers of the fourth-order tribes—or early states—had more power. Moreover, the early states (Papara, Te Porionu'u, Tautira) comprised a number of third-order tribes (Claessen 1988, 81ff.). Against this sociopolitical background, the economic structure of society and state will now be presented.

By and large, Tahitian households were selfsupporting. Practically everything needed was grown in the gardens or could be made at home. With regard to food and goods there was a considerable degree of equality in Tahitian society. And, since the other islands of the archipelago had similar ecologies, there were but limited incentives for trade and markets. There were no sources of raw materials that could be monopolized by the rulers. Long-distance trade to other archipelagoes was no more promising. These conditions are a sufficient explanation for the limited development of the commercial system. This is not to say, however, that trade or exchange were completely unknown in the Society Islands. In the first place, local differences in quality of soil and climate did occur. As a consequence several types of food-producing plants did not come to fruition everywhere in the same period. Oliver (1974, 240) mentions trade in breadfruit because of "local differences in overall annual supply." Voyages were undertaken from Pare to Tetiaroa Atol, 50 kilometers northwest from Tahiti, to obtain specific types of breadfruit. In other months breadfruit was transported from Atehuru to Matavai, and Oliver quotes J. R. Forster, who describes trade between Bora Bora and Tahiti (Oliver 1974, 856).

The Bounty mutineer Morrison tells that a person needing a certain quantity of *tapa* went go to one of the valleys where the material was produced. He asked one of the household heads here to supply him with the quantity needed in exchange for a specified number of pigs. If the other agreed, he received the pigs in advance. If the producer—after having eaten the pigs—did not fulfil his obligations, the "customer" was entitled to plunder his house (Morrison 1966, 134–35). This description is especially interesting, as it indicates local specialization in production, and the occurrence of entrepreneurial activities. Regrettably, Morrison gives no further information on the subject. Other visitors also give incidental pieces of information on commercial activities. Red feathers belonged to the class of most valuable goods. These feathers were connected with the Oro cult and were used, among other things, for the fabrication of the famous *maro ura*, the red feather girdle, one of the highest ranking status symbols in Tahiti (see below). James Cook quickly became aware of the high value attributed to these red feathers, and during his second visit he took care to hold a quantity of such feathers in stock. Tahitian notables went to great lengths to acquire their share of red feathers. Johann Reinhold Forster (1783, 321) mentions that even a man as honorable as his *tayo* (friend) Potatau was willing to offer his wife to Cook (". . . and she appeared as a ready victim. . .") in order to obtain some feathers. Cook, by the way, politely declined the offer. On his third voyage Cook also met with greedy demands for red feathers on Tahiti (Cook 1967, 186, 189). And one of his officers, Samwell (1967, 1066), stated that "red feathers are so valuable here that Otoo (= Tu = Pomare I; HC) gave ten large Hogs for a Tongataboo (= Tongatapu; HC) Head dress made of them" (see also, Samwell 1967, 1052, 1056). The missionaries of the Duff mention a man, a fisherman by trade, "who supplied his neighbours with fish, and received from them canoes, hogs, fruit, roots, and cloth" (Wilson 1799, 192). Maximo Rodriguez, the Spanish interpreter who lived in Taiarapu during 1774 and 1775, gives an account of an exchange of mother-of-pearl shells for hogs (Rodriguez 1775, 205). Banks mentions several times a lively trade at a "marketplace," near the camp of the British. Hogs, breadfruit, and pigs were regularly bartered there (1962, 1:260ff.). There is no evidence for markets in the writings of the other early visitors. Oliver (1974, 540, note 9) states that when marketplaces were established by the British, Tahitians "fell into the practice easily."

Data on trade and commerce in ancient Tahiti are scarce. A possible explanation has already been stated: there was not very much to trade; people were self-supporting. Exceptions were the few luxury items such as red feathers, or mother-of-pearl. This, however, is only part of the explantion. The other part is that here, much of what we now would classify as trade, took place under the name of gift-giving (Oliver 1974, 233, 1083). European visitors, when receiving a "gift," were often surprised to have stipulated exactly what was expected in return. Tahitians repeatedly offered a wide variety of gifts, but at the same time made it patently clear that the return gift was expected to include red feathers.

Such transactions were traditionally arranged between *tayo's*: "friends." Many Europeans were thus invited to enter into such a friendship relation. In this respect the experiences of Wales, the astronomer of Cook's second voyage, are illustrative. After first entering into rather unspecified gift-giving relations, and receiving only insignificant return gifts (except for the promise of *tayo* relationships), he then refrained from giving and started to barter. This gave him more satisfaction—though he never seems to have attempted to figure out the advantages of the *tayo's* he had made (Wales 1969, 799).

The data presented thus far indicate that at the arrival of the Europeans, the inhabitants of Tahiti had clear ideas about value, exchange, obligations, and trade. Though the majority of the transactions went under the cover of gift-giving, it was commerce that was pursued. Many gifts were payments for services rendered, other gifts were exchange for stipulated return gifts, and in the *tayo* relation gifts also had to be reciprocated, though here the return prestation was not usually directly made.

The introduction of European goods made a whole range of new valuables available. In the beginning the Tahitians tried to obtain these by the traditional methods of gift exchange and stealing. Soon, however, barter and trade became dominant in the relations with the foreigners. The British merchant Turnbull, who lived in Tahiti between 1801 and 1804, relates how one evening Pomare II sent a dozen girls to a European ship, to procure by means of prostitution a large quantity of gunpowder (Turnbull 1806, 384). And Moerenhout, living here in 1829–30, also describes commercial activities of Tahitians through prostitution (Moerenhout 1837, 2:223). The missionaries of the Duff tried to explain this indecent behavior in the following way:

> They [the Tahitians, HC] lay the charge wholly at our door, and say that Englishmen are ashamed of nothing, and that we have led them to public acts of indecency never before practised among themselves. Iron here, more precious than gold, bears down every barrier of restraint: honesty and modesty yield to the force of temptation. (Wilson 1799, 342)

Not only iron was required. The Tahitians soon also realized the value of gunpowder, firearms, and liquor. To obtain these goods, Tahitians were willing to pay any price. One may assume, however, that the missionaries greatly overstated the influence of the British on the society's morals. Already De Bougainville, one of the discoverers of Tahiti, informs us that his ship was approached by numerous canoes in which beautiful girls and young women were sitting in the nude, for the men and older women who accompanied them took away their clothes when nearing the French ships (De Bougainville 1966, 185; Caro 1962, 16; Fesche 1929, 2). And Wallis, who arrived in Tahiti in the same period, informs us that from the very beginning of his visit Tahitian girls came on board of his ship in the nude, and invited his crew to partake in sexual activities (1789, 125). Some weeks later he was even obliged to take harsh measures, to prevent his crew from using the nails with which his ship was held together as payment for having sexual relations with Tahitian girls; the ship was in danger of falling apart (1789, 168). The nails for that matter were also used as payment for hogs, breadfruit, plantains, and other kinds of foodstuffs.

With the arrival of European goods, objects of high value were introduced to Tahitian society. Previously the only valuables had been red feathers, and the mother-of-pearl shells used for mourning dress. The red feathers were connected with the Oro cult and its *maro ura*, the red feather girdle (for a description, see Cook 1967, 203). Only in a status conscious society, where the number of status symbols was limited (Goldman 1970), could the introduction of a new cult and new symbols create such an excitement. All *arii* competed for the possession of the Oro image and the right to wear the red feather girdle in the Oro *marae's* (temples). Though at first the right to wear the *maro ura* gave only religious authority, the fact that it was the prerogative of the most powerful leaders to claim the girdle successfully confered enormous prestige on its possession. The Tahitian *arii* competed fiercely; *marae* were built and destroyed, wars were fought, and the image, as well as the girdle, changed hands several times (Claessen 1978, 451ff.). The Oro cult originated in Raiatea and went from there to Tahiti in the beginning of the eighteenth century (Oliver 1974, 667, 677). Some years later a second feather girdle, the *maro tea* (the yellow girdle), also from Raiatea, was introduced on Tahiti. The right to wear the red girdle belonged originally to the *arii* of Vaiari, who lost their claim to the powerful Pomare family of Te Porionu'u. The rulers of Papara were entitled to wear the yellow girdle (Rose 1978). About the time of Wallis' visit to Tahiti, Amo and Purea, who then ruled over Papara, built the enormous *marae* of Mahaiateae in order to have their son Teriirere invested with both *maro's* (Amo could also boast of a claim to the red girdle). It is not clear whether Teriirere was ever inaugurated; the only fact that is known with certainty is that, shortly after the departure of Wallis, a coalition of neighboring polities defeated Parara and destroyed the *marae* as testified by Banks, who visited the ruins in 1769 (Banks 1962, 1:303–05).

The introduction of the Oro cult, and the ensuing competition for power, laid a heavy burden on the income of the rulers. Until then state expenses had been fairly limited. The building of canoes or the construction of a *marae* was only occasionally required. According to Oliver:

> The building of smaller marae would have required little or no craftmanship and energy beyond that of any ordinary man or small group of men. On the other hand, the building of the larger, carefully-faced walls and *ahu* [platforms, HC] called for considerable architectural and supervisory skills, as well as for large levies of labor. There were, in fact, certain men (*tahu'a marae*) who made a specialty (presumably part time) of planning and supervising marae construction. (Oliver 1974, 188)

The question thus becomes: how was the income of the rulers and the state organized? The sources contain numerous references to demands for food, goods, or services by the leaders of the polities. Sometimes such demands give the impression of robbery and arbitrariness. Andia y Varella, one of the Spanish visitors to Taiarapu (in 1774–75), tells that:

> during our stay, this chief [Vehiatua, HC] despatched his messengers to collect from the houses of his subjects a quantity of wraps, parguayes [bark cloth, HC], mats, hogs, fowls, and every sort of provision. This comprises all the tribute they render to the King; and there is no fixed assessment of it, since he calls for it in any quantity and at whatever time he chooses. (Andia y Varella 1775, 264)

De Bovis (1855, 403) states that the chiefs continuously burdened their people with taxation, either in the form of obligatory gifts, or in the form of forced labor, and the Spanish visitor Bonacorsi (1773, 55) points to the fact that the common man "frequently suffers a dearth of food," while "the good and finer fish, of which there is great plenty in the sea" is reserved "for the arii and principal persons." Rodriguez (1775, 20, 23) speaks of houses that *arii* Vehiatua had expropriated to favour the Spaniards, and the missionaries of the Duff relate the following experience with Pomare:

> Wanted plank for the blacksmith's shop; told the king. He said, "Harry-mie, come along." I thought he had some ready; he carried me up the valley, and searching every house took what he liked: many of the people stoutly resisted, but his men would not leave a plank. I told the king, with whom we exercise the most entire familiarity, that he was a thief. "No," says he," it is the custom of Otaheite." (Wilson 1799, 158)

Elsewhere they mention a meeting with Pomare (1799, 200) who is very busy,

> having to collect canoes, cloth, hogs etc. to give away among the different chiefs and arreois, which would attend him to the great feast at Pappara which was to take place in a few days, and for which the island was looking up to him. (Wilson 1799, 200)

Turnbull also stresses the character of arbitrariness and robbery. He tells that when Tahitians return from fishing, members of the royal entourage wait for them in order to confiscate part of their catch as tribute (1806, 270), and elsewhere he says that "these scoundrels" in a most impudent way demand—in the name of their lord—anything they like from the commoners (1806, 323), and that if it happens that a commoner owns something of value, very soon servants of the king come to confiscate it (1806, 366).

To evaluate the data from this anthology of mischief, the facts have first to be separated from the indignation of the reporters. Who were the people that were "robbed" by the *arii* or his courtiers? Were they retainers, working the land or using the canoe of their lord? Or were they independent *raatira* who were pressed against their will to contribute to the household of the ruler?

There are reasons to assume that at least in the majority of cases the "robbery" concerned *manahune*, living on the estate of the ruler. These people were obliged to contribute to the sustenance of the *arii*, and that explains the incidental demands, usually for food. It must be noted, moreover, that there was remarkably little resistance against these demands. If this form of collecting food and goods is compared with the elaborate methods that had to be followed when more encompassing levies were intended, it is clear that here it concerns a different system of taxation.

When major activities were planned, such as the building of a large *marae*, the ruler proclaimed a *rahui* on several types of food in order to have sufficient reserves to feed the workmen once the building started (Henry 1928, 131). A good example of such a *rahui* is the one proclaimed by Amo and Purea of Papara, when they undertook to build the great *marae* for their son (Arii Taimai 1964, 34ff.). They overestimated their power, however, and there were several attemps to break the *rahui*. *Rahui's* were also proclaimed for completely different goals. For example, Bligh relates that

> a stop was put to the sale of hogs in the district of Tettaha [Fa'a'a, HC]. Teppahoo, the earee of that district, told me that they had very few hogs left there, and that it was necessary for a certain time to prohibit every person from killing or selling, that they might have time to breed. (Bligh 1952, 97)

Bligh was not the only visitor hit by such a *rahui*. Cook, during his second visit, was told in Tautira that the few hogs he saw "belonged" to the ruler (Cook 1969, 212, cf. 213 note 1). Once a ruler decided to undertake something important requiring the cooperation and contribution of the population at large—the building of a *marae*, a declaration of war, the fitting out of a fleet—he had to inform his subjects of the decision. This was a complicated matter, for (according to Ellis 1831, 3:117) first the ruler had to ascertain that there was support for the undertaking. This task was effected by friends of the ruler, who went among the *raatira* and *toofa* to hear their opinion. Then he sent around his *vea* (messenger). Both Ellis and the missionaries of the Duff seem somewhat puzzled by the way the *arii rahi* dealt with lower ranking chiefs. They both state that the messenger first informed the *toofa*, who in turn informed their *raatira*, and these then passed the information on to their *manahune* (Wilson 1799, 399; Ellis 1831, 3:117, 121ff.). Or, to put it in other words, every chief was "sovereign of his own district, though all acknowledged the supremacy of the king" (Ellis 1831, 3:119).

Lower chiefs were obliged to contribute to the maintenance of the royal household and to support the large undertakings with food, goods, and services. This implies that there was some pressure on production: a surplus had to be produced to make the required support possible. Captain Wilson of the Duff noted that the farmers had but little interest in producing great quantities, for the surplus would be taken away by the *arii*. They even cultivated mountainous parts, so as to make their gardens not easily accessible (Wilson 1799, 196ff.; Oliver 1974, 255). Not only food and goods were demanded as tax, services were also required: to build the large houses of the *arii* (Cook 1968, 129; Ellis 1831, 3:127), the great canoes (Morrison 1966, 170ff.; Wilson 1799, 399), and the *marae* (Morrison 1966, 149ff.; Henry 1928, 131; Ellis 1831, 3:127). In practice matters were even more complicated, for canoes or houses for the elite sometimes were built under different conditions: labourers were hired and paid for their services. In such cases it is better to speak of a transaction and not of taxation.

The large quantities of food and goods that reached the *arii* as obligatory gifts, or taxation, were in most cases handed out immediately to the notables surrounding him.

> When any of the Chiefs kill a Hog it seems to be almost equally divided among all his dependands and as these are generally very numerous it is but a little that comes to each persons share, so that their chief food is Vegetables and of these they eat a large quantity (Cook 1968, 122).

This observation of Cook is supported by other visitors. Bligh (1952, 50) tells that Tinah (= Pomare, HC) immediately divided the presents he had received "among those who, I supposed, had contributed to support his dignity," and elsewhere he says (Bligh 1952, 90) that Tinah handed out gifts to "some out of friendship and esteem, and to others from motives of political civility" (see also, Bligh 1952, 92). The missionaries Tyerman and Bennet (1831,

1:76) also mention redistribution on a large scale by Pomare, as is also stated by Turnbull (1806, 360). And Wallis (1789, 167) noted that Purea hosted numerous people.

While these examples may give the impression that the greater part of the gifts was redistributed exclusively among the elite, on other occasions the whole population profited from the handing out. This was especially the case after the offerings of the first fruits. Though the term "first fruits" seems a bit out of place on a tropical island (Oliver 1974, 259ff.), there were slight differences in the ripening of breadfruit, taro, and other plant produce. The ritual "consisted primarily of a public offering of food and other valuables to the communities' titular spirits and sovereigns, followed by days of feasting, sports, and other diversions" (Oliver 1974, 259–60). Henry (1928, 177) gives a lively description of such an occasion, and speaks of "contributions of food," that were placed upon the assembly ground "in an immense heap." After prayers and other rituals, the food was divided, and everything that was not especially reserved for the priests or the notables was distributed among the people (Moerenhout 1837, 2:518ff., see also Morrison 1966, 151).

Though it is repeatedly stated that Tahitian rulers handed out enormous quantities of goods, and that the majority of the gifts they received were soon redistributed (Moerenhout 1837, 2:19), there are reasons to believe that they sometimes only reluctantly parted with the valuables they had received from European visitors. Several times one finds mentioned that the Pomares tried to escape the obligation of giving, by leaving their goods on board the British ships, or by hiding them in large chests they had obtained from the sailors (Cook 1967, 222; Bligh 1952, 68; Wilson 1799, 78–79; Mortimer 1793, 61; Bellingshausen 1945, 1:277). It is also mentioned several times that the ruler, because of his obligation to give gifts, is often left empty-handed; in fact he often possessed less than his notables (Oliver 1974, 1007). Ellis describes this situation as follows:

> However abundant the supplies might be which the king received, he was in general more necessitous than many of the chiefs. Applications from the chiefs, for food, for cloth, canoes, and every other valuable article furnished by the people, were so frequent and importunate, that more than was barely sufficient for his own use seldom

remained long in his possession. A present of food was usually accompanied with several hundred yards of native cloth, and a number of fine large double canoes; yet every article was often distributed among the chiefs and favourites on the very day it arrived; and so urgent were the applicants that they did not wait till the articles were brought, but often extorted from the king a promise that he would give them the first bale of cloth, or double canoe, he might receive. At times they went beyond this; and when a chief, who considered the king under obligations to him, knew that the inhabitants of a district were preparing a present for their sovereign, which would include any articles he wished to possess, he would go to the king, and *tapao*, mark or bespeak it, even before it was finished. (Ellis 1831, 3:128)

Tahitian leaders were expected to be openhanded; generosity was a most highly valued quality. This obligation seems difficult to square with their obligations as head of a state. It can be noted, however, that such obligations notwithstanding, Tahitian leaders never failed in amassing sufficient wealth for constructing *marae's*, fitting out war fleets, or entertaining numerous guests. Most Tahitian *arii*—the Pomare's included—present a picture of authority rather than of weakness. Vehiatua, the ruler of Tautira, is mentioned as having banished a number of people "for not having contributed the food supplies due to him"; he destroyed their houses and drove them away (Gayangos 1775, 137ff.; Rodriguez 1775, 27ff.). Elsewhere the Spanish visitors mention "a headman," who was "deprived of his position and lands, and banished" by Vehiatua (Clota and Gonzalez 1775, 325; also Boenechea 1775, 357; Rodriguez 1775, 87). Moerenhout (1837, 1:25; 2:7ff.) is of the opinion that the rulers had nearly absolute power over their subjects, especially on account of their right to declare people, or objects, *tapu*. Other authors assume that the power of the *arii* was based mainly on their armed retainers (Journal d'un voyage 1773, 68ff.; Andia y Varella 1775, 264; Wilson 1799, 229; Henry 1928, 229). It is difficult to decide which of the two power bases was the most effective; but that the *arii* succeeded in having their decisions carried out, if necessary by force, seems without doubt.

Tonga

The Tonga Islands in the west of Polynesia form an archipelago, consisting of several islands and groups of islands (map 12.2).

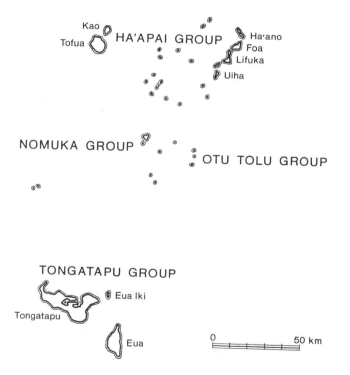

FIGURE 12.2

The Tongan archipelago, excluding the northerly islands of Niuatopu-tapu and Niuafo'ou.

The most important are: Tongatapu, the principal island, the Vavau group, and the Haapai group. Politically the rulers of Tongatapu exercised supremacy over the other islands and groups.

Tongan society can also be analyzed as being based on the concept of the ramage, in which birth order is decisive for the social status of a person. Here, as in Tahiti, several deviations from the basic concept developed in the course of time. In the first place, precedence is given to daughters above sons. This order is continued after marriage. A mother's brother has a lower rank than his sister's children, who have certain rights towards their uncle, the *fahu* rights. They have precedence over him and are free to use his possessions. In case their mother's brother is a high-placed person, this may have political consequences as well. For example, in the case of the *tui tonga*, the sacred ruler, precautions had been taken to protect him against such influences; his sister had to marry a foreigner (a Fijian), and because of that, her children were prevented from holding political office in Tonga. However, they retained their social preeminence over the ruler (Gifford 1929, 80ff.; Kaeppler 1971, 176ff.; Rogers 1977, 158ff.; Bott 1981, 17ff., 32ff.). Cook and his companions give several examples of the *tui tonga*'s respectful behaviour towards his sister's children (1967, 136; Anderson 1967, 954; Clerke 1967, 1309), and some years later the French visitors noted a similar behaviour (Labillardière 1800, 2:126; Dentrecasteaux 1800, 1:290). Also the original ramage structure was affected in other respects. It became customary that younger sons, or younger brothers of leading notables of Tongatapu, were sent to distant villages, or islands, to marry the daughter of the local headmen.

> Once he had managed to land and to get a foothold in the local community, he then married the daughters of an important local title-holder in order to secure the support of the title-holder and his people. The usual rule of patrilineal succession was waived so that the son of the immigrant aristocrat and the chief's daughter could succeed to the leadership position of the old chief. Thus, the local title was either taken over by the immigrant aristocrat, or forgotten, or drawn into the *ha'a* of the immigrant, who was sooner or later granted an official title by the king from whom he was descended. (Bott 1981, 42)

The once existing relation of kinship between a local chief and his group soon disappeared, and foreigners instead of members of the kin group ruled the village. Time and again changes of leadership occurred, till in the end kinship ties between the local group and the ruling elite no longer existed. Within the local groups the ramage structure broke down; only the obligations to the leaders remained (Korn 1978). Broadly speaking, social stratification in the Tonga Islands comprised the following categories: *eiki*, *matapule*, and *tua*.

Of the *eiki*, or notables, the highest rank was occupied by the *tui tonga*, the sacred ruler. His sister, the *tui tonga fefine*, had, in terms of kinship, a higher position, and her daughter, the *tamaha*, an even higher status. Politically the hereditary prime minister, the *tui haa takalaua*, and his hereditary deputy, the *tui kanokupolu*, were powerful competitors of the sacred ruler. The other *eiki* were high born members of descent lines closely related to that of the ruler (Gifford 1929, 35ff.). They exercized efficient control over their own districts and paid allegiance to the *tui tonga* (Cummins 1977, 64). Considerable status differences existed within this category. The most important *eiki* were members of the royal council (West 1865, 261). Their positions were hereditary, and they were entitled to food and goods produced by their subjects, as well as to their labour services (Gifford 1929, 124ff.). From this group the chiefs of the districts, or groups of islands, were chosen (Farmer 1855, 139; Gifford 1929, 48).

The *matapule* were the "titled ceremonial attendants of titled chiefs," though in practice the title was used for all persons who were of *matapule* rank, regardless of whether they held titles or not (Gifford 1929, 140). The rank of the *matapule* depended on the rank of his lord. According to Mariner (1819, 409) this functionary controlled the execution of his master's orders. He oversaw the work and was responsible for the ceremonial duties of his lord. Some *matapule* fulfilled special tasks, such as supervising the building of the large canoes. As a category they held a higher rank than the *tua*—the *tua* were the commoners. They had, according to Dentrecasteaux (1808, 1:309), in fact no privileges at all.

The *tua* are generally described as tenants, the right to the land being vested in the *eiki* (Dumont d'Urville 1832, 4:238; West 1865, 119). "The chief can and frequently does displace the peasants; claiming also an arbitrary portion of the produce of the soil or of the pigs" (Waldegrave 1833, 185; cf. Gifford 1929, 112, 174). Nominally the *tui tonga* was owner of all the land (Waldegrave 1833, 185, 193; Lawry 1851, 53; West 1865, 262; Thomson 1894, 230, 291; Gifford 1929, 171; cf. Gifford 1929, 127, where he stated that the land was owned by the chiefs). The *tua* had many obligations towards the chiefs. Whatever a chief wanted to have, they had to give—at least according to the missionaries of the Duff (Wilson 1799, 238; Lawry 1851, 53); West (1865, 124, 262); the situation was also noted by the French visitor Labillardière (1800, 2:171).

In return for their products and labour service, the *tua* held the right of usufruct to land, almost unrestricted fishing rights, and received food when they fulfilled their labour services (Gifford 1929, 146; Gailey 1981, 88). These arrangements made it possible for the chiefs to exploit their subjects at will, as is testified to by many visitors (Gifford 1929, 104, 124, 127; J. R. Forster 1783, 323; Maurelle 1797, 292, 295; Labillardière 1800, 2:130, 138; West 1865, 263; Wilson 1799, 238; Lawry 1851, 53; cf. however Bott (1982, 71), who states that a chief would not "push his people too far"). It must be added that some form of pecking order existed with respect to the taking of goods. Some of the visitors noted that when members of the *tui tonga* family left their ships carrying the gifts received, members of the *tui kanokupolu* family were waiting on the beach to demand the presents—after which they most politely touched the sole of the foot of the person they had pilfered the moment before (Dentrecasteaux 1808, 1:306, 307; Labillardière 1800, 2:171; cf. Dumont d'Urville 1832, 4:59).

This sociopolitical superstructure was based on an agrarian economy. Its main products were taro, yam, coconuts, bananas, and breadfruit. The work in the gardens was done by men. Women produced mats, baskets, and barkcloth (Cook 1967, 171ff.). The female produce was called *koloa*: valuables (Gifford 1929, 148; Gailey 1981, 90ff.). It was also the task of women to prepare *kava*, the Tongan beverage (Koch 1955, 99ff.). *Kava* was drunk by men at formal occasions, but also for pleasure (Cook 1969, 258; 1967, 140; Anderson 1967, 907–8; Samwell 1967, 1034ff.; Labillardière 1800, 2:136; Mariner 1819, 464). Interestingly, neither Cook, Anderson or Samwell state that women prepared the *kava*; they only speak of "servants." Pigs and chicken were kept by the *tua*, though the flesh of pigs was eaten by the commoners only on special occasions (Waldegrave 1833, 187; Walther 1787, 24; West 1865, 124). Fish was an important addition to the diet. Cook (1967, 169) even stated that "Fish is prefered to hogs and poultry," but Beaglehole explains in a footnote that "hogs were forbidden to commoners" and that all pigs over a certain size "were *tapu* except for chiefs: even their owners could not consume them" (id., note 1). And Cook's companion Anderson states that "the greatest part of their Vegetable diet is Yams, Plantanes and Cocoa nuts: of their animal food the chief is hogs, fowls, fish, of all sorts of shell fish, *and the lower people eat rats*" (Anderson 1967, 942; italics HC).

Though it is questionable whether the term "trade" can be used to describe the exchange of goods in traditional Tongan society, great quantities of goods regularly changed hands (Goldman 1970, 301; Gailey 1981, 90ff.). In these exchanges female goods, or *koloa*, had to be reciprocated with *koloa*. Male goods, such as food, were exchanged in another circuit; they were not interchangeable with *koloa* (see also Mariner 1819, 529; West 1865, 270). Food was given in exchange for other types of food:

> The inland man without a waterfront on which to fish usually had "*tofia* brothers" (men under the same chief) living on the shore who supplied fish in return for yams, fruit, taro, and other inland products. (Gifford 1929, 177)

When a chief wanted a specialist to build a house or a canoe he ordered him to do the work (Gifford 1929, 145). The specialist had a number of relatives as assistants, but the chief could also order commoners to help in the rough and heavy work. In return "he feeds them with the best of foods" (Gifford 1929, 146). The specialist received a handsome present of fine mats and other objects (*koloa*?) for his work. The specialist did not have the right to refuse the order of the chief; there was no free enterprise. Freedom was also limited in other respects. Commoners were not allowed to enter into marriage relations which, because of the ensuing *fahu* obligations, implied the transfer of goods across the border of the district they lived in; that would harm the prerogatives of their chief. Commoners therefore married locally, or within the same district (Gailey 1981, 110).

The chiefs demanded great quantities of food and goods from the commoners. These goods were used to fulfil their obligations to the *tui tonga* and to their relatives. On the other hand, a chief

> was bound by custom as well as by prudence to be generous to his *kainga* in sharing out any provisions he received from outsiders. Hoarding was not practicable with food as a major form of wealth that soon went rotten if not shared. (Bott 1982, 160)

Such a redistribution took place, for example, on ceremonial occasions. Mariner (1819, 127–31) describes such a ceremony, during which enormous quantities of yams and pigs were assembled and ceremonially given to the *tui tonga*. Part of the food was placed on the grave monuments of deceased rulers and the remainder was handed out. A part went to Finau, a part went to Weachi (a son of *tui tonga*'s sister) and other notables, and a part was given to the priests. The recipients in turn redistributed the food among their followers, so that in the end even the lowest of the subjects had gotten some meat and yams to eat (Mariner 1819, 131, 134, 162, 217, where spears were handed out; see also Bott 1982, 102, 128).

To make the commoners produce significant quantities of food to meet the demands of the notables, *tapu's* were laid upon the production, or on part of it. Some types of food were permanently reserved for the notables (for example, pigs), others were temporarily forbidden. Especially when large festivities were to take place, extensive *tapu's* were proclaimed (Mariner 1819, 131, 475, 488; Gifford 1929, 104, 342ff.).

In an interesting section, Kirch (1984, 238–42) describes the complex long-distance trade—or rather exchange—of the Tongans before the coming of the Europeans. In his view the emergence of this long-distance exchange was connected with the development of a complex political organization in the Tonga Islands. The rulers needed prestige goods in order to bind the core islands and outliers to the central polity. Kirch bases his report on Kaeppler's analysis of the exchange pattern between Tonga, Samoa, and Fiji (Kaeppler 1978). Contacts between these islands were already mentioned by Cook (1967, 162–64). From Fiji the Tongans imported canoes, red feathers, decorated barkcloth, mats, baskets, sandalwood, sails, and pottery. To Fiji they exported

whale's teeth, Samoan mats, ornaments, and barkcloth. From
Samoa was imported barkcloth, sleeping mats, and red feathers.
To Samoa the exports consisted of fine mats (Kirch 1984, 239).
Special attention is given to a presumed exchange of women between the three groups of islands (see also Friedman 1981, 286;
1982, 186; Hjarnø 1980). This theory holds that the *tui tonga
fefine* married Fijian chiefs, and that Samoan women were sought
in marriage by high-ranking Tongan males (Kaeppler 1978, 249).
To close the hypothetical circle, Fijian women were supposed to
marry Samoan chiefs. Data to support this hypothesis are rather
scanty, however. In a substantial article on power and rank in
Tonga, Elizabeth Bott (1981) states that only once a *tui tonga
fefine* married a Fijian chief. They founded the Fale Fisi, and it
became customary ever since that the *tui tonga fefine* married a
male of this family. The "titles of the Fale Fisi were regarded as
foreign forever because the original ancestor was a Fijian" (Bott
1981, 32). She quotes only one example of a highborn Tongan
marrying a woman of Samoa: the father of the first *tui kanokupolu*
is reputed to have done so (Bott 1981, 35; elsewhere she speaks
in general terms about Samoan women in Tonga, Bott 1982). The
hau, the secular ruler (first the *tui haa takalaua*, later the *tui
kanokupolu*), usually married the daughter of the *tui tonga fefine*
and the chief of the Fale Fisi (Bott 1981, 34, 56ff.) and not women
of Samoa (Bott 1982, 95). Basing her analysis on recent fieldwork
in Tonga, Kaeppler states that the "pre-eminent Tongan context
for the use of Fijian and Samoan trade goods was, and is, on
ceremonial occasions" (1978, 250), such as weddings, funerals,
and various kinds of state and religious celebrations. Kirch (1984,
240) concludes from this that the foreign goods served the function
of binding local chiefs to the central polity. In this way, he suggests, "the flow of tribute to Tongatapu was balanced by the
distribution of prestige goods to the outliers." Monopolization of
the prestige goods by the central ruler(s) "helped to secure their
power over the system as a whole" (Kirch 1984, 241). This phenomenon clearly belongs to the realm of the political economy.
Data in the sources quoted supporting this hypothesis are scanty.
Elizabeth Bott (1982, 97, 100, 132) relates how at funerals of
notables fine mats (*koloa*) were handed out, while on other occasions *koloa* was also handed out (Bott 1982, 102). Mariner

(1819, 475ff.) speaks about enormous quantities of food distributed during feasts and ceremonies; he also mentions other gifts, but without further specification. When a *tui tonga* is buried large quantities of *koloa*, such as coral, whale's teeth, and Samoan mats, are placed in his grave (Mariner 1819, 483). Mariner also mentions that though Tongans were the better sailors, they preferred Fijian canoes and tried to obtain these at all costs (1819, 513). In this respect one may point to the voyages of the chief "Kow Muala," described by Mariner (1819, 276–85). This chief went to Fiji for sandalwood "das in Tonga ungemein hoch geschätzt wird" (which was valued greatly in the Tonga Islands) (1819, 277), but lost all in Futuna where he was shipwrecked. He then returned to Fiji to get another load of sandalwood. The Fijians demanded from him in return valuable goods, such as whale teeth, barkcloth, fine mats, and the horn of a sting ray (1819, 282). The missionaries of the Duff mention a trip to Fiji "to fetch a spirit," to cure a sick chief (Wilson 1799, 234). Cook (1967, 164, 171) states that the Tongans got red feathers and other articles, such as cooking pots, barkcloth, and dogs, from Fiji (see also Anderson 1967, 958ff.). Information on Samoa was hardly available to Cook (1967, 162; Anderson 1967, 957). Hjarnø (1980, 102, 104, 106, 116, 117), however, maintains that a fairly active trade existed between Tonga and Samoa well before the coming of the Europeans. Articles exchanged included fine mats, red feathers (from Fiji), and whale teeth. Kaeppler (1978, 248) is also more specific on exchanges between Tonga and Fiji than on exchanges between Tonga and Samoa. For Samoa she mentions the sending of daughters, ceremonial attendants, and fine mats; in exchange Samoa received Tongan barkcloth, sleeping mats, and red feathers (1978, 249). In her opinion the articles from Fiji and Samoa were used mainly on ceremonial occasions, where the families of bride and bridegroom displayed and exchanged them in large quantities, depending on their status and wealth (1978, 251). Whether these data are sufficient to prove Kirch's hypothesis correct is doubtful; but surely they are in support of it. In any case, the data do not indicate whether or not there existed a monopoly on prestige goods. As, however, only wealthy chiefs could participate in the voyages and exchanges, there were but few people who could obtain them (see also Gailey 1981, 120, 124).

The foregoing discussion of the political economy of the Tongan early state shows that the majority of the state's income consisted of food, goods, and services. This was usually sufficient to enable the rulers to fulfill their obligations. They rewarded the faithful, maintained their households and their retainers, and, in case great buildings were needed, they applied the labour of their subjects. In that way the monumental graves and forts were build, houses were erected, and canoes were made. The availability of prestige goods made it possible, moreover, to maintain the support of the chiefs of the outlying islands. Occasionally, however, Tongan society as a whole was required to demonstrate their allegiance to the *tui tonga* by presenting him ceremonially with large quantities of food. This happened during the *inasi* festival. There are two descriptions of an *inasi*, of which the one by Cook is the more detailed (Cook 1967, 145–54; cf. Anderson 1967, 913–17, and Clerke 1967, 1306–8). Cook, however, was present at a rather exceptional ceremony, for here the *tui tonga* Paulaho, and his son, Fuanunuiava, both attended the *inasi*. Normally only the ruler presided over the ceremony (Bott 1982, 39ff.). The other description is given by Mariner (1819, 470–76).

The organization of an *inasi* was the duty of the *tui haa takalaua* (Bott 1982, 109). He informed the various chiefs of their obligations. These were often felt as heavy obligations (Mariner 1819, 351, 360). The underlying idea was the offering of first fruits by the *tui tonga*. The aim was to secure a bountiful harvest and the welfare of the country and the people. The *tui tonga*, holding the most sacred title, was to act as the intermediary between the people and the gods (Bott 1982, 39). After the ceremony the greater part of the offerings were divided among the notables, who in turn handed out the food to their followers. Bott stresses (1982, 46) that the *inasi* had both a political and a religious significance.

The normal procedure for taxation ("gifts") was that those commoners who lived near the *tui tonga* presented their gifts directly to him. Farmers who lived remote from the center presented yams to their local chiefs. These chiefs presented a portion of the gift to the *tui kanokupolu*, who presented a portion to the *tui haa takalaua,* who in turn presented a portion to the *tui tonga* (Gifford 1929, 103). In this way, even from faraway islands gifts came to the ruler.

Initially, the arrival of the European visitors did not change the economic pattern of the Tongans very much. There was more barter than before, and more people than previously had the possibility to obtain prestige goods. Cook even felt obliged to organize a kind of market, where the barter could take place (Cook 1967, 125; Samwell 1967, 1026). In this barter only commoners participated; the notables organized their commercial relations with the Europeans on a base of gift giving (Cook 1967). The same pattern is mentioned by the French visitors, some fifteen years later (Labillardière 1800, 2:128, 133). The availability of European goods also led to the development of a kind of prostitution. Samwell (1967, 1042, 1043) mentions receiving female favours in exchange for "hatchets or any thing else that we had," the French visitors complain about the canoeloads of prostitutes, offered by the chiefs (Dentrecasteaux 1808, 1:288; Labillardière 1800, 2:100ff.), and the Italian voyager Malaspina, who was at Vavau in 1793, also mentions women being offered to his crew (1935, 233; on Malaspina: Herda 1987). The Tongan customs described above do not make it probable that the objects obtained in this way remained long in the possession of the women, however.

There are no reasons to doubt that in the early state of Tonga the rulers in the center had sufficient power at their disposal to enforce their decisions. When persons of the lower ranks infringed the rules they were punished without mercy. Clerke (1967, 1310) relates how a man at Eua was beaten to death for having committed adultry with the wife of a chief, and Malaspina mentions the rude behaviour of Vuna, the "governor" of the Vavau Islands and his servants towards the islanders (1935, 230, 236, 241). Beatings were also given when commoners were slow to give way to a notable, and when their canoes lay in the way the notable simply ran them over (Maurelle 1797, 295; Labillardière 1800, 2:96, 99, 175; Mariner 1819, 64, 80, 95; West 1865, 263; Wilson 1799, 100; Cook 1967, 100, 122). Possessions of *tua* were taken without much ado, and no one dared to protest. Fear of disobeying was not limited to the lower ranks. Mariner (1819, 351) tells how his powerful patron Finau, living in Vavau, was once invited to contribute to an *inasi*. Though Finau had great objections to the heavy tax, he did not dare to refuse. He was saved, however, when shortly after the summons had taken place, the *tui tonga* died. Only then did he dare to proclaim Vavau free from obligations to the sacred ruler (Mariner 1819, 360–61). Only after the introduction of firearms and the spread of Christianity did Tongan society begin to change fundamentally (Van der Grijp 1987). It is difficult to guess how the developments in the Tonga Islands would have been if this had not happened. Most probably the long-standing conflict between the *tui tonga* and the *tui kano-kopulu* would have led to a war, and irrespective of its winner, changes would have occurred.

Comparisons between Tahiti and Tonga

It is now possible to compare the economic systems and the political economy of the two Polynesian early states. In many respects their socioeconomic background was identical. The same plants were grown and the same fish were caught. Their technical means were similar, and in both cases the islands were well populated but not overpopulated (Sahlins 1958). The social organization was based on the same ramage structure (Kirch 1984). Though Harris (1968, 4), in view of so many techno-environmental and techno-economic similarities would predict identical cultures, the ethnographical data reveal considerable differences between the two societies. Both were sovereign polities, with a strong central government. The rulers at the center were entitled to taxation in the form of food, goods, and services. Other notables were also entitled to similar forms of sustenance. In view of the existing material culture there were hardly other valuables available for taxation. Where such goods were found—red feathers, whale's teeth, the Oro image—these were reserved for the rulers and reached lower notables only by means of redistribution by the central rulers. The political economy was based on an ideology of reciprocity: taxation was usually represented as a gift, and the receiver in turn handed out food and goods. That, in the given situation, reciprocity was quite asymmetrical is not surprising. The commoners often had to make do with blessings, the guarantee of fertility, or the maintenance of law and order (Claessen and Van de Velde 1987, 12ff.). Occasionally, however, during festivities they received food or goods in return. There is no doubt that the rulers monopolized force: the sources abound with data concerning punishments and beatings. These punishments were meted out by various notables. This was a consequence of the fact that the chiefs in their districts, or islands, had the right—and the duty—to maintain law and order. European visitors repeatedly mention the fact that the commoners accepted the harsh treatment by their chiefs stoically. They accepted the beatings and handed over goods without complaint. Apparently this was the way it should be. When taking into consideration the fact that many commoners lived on land belonging to the chief, and were obliged to produce for his sustenance, it was not so much robbery, as the payment of taxation, or of rent. In turn the local and regional chiefs were obliged to contribute to the maintenance of the central rulers (who also had their own gardens and labourers).

In both cases the structure of the ramage underwent considerable changes. The kinship ties between commoners and notables disappeared. In Tahiti the *arii* formed an endogamous upper stratum, and in Tonga the *eiki* did the same. The commoners were known in Tahiti as *manahune*, and in Tonga as *tua*. In-between are found, respectively, the *raatira* and the *matapule*. These two groups differed considerably. Where the Tahitian *raatira* qualified mainly as lower notables—"a landed gentry"—and were in possession of land, the Tongan *matapule* were known as the "titled ceremonial attendants" of the chiefs. Both categories had different functions to fulfill and occupied a different place in the social organization; on the other hand, both *raatira* and *matapule*, as a category, ranked above the commoners. The *matapule* seem connected with similar functionaries in Samoa (Van Bakel 1989). Another point of difference between the social organization of Tahiti and Tonga, concerns the rank of women. In Tonga daughters ranked higher than sons, and this occasioned several adaptations of the sociopolitical domain in Tonga, for example, with regard to the position of the *tui tonga* versus the *tui tonga fefine* and her children. This was not found in Tahiti.

In view of the heavy demands on production, scarcity of food and goods occurred incidentially in both societies. In order to prevent scarcity when important festivities or rituals were expected, the notables had the right to declare certain products *tapu* for some time. In Tahiti this custom was called *rahui*; for Tonga no specific word was mentioned. The *tapu* of a lower chief could be broken by a chief of higher rank.

Both early states had a subsistence economy. Its main products were yams, taro, coconuts, breadfruit, and so forth, and fish. There was some production of barkcloth and mats. In the Tonga Islands these goods, produced by women, had—because of that— a higher value (*koloa*) than the goods produced by men. The simplicity of the economic base had several consequences. As the great majority of households were self-sufficient, there was but limited need for trade or barter. Occasionally some person produced better, or more, goods than others, and the surplus could be used in exchange for other goods or services. Some people had a better opportunity to fish than others, and some exchange took place. There were specialists who built canoes, houses, *marae*, or grave monuments. They applied local materials and were rewarded with local products. As similar patterns of production were found in the surrounding islands there was little incentive for trading expeditions (Sahlins 1958; Van Bakel 1989). In the Society Islands a rather intensive interisland traffic was found to occur. Often the voyages had an economic goal, for example, to obtain better breadfruit. Other voyages were made for social reasons. The most important result of the contacts with Raiatea was the introduction of the Oro cult in Tahiti, followed by the introduction of the *maro's*. With the introduction of Oro and *maro's* some interesting status goods entered the Tahitian scene, and the leading *arii* competed heavily for these valuables. The long-distance exchange (Kirch 1984) of the Tongans was important and went as far afield as Samoa and Fiji, easily within reach of the *tongiaki* and *ndrau* (Kirch 1984). The aim of this trade was to obtain prestige goods, such as red feathers, whale's teeth, sandalwood, and fine mats. With the help of such goods the central rulers of Tonga tried to secure the loyalty of the chiefs and the outlying islands. Both societies knew various forms of taxation. The obligation to maintain the notables was mentioned already. Taxation usually occurred on a local basis: the goods went to the *raatira*, *toofa*, *arii*, *eiki*, or *matapule* under whose command the region in question fell. Incidentially, however, taxes were demanded by higher authorities such as the *arii rahi*, the *tui tonga*, or his deputy. Usually this was quite an undertaking: messengers were sent in all directions to inform the regional chiefs of their obligations, and these sent word to their deputies, who in turn informed the farmers. The delivery of the goods and food (the usual tax) went in the reverse order: via the local chief and the regional chief to the central authority. Though the system seems more elaborate in the Tonga Islands—occasioned by the fact that people of several islands had to contribute—in Tahiti the same method was found to occur, though on a smaller scale. The Tongan *inasi* in particular was an activity in which the society at large participated. Perhaps this was connected with the fact that the *inasi* also had religious connotations. It was the offering of first fruits to the sacred ruler—a custom that was also found in Tahiti.

The importation of European goods introduced new valuables to both societies. Notables and commoners went to great length to obtain a share of the new goods. In the case of the notables the exchange was conducted mainly on the basis of gift giving. In the case of commoners, barter was more often found to occur. From the beginning the seductiveness of young women played a role in obtaining European goods. The interest in textiles and iron was soon replaced by one in firearms. Though in the beginning the contacts with foreigners did not really change the indigenous culture, after the introduction of firearms and Christianity fundamental changes were soon inevitable (Van der Grijp 1987).

References

Anderson, William
1967   A journal of a voyage made in His Majesty's sloop Resolution (1776–1777). In *The Journals of Captain James Cook; The voyage of the Resolution and Discovery, 1776–1780*, ed. J. C. Beaglehole, 721–986. Extra Series No. 36. Cambridge: Hakluyt Society.
Andia y Varella, Don José de
1775   The journal of ———, while in command of his bark the Jupiter, in which are related the events of a voyage to the Island of Amat and others adjacent thereto. In *The quest and occupation of Tahiti by emissaries of Spain during the*

years 1772–1776, 2:221–318. 2nd Series No. 36 [1915].
Cambridge: Hakluyt Society.

Arii Taimai
1966   *Mémoires d'Arii Taimai*. Ed. H. Adams, trans. S. and A.
Lebois. Publications de la Société des Océanistes, No. 12.
Paris: Musée de l'Homme.

Bakel, Martin A. van
1989   *Samen leven tussen gebondenheid en vrijheid*. Ph.D. Thesis, Leiden.

Banks, Sir Joseph
1962   *The Endeavor journal of* ——, *1768–1771*. Ed. J. C.
Beaglehole. 2 vols. Sydney: Angus and Robertson.

Bellingshausen (Thaddeus)
1945   *The voyage of Captain* —— *to the Antarctic Seas, 1819–
1821*. (Trans. from the Russian.) Ed. F. Debenham. 2
Vols. 2nd Series, No. 91/92. Cambridge: Hakluyt Society.

Bligh, William
1952   A voyage to the South Sea, undertaken by command of
His Majesty, for the purpose of conveying the bread-fruit
tree to the West Indies, in His Majesty's ship The Bounty,
commanded by the Lieutenant ——. In *A book of the
Bounty*, ed. G. Mackaness, 1–110. Everyman's Library
No. 950. London: Dent.

Boenechea, Don Domingo
1773   Narrative of the voyage performed by ——. In *The quest
and occupation of Tahiti by emissaries of Spain during the
years 1772–1776*. Ed. B. G. Corney. 1:284–345. 2nd Series, No. 32 [1913]. Cambridge: Hakluyt Society.

Bonacorsi, Don Raimundo
1772   Voyage to the island of Otayty, performed by Don Domingo Boenechea. In *The quest and occupation of Tahiti by
emissaries of Spain during the years 1772–1776*. Ed. B. G.
Corney. 2:29–63. 2nd Series, No. 36. [1915]. Cambridge:
Hakluyt Society.

Bott, Elizabeth
1981   Power and rank in the kingdom of Tonga. *The Journal of
the Polynesian Society* 90:7–83.
1982   Tongan society at the time of Captain Cook's visits; discussions with Her Majesty Queen Salote Tupou. (With
the assistance of Tavi.) Wellington: The Polynesian Society.

Bougainville, Louis de
1966   *Voyage autour du monde par la frégate La Boudeuse et la
flûte L'Etoile (1766–1769)*. Ed. M. Hérubel. Le Monde
en 10/18. Paris: Union Générale d'Editions.

Bovis, Edmond de
1855   De la société Tahitienne à l'arrivée des Européens. *Revue Coloniale*, 2me Série, 14:369–407, 512–39.
Caro, (J)
1962   Journal du voiage du Tour du Monde fait par le S. ——
            —. In Le lieutenant Caro et sa relation inédite du séjour de Bougainville à Tahiti. Ed. E. Taillemite. *Journal de la Société des Océanistes* 38:11–19.
Claessen, Henri J. M.
1978   Early State in Tahiti. In *The Early State*, ed. H. J. M. Claessen and P. Skalník, 441–67. The Hague: Mouton.
1988   Leiders en lagen op Tahiti. In *Tussen vorst en volk*, ed. H. J. M. Claessen, 79–94. Leiden: Instituut voor Culturele Antropologie [ICA Publication 81].
Claessen, Henri J. M. and Pieter van de Velde, eds.
1987   *Early State dynamics*. Leiden: Brill.
Clerke, (Charles)
1967   Account of Tonga, 1777. In *The journals of Captain James Cook*, ed. J. C. Beaglehole. *The voyage of the Resolution and Discovery, 1776–1780*. 3:1301–40. Extra Series No. 36. Cambridge: Hakluyt Society.
Clota, Geronimo, and Narciso Gonzales
1775   Diary of things noteworthy, that occurred at Amat's Island (alias Otageti). In *The quest and occupation of Tahiti by emissaries of Spain during the years 1772–1776*, ed. B. G. Corney. 2:319–49. 2nd Series, No. 36. [1915]. Cambridge: Hakluyt Society.
Cook, James
1967   The voyage of the Resolution and Discovery, 1776–1780. In *The Journals of Captain James Cook*, ed. J. C. Beaglehole, 3:1–491. Extra Series, No. 36. Cambridge: Hakluyt Society.
1968   The voyage of the Endeavor, 1768–1771. In *The Journals of Captain James Cook*, ed. J. C. Beaglehole, 1:1–479. Extra Series, No. 34. Cambridge: Hakluyt Society.
1969   The voyage of the Resolution and Adventure, 1772–1775. In *The Journals of Captain James Cook*, ed. J. C. Beaglehole. 2:1–682. Extra Series, No. 35. Cambridge: Hakluyt Society.
Cummins, H. G.
1977   Tongan society at the time of European contact. In *Friendly Islands, a history of Tonga*, ed. N. Rutherford, 63–89. Melbourne: Oxford University Press.
Dentrecasteaux, (J. A. B.)
1808   *Voyage de Dentrecasteaux, envoyé à la recherche de la Pérouse*. Ed. E. P. E. de Rossel. 2 Vols. Paris: Nyon l'ainé

Dumont d'Urville, J. S. C.
1832   *Voyage de la corvette l'Astrolabe, exécuté par ordre du Roi,
          pendant les années 1826, 1827, 1828, 1829, sous le com-
          mandement de M. ——, capitaine de vaisseau.* 5 Vols.
          Paris: Ministère de la Marine.
Ellis, William
1831   *Polynesian researches, during a residence of nearly six years
          in the South Sea islands.* 4 Vols. London: Fisher, Son, and
          Jackson.
Farmer, Sarah S.
1855   *Tonga and the Friendly Islands; With a sketch of their
          Mission history.* London: Hamilton Adams.
Fesche, C. F. P.
1929   *La Nouvelle Cythère (Tahiti); Journal de navigation inédit
          (1768).* Ed. J. Dorsenne. Paris: Duchartre and Van Bug-
          genhoudt.
Forster, Johann Reinhold
1783   *Johann Reinhold Forster's Bemerkungen über Gegen-
          stände der physischen Erdbeschreibung, Naturgeschichte
          und Sittliche Philosophie auf seiner Reise um die Welt ges-
          ammlet.* Berlin: Fock.
Friedman, Jonathan
1981   Notes on structure and history in Oceania. *Folk* 23:275–
          95.
1982   Catastrophe and continuity in social evolution. In *Theory
          and explanation in archaeology*, eds. C. Renfrew, M. Row-
          lands, and B. Segraves 175–98. New York: Academic Press.
Gailey, Christine Ward
1981   *Our history is written . . . in our mats: state formation and
          the status of women in Tonga.* Ann Arbor: University Mi-
          crofilm International.
Gayangos, Don Thomas
1775   The official journal of the second voyage of the frigate
          Aguila from El Callao to Tahiti and the islands near-by
          and back to El Callao. In *The quest and occupation of
          Tahiti by emissaries of Spain during the years 1772–1776.*
          Ed. B. G. Corney. 2:103–99., 2nd Series, Vol. 36. [1915].
          Cambridge: Hakluyt Society.
Gifford, Edward W.
1929   *Tongan society.* B. P. Bishop Museum Bulletin 61. Hon-
          olulu: B. P. Bishop Museum.
Goldman, Irving
1970   *Ancient Polynesian society.* Chicago: University of Chi-
          cago Press.
Grijp, Paul van der
1987   Pacificatie van de Pacific: handel en geweld bij de eerste

kontakten tussen Tonganen en westerlingen. In *Sporen in de antropologie*. Eds. P. van der Grijp, T. Lemaire, and A. Trouwborst, 55–78., Nijmegen: Instituut voor Kulturele en Sociale Antropologie.

Harris, Marvin D.
1968   *The rise of anthropological theory*. London: Routledge and Kegan Paul.

Henry, Teuira
1929   *Ancient Tahiti, based on material recorded by J. M. Orsmond*. B. P. Bishop Museum Bulletin 48. Honolulu: B. P. Bishop Museum.

Herda, Phyllis
1987   Documents on Vava'u, Tonga, located in Spanish archives. *The Journal of Pacific History* 22:102–5.

Hjarnø, Jan
1980   Social reproduction. Towards an understanding of aboriginal Samoa. *Folk* 21/22:73–123.

Journal d'un voyage autour du monde, en 1768, 1769, 1770, 1771, contenant les divers événements du voyage.
1773   [Possibly the journal of Dr. Solander]. Traduit de l'Anglois par M. de Fréville. Paris: Saillant et Nyon.

Kaeppler, Adrienne
1971   Rank in Tonga. *Ethnology* 10:174–93.
1978   Exchange patterns in goods and spouses: Fiji, Tonga and Samoa. *Mankind* 11:246–52.

Kirch, Patrick V.
1984   *The evolution of the Polynesian chiefdoms*. Cambridge: Cambridge University Press.

Koch, Gerd
1955   *Südsee gestern und heute; Der Kulturwandel bei den Tonganern und der Versuch einer Deutung dieser Entwicklung*. Braunschweig: Limbach.

Korn, Shulamite R. Decktor
1978   Hunting the ramage: kinship and the organization of political authority in aboriginal Tonga. *The Journal of Pacific History* 13:107–13.

Labillardière, Jaques Julien de
1800   *Relation du voyage à la recherche de la Pérouse, fait par ordre de l'Assemblée Constituante, pendant les années 1791 et 1792 et pendant la 1ère et la 2de année de la République Française*. 2 Vols. Paris: Ministère de la Marine.

Lawry, Walter
1851   *A second visit to the Friendly and Feejee Islands in the year 1850*. Ed. the Rev. E. Hoole. London: Elijah Hoole.

Malaspina, Allessandro
1935   *Allessandro Malaspina; Sue navigazioni ed esplorazioni.*
            Ed. Emma Bona. Roma: Feltrinelli.
Marau Taaroa
1971   *Mémoires de ——, dernière reine de Tahiti.* Translated
            by her daughter, Princess Ariimanihinihi Pomare. Publi-
            cations de la Société des Océanistes 27. Paris: Musée de
            l'Homme.
Mariner, William
1819   *Nachrichten über die Freundschaftlichen, oder die Tonga
            Inseln, von ——, aus der Mittheilungen desselben zusam-
            mengetragen und herausgegeben von John Martin, Doctor
            der Heilkunde.* Neue Bibliothek der wichtigsten Reise-
            beschreibungen, Vol. 20. Weimar: Landes Industrie
            Comptoir.
Maurelle, Don (Francisco Antonio)
1797   Relation d'un voyage intéressant de la frégate la Princesse,
            de Manille à Saint Blaise, en 1780 et 1781. In *Voyage de
            la Pérouse autour du monde, publié conformément au Dé-
            cret du 22 avril 1791,* rédigé par M. L. A. Milet-Mureau,
            1:261–350. Paris: Mérigot.
Moerenhout, J. A.
1837   *Voyages aux îles du Grand Océan, contenant des docu-
            ments nouveaux sur la géographie physique et politique, la
            langue, la littérature, la religion, les moeurs, les usages et
            les coutumes de leurs habitants.* 2 Vols. Paris: Bertrand.
Morrison, James
1966   *Journal de ——, second maître à bord de la 'Bounty'.*
            Traduit de l'Anglais par B. Jaunez. Publications de la
            Société des Océanistes, Vol. 16. Paris: Musée de l'Homme.
Mortimer, George
1793   *Waarnemingen en aanmerkingen aangetekend geduurende
            eene reize naar de eilanden Teneriffe, Amsterdam, Marias
            eilanden bij van Diemens-land, Otaheite enz. in het bri-
            gantijnschip de Mercurius.* Uitgegeven door ——, Lieu-
            tenant onder de zee-troepen. Vertaald door J. D. Pasteur.
            Leiden: A. Loosjes.
Oliver, Douglas
1974   *Ancient Tahitian society.* 3 Vols. Honolulu: University of
            Hawaii Press.
Rodriguez, Maximo
1775   Daily narrative kept by the interpreter —— at the Island
            of Amat, otherwise Otahiti, in the year 1774. In *The quest
            and occupation of Tahiti by emissaries of Spain during the
            years 1772–1776.* Ed. B. G. Corney. 3:1–210. 2nd Series,
            No. 43. [1919]. Cambridge: Hakluyt Society.

Rogers, Garth
1977   The father's sister is black: a consideration of female rank
            and power in Tonga. *Journal of the Polynesian Society*
            86:157–82.
Rose, Roger G.
1978   *Symbols of sovereignty; feather girdles of Tahiti and Ha-
            waii*. Pacific Anthropological Records, No. 28. Honolulu:
            B. P. Bishop Museum.
Sahlins, Marshall D.
1958   *Social stratification in Polynesia*. Seattle: American Eth-
            nological Society.
Samwell, David
1967   Some account of a voyage to South Sea's in 1776–1777–
            1778. In *The journals of Captain James Cook*, ed. J. C.
            Beaglehole. 3:987–1300. Extra Series, Vol. 36. Cam-
            bridge: Hakluyt Society.
Thomson, Basil
1894   *The diversions of a prime minister*. London: W. Blackwood
            and Sons.
Turnbull, John
1806   *Reise um die Welt, oder eigentlich nach Australien in den
            Jahren 1800, 1801, 1802, 1803 und 1804*. Bibliothek der
            neuesten und wichtigsten Reisebeschreibungen. Vol 29.
            Weimar: Landes Industrie Comptoir.
Tyerman, Daniel and George Bennett
1831   *Journal of voyages and travels by the Rev. ——, and
            ——, esq., deputed from the London Missionary Society*.
            Ed. James Montgomery. 2 Vol. London: Chapman.
Waldegrave, W.
1833   Extracts from a private journal kept on board H. M. S.
            Seringapatnam, in the Pacific, 1830. *Journal of the Royal
            Geographical Society of London* 3:168–96.
Wales, William
1969   Journal of ——. In *The journals of Captain James Cook*,
            ed. J. C. Beaglehole, 2:776–869. Extra Series, Vol. 35.
            Cambridge: Hakluyt Society.
Wallis, Samuel
1789   Relation d'un voyage fait autour du monde dans les années
            1766, 1767, 1768, par ——, commandant la vaisseau du
            Roi le Dauphin. In *Relation des voyages entrepris par ordre
            de sa Majesté Brittanique, etc.*, ed. J. Hawkesworth, 3:5–
            248. Paris: Nyon and Mérigot.
Walther, Frederik L.
787   *Natuur-en aardrijkskundige beschrijving der Vriendelijke
            Eilanden in de Grote Zuidzee volgens de nieuwste ontdek-
            kingen*. Amsterdam: J. van Meurs.

West, Thomas
1865   *Ten years in South Central Polynesia; Being the reminis-
               censes of a personal mission to the Friendly Islands and
               their dependencies.* London: James Nisbet.
Wilson, James
1799   *A missionary voyage to the southern Pacific Ocean, per-
               formed in the years 1796, 1797, 1798, in the ship Duff,
               commanded by captain James Wilson.* London: Chapman.

List of Contributors

MARTIN A. VAN BAKEL. Institute of Cultural and Social Studies. University of Leiden. The Netherlands

ELIZABETH M. BRUMFIEL. Department of Anthropology and Sociology. Albion College. Albion, Michigan, U.S.A.

HENRI J. M. CLAESSEN. Institute of Cultural and Social Studies. University of Leiden. The Netherlands.

RONALD COHEN. Department of Anthropology. University of Florida. Gainesville, Florida, U.S.A.

FREDERIC HICKS. Department of Anthropology, University of Louisville. Louisville, Kentucky, U.S.A.

PATRICA J. O'BRIEN. Department of Sociology, Anthropology and Social Work. Kansas State University Manhattan, Kansas. U.S.A.

JOANNA PFAFF-CZARNECKA. Ethnologisches Seminar. University of Zürich. Zürich, Switzerland.

RIEN PLOEG. Department of Archaeology, Government of Belize. Belmopan, Belize.

327

M. ESTELLIE SMITH. Department of Anthropology. State University of New York at Oswego. Oswego, New York, U.S.A.

AIDAN SOUTHALL. Department of Anthropology. University of Wisconsin. Madison, Wisconsin, U.S.A.

ALBERT A. TROUWBORST. Department of Anthropology. Catholic University. Nijmegen. The Netherlands.

MICHAL TYMOWSKI. Historical Institute. University of Warsaw. Poland. (Temporarily Director of the Polish Institute of the Sorbonne University, Paris, France).

PIETER VAN DE VELDE. Department of Archaeology. University of Leiden. The Netherlands.

Index

Narrowly connected words such as *legitimacy, legitimation*, etc. have been subsumed under one heading. Words such as *state* or *economy*, which appear on practically every page, have been omitted, except for places where definitions are given.

329

www.ingramcontent.com/pod-product-compliance
Ingram Content Group UK Ltd.
Pitfield, Milton Keynes, MK11 3LW, UK
UKHW041840280225
455677UK00010B/272